Issues Confronting City & State Governments

Issues
Confronting
City & State
Governments

A guide to improving
& understanding local governments
of all shapes & sizes,
from towns to counties
to state agencies

ANDY OAKLEY

P.O. Publishing Company

Box 3333
Skokie, Illinois 60076-6333

FIRST PRINTING
Library of Congress Catalog Number 93-85469
ISBN 0-944146-01-5
224 pages

Copyright © 1994 by P.O. Publishing Company

Publisher's Cataloging in Publication

(Prepared by Quality Books Inc.)

Oakley, Andy.
   Issues Confronting City & State Governments : A guide to improving & understanding local governments of all shapes & sizes, from towns to counties to state agencies / Andy Oakley.
   p. cm.
   Includes index.
   Preassigned LCCN: 93-085469.
   ISBN 0-944146-01-5

   1. Local government--United States. 2. State governments--United States.   I. Title. II. Title: Issues Confronting City and State Governments.

JS3.A1O35 1993   352
                                              QBI93-1110

May Glen read this book carefully before giving up hope and becoming a nihilistic revolutionary like his father.

Acknowledgments

This book would not have been possible without the support and vision of *City & State* Publisher Dan Miller, a renowned journalist and top administrator who agreed that this project would benefit local governments for years to come. Reporters on the staff at *City & State,* as well as some free-lance writers, were instrumental in sharing their knowledge of government. A special thank you goes out to Gary Enos, whose abilities as a *City & State* staff writer made a large part of this project a pleasure; he easily is one of the top reporters in the United States. Len Strazewski was responsible for translating information-technology gobbledygook into lucid prose. Other invaluable people who contributed their talents were Joseph Winski, Todd Sloane, Rodd Zolkos, Ellen Perlman, Dorothy Parr Riesen, Becky Myers and Evelyn Dorman. Editors whose abilities were a godsend included David A. Gorak, Bradley Webber, Sue Kapp and Ann Arellano.

—Andy Oakley, Editor

Table of contents

Introduction

The problems facing state and local governments are documented *ad nauseam* in national daily newspapers, nightly television news shows and local weekly papers. Unfortunately, most government problems — budget deficits, overflowing garbage dumps, antiquated record-keeping procedures, ineffective police departments, negative public perception of elected and appointed officials, skyrocketing cable television rates and so on — are rarely accompanied by logical solutions. No central source of information even attempts to answer the complicated questions that plague communities and their residents — until now.

Each chapter of this book examines government woes and details solution-oriented approaches that have worked for other governments. The idea is for local administrators, community activists, politicians, would-be politicians and average citizens to learn from each other in their searches for answers to complex questions. Be forewarned that just because a program works for one government does not necessarily mean it will work for another, but most successful programs outlined in this book can be molded to benefit local governments from around the country.

Unlike other works that deal merely with the structures of federal, state and local governments, this book is a hands-on guide to problem-solving for state agencies, cities, counties, towns, villages, sewer districts, municipal utilities, school districts and other non-federal governments that serve U.S. citizens at the grass-roots level. The information within this book draws upon thousands of interviews and hundreds of stories completed by Chicago-based *City & State,* a national newspaper that covers the operations and politics of state and local governments. Each chapter is written so that a layman can understand it, but the advice is detailed enough to be of use to top-level bureaucrats and politicians. In addition, this book strives to remain objective and declines to endorse any person's or political party's philosophy of government.

The following types of government are covered in this book:

■ **State:** A state is one of the 50 territorial and political units that constitute the United States. Taxpayers usually consider states too large to be local governments. This is untrue, however, of most of the agencies within state governments that deal directly with certain regions or constituents; those departments include agriculture, community development, international trade, small-business and revenue offices. The population sizes of states range from about 454,000 people in Wyoming to nearly 30 million in California. The sizes of state government budgets range from barely over $1 billion in Vermont to about $55 billion in California.

■ **Municipality:** This general term, although used regularly as a synonym for city or town, refers to any form of local government, including counties and school systems. The term municipality commonly is used to describe governments that fall below state governments in terms of power and size.

■ **City:** This term describes an incorporated government whose boundaries and powers are defined by state charter and the state constitution. Cities, whose populations can range from a couple hundred to millions of people, are responsible for a wide range of basic public services, most notably police and fire protection, street repair and zoning control. The services cities provide to taxpayers differ tremendously from one government to another. Some cities are limited in function and depend on other local entities — especially counties — to provide services. Others possess expanded powers, overseeing bus lines, city hospitals or other operations normally controlled by businesses or separate governments.

The most popular form of city government is mayor-council, where the governing board (usually called the city council) consists of anywhere from two to 50 representatives elected by voters. Two setups can exist: strong mayor-council and weak mayor-council. The strong mayor is elected directly by the people and given broad administrative powers, including appointing department heads and drawing up the annual budget with the help of city staff members. Under a weak-mayor system, the mayor is a member of the city council chosen by fellow council members. Power is fragmented — most is held by the council — and, in some cases, voters get to choose department heads responsible for city operations.

The commission form of city government usually consists of five elected officials, each heading a department of the city. In some cities, one of the commissioners is named mayor, but that person is vested with few additional powers.

Council-manager government is most popular in cities with populations ranging from 10,000 to 200,000 people; among the largest exceptions are Dallas, Oakland, Phoenix and San Diego. The city council and mayor are elected by the people, and they appoint a professional manager to run the day-to-day affairs of government. The council sets broad policy and the mayor's seat generally is ceremonial (banging the gavel at council meetings and attending ribbon-cutting ceremonies). The city manager takes care of the details of government, with some direction from elected political leaders. Supposedly such an arrangement keeps the manager out of politics; however, when a new council is swept into office, or when the political winds shift on the old council, the city manager can find himself blown out of office with a simple majority vote of council members.

City and county operations often overlap because cities fall within the regional jurisdictions of territorially larger counties. For instance, Houston lies within the purview of Harris County, Texas, and the county provides the lion's share of social services to residents. In a handful of metropolitan areas, such as Indianapolis (Marion County), The City and County of Denver, and Columbus (Muscogee County) in west-central Georgia, city and county governments have merged to form all-powerful regional governments. Some cities, such as St. Louis, Baltimore and Richmond, Va., are entities unto themselves and are not part of counties; that means the city of St. Louis and St. Louis County border each other and share the same name, but they do not cover the same geographic area.

The sizes of city budgets range from $31 billion-plus for New York City to tiny governments with yearly revenue in the tens of thousands of dollars. There are some 19,200 city governments in the United States.

■ **County:** In most states, the county is the largest local government subdivision with taxation power. Louisiana counties are called parishes, and in Alaska they're called boroughs. In a handful of regions, particularly Connecticut and Rhode Island, counties have few duties and are almost extinct forms of government. Traditional services provided by counties are road construction and maintenance, property assessment, tax collection, law enforcement and voter registration. Counties in urban areas have expanded their services to include health care and social services. D. Michael Stewart, a commissioner for Salt Lake County, Utah, and former president of the National Association of Counties, once repined that counties must spend large sums of money to provide up to 104 different services to the public, compared with cities' 10 to 12 services.

The duties of counties vary considerably from state to state. In Maryland, for instance, counties oversee financing of schools, sewers and parks. But in Illinois, separate government taxing

3

entities, including school districts, park districts, forest preserve districts, and water and sewer districts, relieve counties from such services. In fact, many Illinois counties don't even have to worry about controlling insect infestations, thanks to tiny mosquito abatement districts.

The most prevalent form of county government is the commission, with the board usually consisting of five to seven elected officials called commissioners, supervisors or freeholders. Cases do exist where the board contains 50 or more members. Larger boards consist of township officials, while smaller boards are directly elected by voters. Oftentimes county clerks, sheriffs, treasurers, health officers, coroners, animal control officers and surveyors find themselves on the local ballot during election season.

An elected county executive controls county operations under one form of government most often found in urbanized areas. The executive-politician depends on professionally trained assistants to keep tabs on county finances and services, or on a chief administrative officer appointed by other elected county officials.

The county government with the largest budget is Los Angeles County, Calif., which oversees revenue and expenditures of more than $7.5 billion a year. At the other end of the spectrum are rural counties whose budgets run into the tens of thousands of dollars. Some 3,042 counties exist in the United States; about 80% are rural.

■ **Village:** This term refers to quaint unincorporated communities with a smattering of houses somewhere in the countryside. More technically, a village is an incorporated municipality whose powers are defined by state charter and the state constitution. Generally speaking, a village's powers are slightly limited in comparison to the powers of a city within the same state. In states where village governments exist, statutes spell out the differences between villages and cities.

■ **Towns, townships:** About 16,690 towns and townships exist in 20 states in the Midwestern and Eastern United States. Some have powers that don't go far beyond distributing aid from the federal government, while others are so strong that they virtually render county government useless. Even more so than counties, towns and townships are considered to be the government "closest to the people." The New England town meeting is the stuff of legend, revered in the United States as the pinnacle of Democracy. In the Northeast, the town is the principal form of non-city government, carrying out the duties of a county or school district for a region of villages and unincorporated land. In Connecticut, for instance, towns and cities are the premier forms of government, and counties have depreciated to merely running local court systems. Residents in many towns still can attend town meetings and vote directly on local issues simply by raising their hands. Like counties, each town has its own slate of officials: three to five members of a board of selectmen, treasurer, town

4

clerk and assessor.

Towns and townships were formed as rural governments to serve farmers and settlers during an earlier period in U.S. history. The weaker a town or township government is in relation to other local governments, the more likely the township is used as a behind-the-scenes patronage bastion by political bosses.

In Iowa, townships operate mostly as fire protection districts. Michigan townships flex more muscle, occasionally rivaling the powers of the counties; townships in this state have the ability to oversee major road construction projects and run their own police departments. In Illinois, where a grass-roots movement has been active in trying to abolish the 1,435 townships as worthless and repetitive institutions, local officials mainly distribute money for social programs and road repair, and they also act as headquarters for voter registration. The trend in Ohio, on the other hand, has been for state legislators to try to swing more power to township officials, who primarily have been caretakers of roads. The Kansas Legislature has whittled away at the duties of its 1,360 townships in recent years, but they're still responsible for a variety of services, ranging from ambulance service to bridge repair to prairie-dog eradication to weed control.

■ **Special districts:** A special district is a unit of government that, in general, is established to perform a specific function for a region, such as financing the local education system, operating pipelines to provide drinking water to homes, overseeing the public transit system or maintaining cemeteries. The most prevalent governments of this type are school districts, fire protection districts, housing agencies, drainage and flood-control districts, and water supply districts. Larger special districts serve areas that take in several municipal governments. For instance, the monolithic Metropolitan Water Reclamation District of Greater Chicago, which is a special district providing sewer services, covers every city, village and township in the Chicago suburbs. The Massachusetts Municipal Wholesale Electric Company in 1976 became a public corporation with the power to buy, build and finance facilities to generate electricity for municipal electric systems in Massachusetts; by the early 1990s, 34 local governments were members of the operation, and another 12 maintained contractual links with the district. An irrigation district, such as the 80-year-old Imperial Irrigation District in Southern California, might cover several counties. A government like the Dallas-Fort Worth International Airport Board might be in charge of the operations of a single facility, in this case the main airport serving the Dallas-Fort Worth metropolitan area. A public hospital district often will serve at least one city and the surrounding rural area.

In comparison, special districts also can be parochial in nature, covering neighborhoods of fewer than 100 homes. The best examples of this phenomenon are the Municipal Utility Districts

5

(MUDs) in Texas. MUDs are created by developers to bring water and sewer systems to new subdivisions that for one reason or another cannot be served by a local city, county or other government's established water and sewer operations. A developer will produce a MUD for his housing project (with approval from the county and other nearby governments), borrow money to build water and sewer lines for the homes, and then tax the residents who move into the new homes so he can accumulate enough money to pay off his water-sewer loan. When the bottom dropped out of the Texas real-estate market in the middle and late 1980s, some MUDs defaulted on their loans because no one was moving into the new subdivisions; thus, no property owners were around to pay off the developer-initiated loans. Today, however, MUDs are considered stable forms of limited government — as long as developers do not overbuild and as long as the economy remains stable.

The U.S. Census Bureau reports that about 7,000 special districts exist in the United States. Other people argue that tiny groups such as neighborhood and condominium associations also count as special districts, bringing the total to 28,000. These associations generally have no taxing capabilities; they merely collect monthly dues or other payments for special projects such as plowing snow on private roads that run through apartment complexes or building new swimming pools for condominium inhabitants. Special districts continue to proliferate. In August 1990 in Missouri, for example, state voters approved an amendment to the Missouri Constitution authorizing cities and counties to create neighborhood improvement districts that could borrow money to pay for improvements — mainly new streets and parks — within those districts. Under the initiative, the districts could be created by a city or county upon approval by a four-sevenths majority of the property owners in the proposed district. If the district were to borrow money in the municipal bond market, the bonds would be repaid through a levy assessed against the real-estate owners in the district.

Warning: Local governments are dynamic, despite publicity to the contrary, and officials quickly move up and down the administrative ladders of municipalities, or they jump from one government to another, or they unexpectedly get voted out of office. Thus, some of the titles of officials within this book may already be outdated. But since most of the book's information comes from data compiled in 1992 and 1993, the ideas remain fresh.

Officials from all parts of the political spectrum — Democrats, Republicans, Libertarians, Socialists, independents and others — have pieced together solution-oriented programs or pushed through legislative packages that enable governments to serve their constituents better. Their ideas appear on the following pages. The bottom line is that governments will run more efficiently once their leaders peruse this book.

Budgets & finances

If a local government is to serve the interests of its residents, it must make good use of its primary resource — money. If revenue from sales taxes, user fees, property taxes, state revenue-sharing programs and other sources is not distributed properly by government officials, even the simplest program or public service will fail to meet its goals.

For instance, the village of Skokie, Ill., in 1990 had an ordinance limiting each house to only one small "For Sale" sign in its yard. The village government, however, believed it lacked the money to hire someone to enforce the limitation. Thus, real-estate salesmen tended to post giant "For Sale" signs, wildly colored streamers, pennants and other outlawed paraphernalia on property throughout Skokie. In essence, the village had a law that trustees and the mayor thought would keep yards from becoming unsightly, but the law was useless without money to provide enforcement. Officials overcame the problem a year later by loosening their ordinance to allow more "For Sale" signs and by rearranging their resources so that an employee already working for the village would devote more of his time to enforcing the sign ordinance.

To ensure that special programs work and that traditional public services like police protection and street repair are carried out, local governments must budget their money carefully. "The budget document should be prepared so that it facilitates public study and effectively communicates key economic issues and fiscal policies," reported the Chicago-based Government Finance Officers Association in a booklet, "An Elected Official's Guide to Government Finance." The booklet noted that some governments "require their finance officers to prepare budget documents that are so detailed that they do not communicate effectively with the public. Elected officials should not allow details to stand in the way of having a budget that communicates the government's policies and plans. Concise summaries of key information help the public and the press. Charts and graphs are particularly useful."

Three basic types of budgets exist for governments: line-item, program/performance and zero-based. About 60% of all cities use line-item, 10% favor performance, 9% go with zero-based and 20% use a combination of either line-item and program/performance or line-item and zero-based, according to the National League of Cities, a lobbying group for city governments based in Washington, D.C. Descriptions of the three budget types follow:

■ **Line-item budget:** The simplest and longest-used form of financial planning, the line-item budget organizes expenses by department (such as public works department, finance department and planning department) and by objects purchased or money spent (such as salaries, pencils, consultant advice and tar for road repairs). These budgets, produced on a yearly basis, rarely show more than where the government's money is going. There is no indication, for instance, of how successful a program initiated by several departments may have been; instead, only bits and pieces of the project's expenditures are detailed. Line-item budgets work well for smaller governments with uncomplicated finances, but larger governments tend to lean toward other budget forms.

■ **Program/performance budget:** Department expenditures are listed by program or project in a program budget, making it easier to follow the success of sewer construction, snow-removal, welfare aid and other activities. Under a program budget, a layman can more easily determine whether a project is costing a government more than originally expected. Average day-to-day expenditures for government are easier to follow, too. For instance, a sanitation department might have separate expenditure categories for trash removal, recycling and garbage dump fees; each of these three categories would be broken into line items such as garbage-truck repair, salaries and administrative costs. If the government's recycling program is relatively new, an average observer can determine whether recycling is cutting the costs of trash collection.

A performance budget is a refinement of the program budget. To keep tabs on productivity and service levels of programs, the government can set performance standards and evaluate the programs during the budgetary process. The National League of Cities warns, however, that because a performance budget emphasizes a government's actions over its purchases and revenue collections, performance budgeting is costly to implement and needs a highly skilled staff for implementation. In addition, government officials have a hard time developing tangible standards and goals for measuring the success of programs.

■ **Zero-based budget:** The most time-consuming type of budgeting for government staffs is zero-based budgeting. All departments are expected to discard details of the previous year's budget and start from zero. Whereas department heads in some governments might simply add 4% or so to their line-item spending requests from one year to the next, officials who deal with zero-based budgeting start with nothing and must be able to defend all proposed programs and spending levels. For this reason, it is a time-consuming process. At the same time, it discourages lazy budgeting practices and prevents entrenched bureaucracies from forming because every program and staff position must be re-evaluated annually.

Inaccurate revenue forecasting means troubled budgets

Each government strives to finish its budget for a fiscal year at least a couple of weeks before that year is scheduled to begin. In Albuquerque, N.M., for example, fiscal 1991 began on July 1, 1990, and ended on June 30, 1991. Albuquerque officials worked to finalize their budget prior to the July 1, 1990, start of the budgetary year, meaning they had to estimate how much tax money and other revenue they would receive during fiscal 1991. By the end of that fiscal year, officials discovered that their revenue estimates for the general fund (the government's main operating fund) had been within a remarkably accurate $800,000 of the $204.2 million they actually received. In other words, budgeting in Albuquerque and every other locality around the country is a game of educated guesses. If Albuquerque's economy had improved suddenly and unexpectedly during fiscal 1991, the city government would have received much more revenue than anticipated due primarily to greater sales tax revenue from expanded business sales activity. On the other hand, if the area economy had plummeted, the city would have received far less money than expected, leading to a deficit and the possible need to cut back programs and lay off public employees.

When compiling budgets, officials generally tend to put on rose-colored glasses and go for broke — sometimes quite literally, as it turns out. Especially on the state government level, budget officers tend to miss the mark in good years and bad, noted Tony Hutchison, senior fiscal policy analyst in the Denver office of the National Conference of State Legislatures (NCSL). In flush years they underestimate to build up their reserve funds, and "in poor years they pick the higher estimates, even though they know they're likely to come up short," Mr. Hutchison said.

Robert J. Froehlich, vice president at Van Kampen Merritt Investment Advisory Corp. in Lisle, Ill., added, "It's more politically expedient to adjust revenue up than to cut expenditures."

Mr. Hutchison stresses that budget projections often provide ranges rather than precise figures. "Forecasters need to explain to budget officials ranges of predictions and include the statistical error," he said. "Officials involved in the budget process want to pick one number and budget to the penny; they don't want to work within a range."

Then there's politics. Rather than work with estimates, each group latches to revenue estimates that reflect a viewpoint or political agenda rather than economic reality, Mr. Hutchison said.

The standard for error in revenue forecasting is plus or minus three percentage points, which in numerous cases translates to millions of dollars in the budgets of larger cities or states. "In a $1 billion budget, if you're anticipating a 2% surplus ($20 million) but you're 3% off, it could mean either a $50 million surplus or a $10 million deficit," explained Mr. Froehlich.

To protect themselves from such swings after the crash in oil prices in the mid-1980s, several states whose economies are dependent on the oil industry passed constitutional amendments limiting how much of each year's revenue can be appropriated. Oklahoma legislators can plan to spend only 95% of the year's revenue estimate. Any incoming revenue between 95% and 100% of the estimate is held until the following year as a cash balance. Revenue over 100% of the estimate is transferred into a revenue reserve account called the rainy-day fund, explained Nancy Tarr, senior revenue analyst, Oklahoma Office of Management and Budget.

In most states, revenue estimates now rely on econometric models. These models are computer-generated scenarios incorporating national trends for income growth, population growth and inflation to help predict government revenue growth. While these computer-generated models are significantly more sophisticated than older methods of prediction, they also aren't foolproof, said George Leung, vice president for state ratings at credit-rating agency Moody's Investors Service Inc. in New York. The problem is that many of these assumptions reflect national trends, and applying them to forecasts of state revenue can be tricky. In addition, models work best with recurring, somewhat recession-proof revenue like personal income taxes but have a hard time accounting for variables like taxpayer behavior or the strength of the service sector. Corporate income and sales taxes are more volatile, Mr. Leung said, particularly if the sales tax base is narrow and the corporate tax is based on profits rather than assets.

In some governments — and at the federal level — the executive and the legislators produce independent estimates and then haggle over whose numbers will prevail. "When estimates are part of the political process, you're going to see wide variations in the numbers," Mr. Froehlich said. He believes that an independent agency or bipartisan group should be responsible for generating forecasts. "Estimating should be a financial skill, not a political one."

Florida is a classic example of what experts refer to as "consensus revenue forecasting." Elected officials are specifically excluded from sitting on the revenue estimating board. Instead, the board consists of legislative staff members and members of the governor's staff who start with separate estimates but work toward a consensus. Appropriations (money set aside for specific purposes) aren't considered until a consensus is reached on the revenue side. This doesn't guarantee that the estimate is right, just that there will be less mudslinging and political fighting, Mr. Hutchison said.

Governments like Needham, Mass., are turning to software that automates the otherwise dreary process of forecasting revenue and expenditures. "In a fairly painless way it lets you manipulate the numbers," said Needham Administrator Carl F. Valente. "It allows us to look at various assumptions underlying our revenue and expenditure projections."

In December 1991, the Massachusetts government began offering free forecasting software to all 351 local governments in the state as a financial management tool. The software, which runs on a personal computer, was developed by Massachusetts in conjunction with Needham officials. The software stores years of data in one place and, using percentage changes in that data, enables localities to forecast revenue for future years.

The ability to note changes in forecast-related numbers and to obtain instant data can improve the budgeting process and help communities that don't have the resources to develop software themselves, said Rick Kingsley, section chief for technical assistance in the state Revenue Department's Division of Local Services. "It allows you to do the what-ifs" of forecasting, Mr. Valente said. "It lets policy-makers ask, 'If we do this, what's the impact over five years?' " Manual forecasting was time-consuming, the lag time was tremendous and "it's static," Mr. Valente explained. "If we discovered gold in our town tomorrow and want to figure out the revenue, manually it would be very difficult."

The state accumulates an array of information from the cities and towns — including revenue, expenditures and cash reports — and puts it into a data base. Ultimately, the software can accommodate up to 10 years of data, Mr. Kingsley said. The Division of Local Services copies information onto a floppy disk that is sent to any city or town that requests it. The division also helps local staff members with the software and forecasting needs. "It was our desire to provide a service and give the information back to communities in a preprogrammed way so they could use it immediately without having to develop the formulas," Mr. Kingsley said. Although cities and towns with money and professional staff could do the work themselves, fund-balance analyses are sophisticated and many communities do not have the resources, he said.

State officials report it takes up to two weeks to process information requests because the package usually contains 2,000 or so items of data. Although knowledge of Lotus 1-2-3 spreadsheet software is helpful, newcomers also are able to handle the software, Mr. Valente said.

Assessments vary widely in determining tax value of property

Property taxes are clearly the backbone of most local revenue collections, accounting for more than $157.4 billion in local revenue nationally, according to the U.S. Census Bureau. Yet despite the property tax's uniform importance — nearly three of every four local tax dollars come from property taxes — the way property is assessed varies as much across the country as the scenery. And the property tax revolt movements that crop up periodically show that property taxes and their underlying assessments aren't just important issues for government officials . . . the voters take them seriously as well.

Typically, property assessments are completed by the county government. Assessed values in some locales are set annually, elsewhere every two or three years and in some regions less frequently. Except in California, property taxes are based on taxing some percentage of the "current value" of property.

The granddaddy of all property tax revolts, California's Proposition 13 in 1978, set that state's assessment method apart from the rest of the United States. It was the first time a state made an effort to cut assessments loose from a current value system. Trying to curb soaring property tax bills, Proposition 13's creators established a method of basing property taxes on a percentage of a property's most recent purchase price.

Assessments in many jurisdictions are based on property's "full market value," its real value on the open market. Sometimes the assessment is a percentage of that market value, and in some states the tax roll is split, with different classifications of property (residential, commercial, industrial, etc.) assessed at different percentages of full market value (33% of market for residential, for example, and 50% for commercial).

According to Mark S. Gardiner, managing director in the Portland, Ore., office of the Public Financial Management Inc. government financial advisory company, "The closer you are to true market value, the better off you are. The farther you get away from 100% pure cash value, the more any mistake in assessment tends to be magnified."

Property tax assessment increasingly has become a mass appraisal task, differing from the individual appraisal system used by mortgage companies. Instead of relying on individual physical examination of each property, mass appraisal compares property with actual residential market sales from the same area and throughout the county. New homes, additions and remodelings are valued on the basis of individual characteristics, their costs and the value that the work adds to the existing property.

Mass appraisal certainly offers cost advantages to local governments, according to Annie Aubrey, director of communications for the Chicago-based International Association of Assessing Officers. "A single property appraisal costs about $300," she said. "With mass appraisal they're doing it for about $10 to $15 a parcel." And mass appraisal doesn't have to be less accurate than individual appraisal. "When you have computerized mass appraisal, a number of different factors are considered to try to determine value," she said. "We favor full market assessment. It's much less confusing for the taxpayer than fractional assessment. Annual appraisal cycles are best, but sometimes it's not economical for jurisdictions to do that, so up to four years is permissible, assuming there's some sort of indexing or updating in between."

In Oregon, counties assess property at 100% cash value based on physical appraisal every six years, with computerized adjustments reflecting real-estate values in the years in between. But assessments lag even with computerization, said Mr. Gardiner, who is the former director of fiscal administration for the city of Portland. Contrary to what has happened elsewhere in the country, Oregon's real-estate values have gone up, causing some problems from an assessment perspective. Because commercial property values have not increased at the same rate as residential property, a greater portion of the property tax burden has been shifted to residential property owners. To offset that trend, talk has circulated of splitting Oregon's tax roll, assessing residential and commercial property at different percentages of their actual cash value. Such a move could cause problems in the long run, Mr. Gardiner conceded, taking assessments in the state away from the more ideal, and accurate, full market value.

Minnesota uses a multiple class property tax system, where assessed value is based on established market value determined by the county assessor, according to Brian Ducklow, assessor of Ramsey County, which covers St. Paul. Rates for each class established by the Minnesota Legislature are applied to the established market value to determine the basis of figuring property tax liability. As in many states, residential property that fits statutory guidelines as "homestead" property benefits from preferential rates. Minnesota law requires that 25% of the parcels of property in the county be reassessed each year. In the interim years, market values of property not scheduled for reassessment can be adjusted by using value trend and market analysis.

According to William H. Cook, assessor of Santa Barbara County, Calif., 80 miles northwest of Los Angeles, an ideal assessment scheme would be like Minnesota's, beginning with an ad valorem system that uses a property's market value as its basis, with a periodic reassessment to keep that value figure accurate. A check on the tax rate along with an ad valorem system would be the ideal, Mr. Cook indicated, so that "if assessments went up, the tax rate would come down." The optimum reassessment cycle would be determined by the rate of inflation, Mr. Cook explained.

In times of rapid inflation, it would be best to reassess every three years, "and you're certainly capable of doing that with our computers and our analysis of properties. Annually could be accomplished, but I think that is overkill. Besides, you don't want to get property owners upset every year."

Unhappiness among California property owners, fueled by the lack of a check on tax rates and changes in assessed value, led to California's Proposition 13. Property tax bills skyrocketed as property values and assessments increased dramatically. "If you would follow California's property tax system for the years I've been involved in it, one could see very readily what was happening," Mr. Cook said. A study prepared by Mr. Cook showed property taxes rising from between 2.5% and 3% of the average household income to more than 10% in the period between 1960 and the mid-1970s. Approved in 1978, Proposition 13 rolled back property taxes to 1975 levels and limited any future property taxes to 1% of purchase price, with just a 2% annual tax increase for inflation.

Essentially, Proposition 13 provided that the assessed value of property in California no longer be adjusted every year to reflect market value. Instead, the purchase price became the new assessed value, adjusted with each change of ownership. Because assessed value can be moved upward a maximum of only 2% a year as California housing prices increase dramatically (25% or more in some years since Proposition 13's passage), assessed values in the state typically lag far behind actual market value. Huge discrepancies have developed between the amount of taxes paid on similar property, depending on when the property was purchased. Those discrepancies led several property owners to challenge the measure in court.

On June 18, 1992, the U.S. Supreme Court upheld Proposition 13 by a vote of 8-1. The plaintiff in that case, Stephanie Nordlinger, bought her first home in southwestern Los Angeles in 1988 for $170,000. Under the terms of Proposition 13, her initial property tax bill was 1% of that amount, or $1,700. Her neighbors, who bought virtually identical homes in the 1970s, had tax bills averaging only $376 per year. That tax treatment was unfair and unconstitutional, Ms. Nordlinger charged. After California state courts dismissed Ms. Nordlinger's complaint, the U.S. Supreme Court sanctioned Proposition 13's ironically named "welcome stranger" provision that had forced some home buyers to pay as much as 17 times more in taxes than neighbors who purchased before 1978. While California's property tax system — which has yielded about $17 billion a year in revenue — is considered unique, the court ruling encouraged other states to consider similar plans. Justice Harry A. Blackmun, writing for the court, said the system "is not palpably arbitrary" even though it may seem unfair to younger prospective buyers. He said the system reasonably operates to further "local neighborhood preservation, continuity and stability." Mr. Blackmun also said it is reasonable for

14

the state to give a tax break to existing owners over new owners because "a new owner has full information about the scope of future tax liability before acquiring the property, and if he thinks the future tax burden is too demanding, he can decide not to complete the purchase at all."

Revenue officials clamp down on tax delinquents

State and local officials periodically launch programs that go after tax delinquents who are cheating governments out of millions of dollars. The programs are especially popular when government revenue drops during uncertain economic times.

Automation has enabled many revenue departments to operate at higher levels of efficiency in tracking down tax deadbeats. "They're working a lot smarter" than in years past, said Verenda Smith, head of intergovernmental relations at the Federation of Tax Administrators, Washington.

Illinois is responsible for collecting 62 types of taxes, the largest being income and sales taxes, said Kevin Johnson, state Revenue Department spokesman. The department intends to start several pilot projects. One would allow delinquent taxpayers to pay with credit cards. Another would transfer tax payments electronically to state coffers from taxpayers' bank accounts. In January 1992, Illinois started a program using its lottery commission to enforce payment of taxes. When a retail outlet owes back taxes, the state suspends the lottery license and withholds lucrative lottery terminals until the store forks over the money. Other state agencies also work with the Revenue Department. For years, Illinois officials have embraced similar tactics with liquor licenses and corporate charters. "We're trying to leverage the taxpayers into paying us before they pay other creditors," explained Paul Wiley, accounts receivables program administrator for the Illinois Revenue Department. "In trying times, to meet payrolls and continue the business, people let their tax liabilities slide. They'll pay suppliers first. We sometimes sink three or four notches down the totem pole. We use any element that would affect the business and get them to pay."

The state of Louisiana, which administers 26 taxes, has saved work and money by turning over responsibilities for out-of-state collections to a Pennsylvania-based firm that gets a cut of whatever it collects, said Jane Dupuy, supervisor of the enforcement section of the Collection Division of the Louisiana Department of Revenue. The state has run newspaper and radio advertisements warning debtors of the long arm of the law. Whatever the state government gets is gravy because the collection agency receives payment from the delinquent taxpayer.

A Maryland tax consultant has dusted off a statute that is helping that state recover money from out-of-state delinquents. The statute, which allows Maryland to file its tax liens in other states under reciprocal agreements, received $19,000 from one tax

15

cheat who moved to New York, said Stuart Cordish, tax consultant with Maryland's Income Tax Division. "It could be a real big source of revenue," he said. "Before this, we've been stopped at the border. Forty-four states have reciprocal statutes, but no one uses it because tax departments have never heard of it." Maryland's statute has been on the books since 1950, he added, but had not been used effectively until 1992.

New York City officials have attempted to go after large property owners' personal assets rather than foreclosing on property, which dumps landlord responsibilities onto city government. "With a budget crunch, we search out every possible way we can to increase revenue," said Joseph Dunn, spokesman for the city's Department of Finance. In the first three quarters of fiscal 1992, property tax owners owed the city $563 million, a 15% jump over the previous year. "A lot of these people do not pay on time and sort of use the city as a bank. They do pay interest, but they don't mind that," Mr. Dunn said.

Since much tax delinquency stems from ignorance, many officials agree an education program that teaches compliance is one of the most effective ways to get taxes paid. "One thing we're trying to do is more effort in the customer service area. We want to get information to businesses as early as possible so they understand their tax liability," said Dwight E. Lahti, assistant commissioner of the Minnesota Department of Revenue. "The longer you wait, the more expensive to collect."

Florida officials agree they need to educate new residents about their state's taxation methods. Although Florida doesn't have an income tax, it levies a variety of other taxes, such as a tax on stocks and bonds. Jere N. Moore, director of the Department of Revenue, said the Florida government would collect another $1 billion a year in taxes if it received everything it was owed. More than half is from people who don't know they owe, he said.

GAAP gives constituents a clearer picture of the budget

Generally accepted accounting principles, better known as GAAP (pronounced "gap"), are encouraged by the Governmental Accounting Standards Board of Norwalk, Conn., a self-regulatory organization that works to standardize practices in financial reporting for local governments across the United States. The board possesses no enforcement powers but is respected by Wall Street and government officials for its pronouncements and suggestions on financial matters. GAAP uses so-called accrual-based accounting, considered by most experts to give a more accurate picture of a government's financial condition than cash-based accounting. Under the accrual system, expenses and income are recorded and apportioned for the period in which they take place — regardless of whether the revenue has been received or the check has been written.

For example, if the fiscal year for a government using cash-based accounting ends on Dec. 31, and if an official with that government on Dec. 27 receives a large bill for, say, sewer system repairs completed by a local business, that official could wait until Jan. 1 to pay the bill so the expense would be recorded in the next fiscal year instead of the current fiscal year; the temptation to hold off on paying the bill would be especially strong if the government were anticipating a deficit for the current fiscal year. Under accrual reporting, however, the bill would be recorded as a government payment on Dec. 27 (the day the bill was received) even if the official were to wait until the next fiscal year to write out a check to pay the amount.

But not every official believes GAAP is necessary for government. As the Government Finance Officers Association's booklet warns, "Opinions differ regarding the need to adopt budgets that follow GAAP. This lack of professional consensus can result in elected officials and the public receiving inconsistent information. The budget may contain numbers presented on a budgetary basis, while the financial report contains numbers prepared on a GAAP basis. Consequently, administrative personnel sometimes are accused of 'keeping two sets of books.' If complete integration of formats is impossible, budget and accounting officers should be encouraged to reconcile and explain differences in their reporting bases."

Many state and local governments have avoided moving to GAAP because their books will show negative balances during the first year of the new accounting system. Not so in Wyoming. Changes in Wyoming's accounting practices, spurred in large part by two national magazines' reports in 1992 criticizing the state government's financial management, were expected to produce a one-time windfall of roughly $180 million over a two-year period, Gov. Mike Sullivan and state Auditor Dave Ferrari said. But the Democratic governor warned that the state's financial problems should not prompt legislators to try to tap the windfall. "This one-time bulge in state funds should not be used for ongoing operations and should not be viewed by either the citizens or by the Legislature as a way to get away from the serious problems that we have with respect to revenues and expenditures," Mr. Sullivan said. Instead, the governor wanted to see the money spent on one-time needs, such as on capital construction projects and investments or to address deferred maintenance.

Wyoming's financial reporting changes were expected to require about 18 months to take hold. They would move the state from a cash-based accounting system to one that tracked accrued revenue. For instance, whereas in the past some revenue was collected during one fiscal year but not accounted for until distributed the following year, the new system would account for the money as soon as it was collected. As a result, dollars from sales and severance taxes and mineral royalties would be credited to the period in which they were earned rather than building up for as much as six months before being credited as income.

"What we're trying to do is give the public and the people of Wyoming a more accurate and clearer picture of revenues and expenditures in the same year," Mr. Ferrari said.

The move to accounting principles recognized by the Governmental Accounting Standards Board was motivated in part by an article in *Financial World,* a national magazine, that called Wyoming the worst-managed state in the country because it spent almost all of its budget reserve account, had poor employee and program performance evaluation systems, and did not follow GAAP. A similar survey by *City & State* newspaper placed Wyoming in a tie with Wisconsin for fifth place among the best-managed state governments but also warned that Wyoming was not on GAAP.

When Mr. Ferrari took office in 1991, he listed among his objectives the need to bring the state accounting system in line with GAAP. "Wyoming is one of the few states that does not now have GAAP accounting," the auditor said. "This state does not want to have the reputation of being in the Dark Ages."

Messrs. Sullivan and Ferrari explained that the changes would produce a one-time infusion of $215.9 million at the end of the fiscal 1993-1994 biennium; roughly $180 million would accrue for state government and most of the rest would go to local governments around Wyoming.

Finance officials are wary of potential bank failures

Guardians of government revenue have grown cautious over the health of the banks with which they do business.

"California has more than its share of banks on the danger list," said Dan Daly, chief investment officer for San Francisco, which in the last four years has seen the closing of two banks that held a small portion of city funds.

Indeed, experts say concern over tighter banking regulations is most pressing in California, where banks are saddled with bad real-estate debt and public officials have not yet been exposed to the bank crises that awakened officials in Texas, the Farm Belt and New England in the early 1990s.

On Dec. 19, 1992, a key provision of the 1991 Federal Deposit Insurance Corp. (FDIC) Improvement Act kicked in, requiring regulators to take tougher measures against banks that maintain low ratios of capital to assets. Measures could include closings of the weakest banks in that group. Banking officials insist banks are getting stronger overall, but people like 1992 independent presidential candidate H. Ross Perot and U.S. House of Representatives Banking Committee Chairman Henry B. Gonzalez, D-Texas, have claimed that bank woes could develop into a major crisis.

Whoever is right, local government officials are approaching the investment of public funds with a new vigilance. Many are seeking the advice of financial rating companies and shunning relationships with banks that rank low on the agencies' measures of relative strength.

"Public treasurers should be concerned," said Earl R. Hoenes, director of cash management services for Sheshunoff Information Services Inc., Austin, Texas. He pointed out that, as of Dec. 19, 1992, federal regulators were required to move faster against weak banks, and they were not required to pay uninsured deposits. The FDIC insures deposits of up to $100,000 at each federally insured bank. But while it used to be understood that depositors at failed banks also would recover their uninsured money in full, the FDIC Improvement Act makes it more likely for large depositors, including local governments, to suffer some losses.

Sheshunoff and other rating agencies offer clear advice to their public sector clients: No matter what social goals they try to accomplish in investing public funds, safety should come first.

"Public officials have got to have more information about banks than they've had because of the political risk involved," said David C. Cates, chairman of Washington-based Ferguson & Co., which administers the Cates Bank Rating Service. "Citizens will ask if a government has deposits in a troubled bank."

The city of Southfield, Mich., near Detroit, tries to balance the safety of its investments against its goal of rewarding community-oriented banks. City Treasurer Roman Gronkowski said banking decisions are based first on an institution's rating, then on how the bank is meeting requirements under the Community Reinvestment Act and finally on whether the bank offers the kinds of services the city needs.

In many states, local officials are heartened by state statutes requiring that all municipal deposits be collateralized; in other words, the deposits must be backed by bank securities of similar value. But bank rating firms urge officials to study those statutes because not all collateral agreements are created equal. Mr. Hoenes said it is not enough for a state simply to require collateral for government deposits. The Government Finance Officers Association offers guidelines for collateralization, including a recommendation that the collateral be held by a third-party bank, but some states ignore the advice. Mr. Cates said collateralization requirements do not always ensure next-day access to funds if a bank closes. According to Mr. Daly, San Francisco waited 10 days for interest payments after a minority-owned bank in Oakland failed in 1988. The San Francisco government was paid interest for the 10-day period.

Officials in Overland Park, Kan., near Kansas City learned in 1992 that governments need to monitor the status of their collateral. On two occasions, officials found that a bank with which they did business traded a portion of the city's collateral, once leaving the city's account underpledged by $1 million. "Some of our banks don't seem to take this as a serious concern, so now we monitor our collateral daily," said Dave Scott, Overland Park's manager of finance and accounting. A large thrift in the Kansas community appeared on a list of banks that on June 30, 1992, had capital ratios that could have triggered corrective action. But Overland Park taxpayers didn't need to worry; the city avoided investing in the savings and loan because of its low ratings from outside agencies, Mr. Scott said.

Some communities feel more secure about collateral agreements for their funds. David Schuler, cash manager for Garland, Texas, in Dallas County, said city policy requires that collateral for municipal deposits be placed in a third-party bank.

Today's uncertain times would seem to dictate the need for more flexibility in a city's investment options. However, many communities adhere to rigid practices that limit their ability to invest outside the city. For day-to-day banking, about 85% of local governments require by policy or statute that deposits be made with local banks, Mr. Hoenes estimated. That certainly is good community policy, he said, but it must be weighed against safety, especially in small communities where "local-only" requirements limit one's options. "If only one bank in town has the machinery allowing you to clear checks and negotiate wire transfers, maybe you should reconsider the local-only policy," Mr. Hoenes said.

Merger mania is a factor that requires public treasurers to study banking trends. According to Mr. Scott, constant rumors about Missouri banks buying out their Kansas neighbors require a closer look at bank rating data.

For many communities skittish about their investment options, there is an alternative: local government investment pools managed either by states or private companies. At least 28 states manage pools in which municipal cash is invested jointly and earnings are paid out proportionately. Many of the pools invest in a wider variety of instruments than the individual local governments, which traditionally keep much of their money in bank certificates of deposit. Connecticut's state pool, for example, which carries about 100 municipal accounts, invests in government securities, certificates of deposit, commercial paper and repurchase agreements.

Officials often assume that since the local bank has been around for years and its president seems optimistic about the future, nothing can go wrong, Mr. Hoenes warned. "They should be looking beyond that," he insisted.

Information technology

Information technology — computers, telecommunications and the like — are changing the world of government, usually for the better. Technological advancements are allowing state and local officials to serve their constituents more efficiently in a variety of areas, from providing access to government information to repairing potholes to passing out welfare benefits.

Unfortunately, financial problems are forcing governments to cut budgets on information technology, one area where cost savings can be substantial. Do more with less — that's the message state, county and city budget officials are sending to information technology directors around the country. As more jurisdictions post deficits, management information system departments and other information technology bureaus are being forced to cut staff, trim budgets and pick up the slack with more efficient uses of technology.

"There's no question that budget cuts have become endemic to government information technology departments," said Roderick Chu, worldwide director of the Andersen Consulting government practice in New York. "When there are 35 or so states with substantial budgetary deficits, there's no question that those deficits are going to affect the way government uses technology. Everyone is being forced to do more with less. Most jurisdictions are trying to increase tax revenue with more technology and less manpower and become more efficient in providing services with automation. But, at the same time, their ability to expand technology is being curtailed."

Jeff Held, partner in the national strategic planning division of Ernst & Young in Vienna, Va., agreed: "Governments are chopping information technology budgets and, in many cases, undermining the most important resource they have for long-term savings. Cutting information technology budgets is like shooting yourself in the foot."

Support is lacking for states' high-tech operations

In a report to the National Association of State Information Resource Executives (NASIRE), Lexington, Ky., 10 state governments in the association's Eastern region reported budget, salary and staff cutbacks in information technology departments. Though budget cuts are a national problem for state governments, according to the NASIRE, the Eastern region was hit particularly hard. In Rhode Island, for example, state employees took a 14% pay cut as part of a deficit reduction plan and the state information technology agency cut staff by 10%. In other Eastern states, Delaware's information processing agency returned $500,000 from its budget by eliminating vacancies, cutting expenditures and suggesting early retirements. Pennsylvania's centralized information processing department had its $250 million budget cut by 20%. Vermont reorganized its information processing activities, transferring some of the staff directly to other agencies.

Some financially struggling states, however, reported support for new technology or ongoing information technology initiatives that promised long-term cost savings. In Connecticut, where only essential state services were being funded, the state budgeted for a 400-mile fiber-optic network projected to save $120 million over a period of several years.

In Texas, state officials consolidated some information technology areas and expanded others, reported Ann Baker, associate deputy director of strategic planning and policy. Following recommendations taken from an in-depth study of state operations conducted by a blue-ribbon panel and state information technology staff, Texas expected to save at least $3 million in the 1992-1993 biennial budget. Report recommendations included long-term commitments to an open systems environment (in which all state computers would be compatible), shared software and data bases, and a statewide shared geographic information system (GIS), according to Ms. Baker. "In the short term, many of the recommendations will cost the state some money," she said. "In the long term, we will save money by providing a more efficient information technology environment."

"You've got to spend some money to save money," agreed Loleta A. Didrickson, director of the Illinois Department of Employment Security. The department earned dividends from automation developed during the mid-1980s when extended unemployment benefits went into effect in November 1991. According to Ms. Didrickson, the department generated more than 65,000 letters to potential recipients of the expanded benefits in fewer than 48 hours. The automated system also helped the state create a self-certification form that reduced the load on the department's staff. "The cost of this project will be somewhere between $4 million and $7 million," she said, "but by using the unautomated procedures of several years ago, it would've cost the state $20 million or more." Automation also helped the department reduce staff to 3,000 from more than 6,000 employees in the 1970s and eliminate a $2.5 million deficit recorded in the mid-1980s.

Many local governments are trying to use technology internally to reduce costs and improve service while cutting back on personnel, according to consultants and information technology department heads. However, out-sourcing (entering into a contract with private industry to provide some services) seems to be losing popularity. "If you are taking work from a poorly run department and giving it to an efficient contractor, out-sourcing works," Mr. Held said. "But if you try to take work from a relatively well-run department, out-sourcing will cost you money in the long run, regardless of the contract cost. The first years will show savings, but expect costs to go up."

Working internally, "local governments basically have two directions," said Mr. Chu, who was New York's tax commissioner from 1983 to 1985. "They can use technology to maximize tax and investment revenue in the treasury department and reduce expenditures in other departments by providing more efficient service."

For example, in Merced County, Calif., east of San Jose, the Human Services Agency automated welfare eligibility operations in 1990 with its Merced Automated Global Information Control System. The agency used "expert system" software that evaluated benefit applications according to a series of rules developed by agency staff and Andersen Consulting, removing much of the clerical and evaluation responsibilities from staff caseworkers. The result, according to Rita Kidd, director of the system, was an annual savings of $4 million and successful compliance with the county's employment attrition program. The agency immediately absorbed a 30% staff reduction, thanks to the greater efficiency of automation. The greatest achievement of the system was the improvement in accuracy, Ms. Kidd added.

At the city level, finance departments are turning to automated procedures to maximize returns on investments. In Dallas, Robert Dulaney, cash and debt administrator, began using TRACS, an online service based in Salt Lake City, Utah, as the Dallas city government's key investment monitoring tool. "Like all municipalities, we have to be more efficient in our cash and investment management," Mr. Dulaney said. "By using TRACS, I can keep closer watch on our investments and work smarter. We need a system that is fast and comprehensive and doesn't require a lot of analysis at our end." The service provides 24-hour-a-day investment monitoring and cash-flow forecasting, he said, maximizing returns on funds used for public programs.

Making public access work for governments

As more state and local government agencies offer public information to constituents through online computer access systems, information systems managers should heed a warning and some advice: There is such a thing as too much access, but in the long run it can work for you.

In Montgomery County, Pa., north of Philadelphia, online access to property information, real-estate records, court calendars and registered trademarks has been available for years, but usage of the system ballooned in the early 1990s — almost beyond the county's ability to manage it. The county began offering local law firms and corporations access through teletype systems in 1982 and later through personal computers and telephone modems. The number of information transactions eventually increased to 350,000 from 3,000 per month, reported Ray Seidel, executive director of the Montgomery County Information Systems. "We started out with two telephone lines and telex machines, answering questions about land records transmitted to our offices here in Norristown," he explained. "A few thousand transactions a month was manageable and everyone in the county liked the idea of not having to come to the courthouse for routine information."

In 1983, the county added information from the Montgomery County Court Administrator's Office, including schedules for the county's 16 judges, trial assignments and arbitration case schedules. The new data base was extremely popular with local attorneys because it eliminated the need for multiple courthouse trips to check dockets, Mr. Seidel said. By 1987, the information system was so popular that transactions increased to 50,000 per month through 25 telephone lines. The data needs spurred the county to expand its mainframe computer system at a cost of $5 million in 1988. In 1990, usage reached 340,000 transactions over 36 telephone lines, and the county was ready for a change in procedures, Mr. Seidel recalled. "About 10% was entertainment usage, people just browsing through the system looking around at what we had, not transacting any real business," he said. "We had to do something to identify users and control activity."

The solution was an information gateway service from Bell Atlantic Corp. in Philadelphia, parent of the county's regional telephone carrier, Bell of Pennsylvania. In October 1991, Montgomery County switched its online service from its own computer bulletin board and telephone lines to Bell Atlantic's Intelligate Business Service, a network switching service regulating access to public and private information data bases. Among other services available through Intelligate were the Trademark Register, a data base of 800,000 U.S. registered trademarks; Accurate Realty, allowing

real-estate buyers and sellers to analyze property values in Philadelphia and its suburbs; and *USA Today* news stories. Intelligate
required users to register with the service, submit to a credit
check and use special software with their personal computers.
Intelligate charged 10 cents per minute for access time, returning
about 80% of the charges to the county.

"We reduced entertainment use to almost nothing in the first
full year and we reduced overall usage by about 30%," Mr. Seidel
said.

Though many users were surprised and disturbed by the
changes, most regular users adapted quickly to the new requirements. By August 1992, total monthly usage was back up to more
than 350,000 transactions.

"Because of the gateway service, volume and the telephone
company's billing system, we are recovering part of our costs,"
Mr. Seidel said. The service generated about $150,000 per month.
The revenue was used to offset the $200,000 monthly cost of the
service. The lesson, according to Mr. Seidel, was this: "It will not
be long before all county, state and municipal governments will
be offering comprehensive information from their courthouses
and other agencies. They should start planning now."

Neighboring Bucks County, Pa., which began using the Intelligate system in July 1992 to control online access to deeds and
land parcel information, recently added civil courts information,
according to Jim Kelly, county project manager. "What we were
trying to do is come up with a mirror image of Montgomery
County," he said. "Online access to data has become very big with
attorneys and real-estate agents in Philadelphia and has created a
big demand for information. Our data base is the key to closing
the title search loop." Though Bucks County has maintained a
computerized data base of land information since 1980, it began
experimenting with online access only in 1991 — developing a
client base of about 90 corporate or law firm users. "It's certainly
cheaper to dial up the data than to send a paralegal or an attorney
to Doylestown (the county seat) to pick up hard copy," Mr. Kelly
said. Bucks County now averages about 160 calls per month, representing 95% of the title information requests, he said. "About
5% of cases require personal attention or hard copy from the
courthouse, but the online connection now replaces most of the
visits," he said.

Under surveillance: Public files open privacy debate

*"The murderer tracked his victim to his new address using
records obtained from the State Department of Motor Vehicles'
computer data base."*

— *Television anchorman*

Murder by government data base hasn't happened yet, but one
tragedy, such as the fictionalized news account above, is all it

would take to turn the issue of privacy and government records into a national crisis, said Iowa state Sen. Richard Varn, chairman of a National Conference of State Legislatures task force on information policy.

"Privacy is a growing concern for many Americans," the Democrat said, "an issue waiting to become a crisis, depending upon circumstances. As soon as someone is hurt or killed because of government information revealed about that person, it will become a crisis. We should be dealing with this concern in a systematic way before the issue turns into a crisis."

Advances in information technology, including long-distance computer networks, powerful data base software and GIS, are making it hard for state and local governments to keep up with their evolving responsibilities, Mr. Varn said. New storage media such as compact disks and electronic transfer of data over telephone lines have replaced paper printouts and made government data more easily accessible to a wide variety of potential users. "Our task force is just beginning to look at the issues involved," he said, "and they are complex."

Government information technology managers and industry consultants agree that privacy issues are becoming more complex with every new data processing and telecommunications development. Three questions are key:

- What information should be available to the public?
- In what form should information be provided?
- How much should a local government charge for access to the information?

"Local government has a responsibility for stewardship of data that goes back 200 years, and there is an implied responsibility for confidentiality in that relationship," noted Michael A. Mische, principal at A.T. Kearney Inc., Chicago, and an expert in data privacy issues. "But as local governments' ability to gather and manipulate data increases, the data is becoming a powerful asset. It can be an asset for better government, but it also can be a powerful commercial asset." As a result, local governments often are asked to provide government-collected data to companies that use the data for commercial development or marketing mailing lists. "Governments could aggregate the data they make available to obscure personal information, but it is not clear that commercial users shouldn't have the right to the more specific data. It all depends on state laws," Mr. Mische said.

GIS technology poses special privacy problems, added Larry Engelken, principal at United Graphics Consultants in Englewood, Colo., a GIS consulting company. As state and local governments develop huge shared data bases that contain digitized maps and individual land record information, they are under pressure to make this information available in computer formats to real-estate development companies and data resellers. "Tax assessors, for example, are always receiving requests for public map data and the specific individual information that accompanies those data sets," Mr. Engelken explained. The opportunity to charge commercial users for this data is attractive, he added, as agencies seek to recover the expense of gathering and digitizing the original data. Mr. Engelken believes that when an agency does charge for data, government should charge a fair price that can offset some of the expense of data-gathering and maintaining a computerized system.

But it is not always clear what data should be made available and how much should be charged. "The result is a constant balancing act between the public's right to know, which includes commercial entities, and the government's fiduciary responsibility toward information gathered from individuals," Mr. Engelken said. "The best advice I can give is to organize your activities the best you can according to your statutory responsibilities and keep as much as possible to the purpose for which the data was intended."

In many states, however, statutory responsibilities may not be clear under local public records acts. According to a survey conducted by Nevada state researchers for presentation to a legislative subcommittee on laws governing public records, only 29 states have detailed provisions and deadlines for controlling access to government data, and only nine states have laws that acknowledge electronic distribution of information. Fred Dugger, manager of information systems for the Nevada Legislature and chairman of the information policy committee of the NASIRE, said the survey reveals that most state public records laws are "antiquated and badly in need of an update." Many states simply have not kept up with the changes in data maintenance and accessibility wrought by technology. Those that have, including Alaska, California, Illinois, Indiana and Minnesota, need to share their perspectives with other states, Mr. Dugger said. As an organization, the NASIRE is beginning to take steps to create a forum for these issues through the information policy committee.

Despite concerns about the privacy of individual data, most states aren't looking at restricting public information. But many states are examining their policies on the packaging of information and the recovery of costs involved in providing data to commercial users. Most state information technology executives agree that local governments have the right to recover costs from commercial concerns that request data in special electronic formats, but the definition of costs is not clear. Costs may include a portion of the investment local governments must make in gathering and computerizing their data as well as the expense of providing that data to users.

In Florida, a state that already has revised its statutes to cover electronic access to data, local governments are developing a strong service attitude toward the delivery of their information, said Manuel Garcia, director of computer systems and information technology in Dade County. "I feel very strongly about my responsibility as a public administrator," Mr. Garcia said, "and ensuring the citizens' right to access public information is fundamental to my job." Ensuring access for an individual, however, is not exactly the same as ensuring access for a profit-making enterprise. "The Florida public records law is very liberal. With the exception of criminal histories and the personal addresses of police and court officers, virtually all of the data collected by local governments is available," Mr. Garcia said. State law allows local governments to charge commercial fees that can recover a prorated portion of the expense of gathering and delivering the data, Mr. Garcia noted, and Dade County has developed, and charges for, an online communications service that provides subscribers with computerized data via telephone modem. The service, which has about 200 users, costs $175 for installation and $75 per month.

Mr. Garcia, chairman of the Urban Consortium Telecommunications and Information Task Force, an ad hoc group of large local government information technology executives, believes that more local governments should take advantage of the rising demand for public data. He recommends local governments turn the delivery of the data into a revenue stream that can help pay for technology upgrades and the development of new government services.

Mr. Chu of Andersen Consulting added, "Changing information technology is leading to a whole philosophical change for local governments in the way they deal with public records." The evolving power and value of government information should lead local governments to take a "customer service-oriented approach" to information management. Local governments should create systems that can provide commercial information users with the data they seek, "and there is no reason why the cost of developing those systems and gathering that data should not be 100% recoverable," Mr. Chu said.

Still, local governments also should continue to serve the privacy needs of individuals by making government data reviewable and changeable by the people it represents, he said. Mr. Chu suggested that the same advances in information technology that have expanded the data collected by local governments also be used to ensure privacy and accuracy. Public access kiosks, for example, could allow individuals to review government records and request changes in inaccurate information.

Minnesota voter network speeds election results

Crowds, confusion and nail-biting into the wee hours of the night have always been a part of the romance of Election Day. Voters line up to cast their votes. Election judges scramble to check registrations. Everyone stays up late to watch the results.

During the 1992 election season, however, the old-fashioned

romance began disappearing in Minnesota, overtaken by speed, efficiency and sophisticated online automation. During the state's primary on Sept. 15 of that year, Minnesota election officials unveiled the latest development in their multiyear, multimillion-dollar voter registration and election results automation project. Using the 1500-terminal online network that linked the state's 87 counties and 2.7 million voters into a central voter registration data base, the state began online reporting of election results. The technique was designed to improve the reporting process and speed up returns — delivering some results within minutes after the polls closed, boasted Joe Manski, Minnesota's director of elections. "Our goal is to have everyone home and in bed by 12:15 on election night," Mr. Manski said.

The state voter network, which operated on a Unisys 2200 mainframe computer using MAPPER fourth generation programming language, began with a 1987 mandate from the Minnesota Legislature to improve statewide voter registration, explained Tim Hanson, director of information services for the Secretary of State's Office. "Most voter registration takes place at the county level. Some wanted a network that could be used jointly by the state and the counties, a system that would allow counties to accumulate the voter data as they had been doing, but enter the information into a data base that could be shared with other counties around the state," he said. "That's why we chose an online network model."

The mainframe data base and the statewide communications network went online in May 1988, allowing county officials to dial up the system in the state capital of St. Paul from terminals linked to their own host computers. They then could enter voter registration data. Once the information was in the data base, the system worked in several ways:

■ Updating records whenever a voter registered at a new address and notified local officials of the change.

■ Printing voter verification cards, which were mailed from a central location.

■ Checking for duplication and eliminating names of deceased voters.

According to Minnesota Secretary of State Joan Growe, the system generated 270,000 verification cards in 1991 and produced more than 500,000 cards for the 1992 presidential election. Since as many as 20% of Minnesota's voter records change each year, the online network has eliminated vast amounts of manual filing, mailing and other record-keeping at the county level, she said.

After the 1990 U.S. census, the state found another use for the system — redrawing district boundaries. Using the flexibility and graphics of the MAPPER computer language, the state was able to directly compare voter data with the geographic information from the GIS that the state used to redraw district boundaries, Mr. Hanson said. Data from both systems was loaded into a precinct-

29

finder program that automatically reassigned voting precincts and election districts.

"To my knowledge, no state has attempted to do what we are doing," Mr. Manski said. "We will not only have better and more accurate geographic records between census years, but the legislative and local jurisdictions will have a much easier time in doing what they have to do."

The power of the online network generated the election brainstorm, Mr. Manski added. "Since 1984, Minnesota has been using some computerization for reporting of election results, but the automation has never been used statewide. It occurred to us that, with this statewide network in place, we also had a tool for election reporting." For the Sept. 15 primary, county election officials in 82 of the state's 87 counties used the network to enter local results, which were tabulated as part of the statewide totals. Five counties transmitted results directly from voting equipment, using optical character scan voting systems already in place. The primary test indicated that the statewide network could generate returns faster and more efficiently than manual reporting of results by telephone, Mr. Manski said. "In some cases we had results from precincts within 15 minutes after the polls had closed. As we expand the number of counties that have their voting equipment online, we can greatly speed up the process and get our results complete by the evening news."

The September trial received national attention. Representatives from several states, including Georgia, Tennessee and Texas, were on hand for the primary and a seminar on the system the next morning. "What makes Minnesota's system unique is that it is online," said Dick Molpus, Mississippi secretary of state and president of the National Association of Secretaries of State. "We are entering a new era in which state election officials need voter information that is both reliable and cost-efficient. That's why I think you'll see states across the country looking with very keen interest at the system in Minnesota."

Computerized maintenance hits the road in Arizona county

For years, information on the roads maintained by the Maricopa County (Ariz.) Highway Department was as far-flung as the roads themselves — scattered over more than 9,000 square miles of territory. But a computerized transportation management system being developed by the department soon will put an end to that problem. The system will bring information now contained in several data bases together into a single GIS that holds the potential for millions of dollars in savings in highway maintenance costs.

In the past, Maricopa County used a non-geographic data base that included information such as width of roads, pavement types and pavement depths, according to Frank Harrison, GIS manager with the Maricopa County Department of Transportation. The county also possessed data bases on accidents, traffic volume and sign types. "We've been maintaining those things for a long time but, unfortunately, they're in different data bases, they aren't able to be used with one another and they aren't geographic," Mr. Harrison lamented.

When completed, the new system — the largest GIS in the country, boast Maricopa County officials — will provide an index at any point on the GIS map to all known road information about the site. If, for example, county officials wanted to look up pavement type, traffic volume and accident rate information at a specific site, they would be able to do so with a single query. As things stand now, "we'd have to make three separate queries and correlate all the information," Mr. Harrison said.

Officials in Maricopa County, which covers the Phoenix metropolitan area and beyond, began the project by acquiring an Arizona Department of Transportation computerized data base identifying vehicle accident locations. The next step will be to tie the different data bases together through road name and mapmatching. Adding graphics to the raw data will allow the information to be more easily displayed.

Besides providing easy access to the full range of data for any spot in the county's 3,000-mile road network, the GIS will generate visual presentations to accompany funding requests. The system should enable county officials to maintain their roads more efficiently, generating an estimated $100 million in savings over the first decade, county Supervisor Tom Freestone estimated. The comprehensive data base will save the county money by enabling Maricopa County highway officials to better coordinate maintenance functions. "We don't like to admit it, but at times we have a striping crew coming down the road in one direction and a paving crew coming up the road the other way," Mr. Harrison said. The county will make more efficient use of road crews sent to remote areas for specific road repairs by using the system. Before a crew leaves a specific location, county officials will be able to identify other work the crew might be able to do in the area on the same trip. "The other big saving will be in just knowing what we have and being able to coordinate how we use our money," Mr. Harrison said.

The transportation management system ultimately will cost Maricopa County about $550,000 to develop. The price tag covers consulting, labor, hardware and software. The cost has stayed low because much of the work has been kept in-house. The system is based on ARC/INFO GIS software by Environmental Systems Research Institute Inc., Redlands, Calif., operating on a hardware platform of UNIX workstations and networked personal computers. Once in place, the highway data base should be of use to other county departments and state agencies that rely on information based on street addresses. Maricopa County officials also might share the system with municipalities located in the county.

Child protection: Social worker in a computer

It was late at night when the police picked up a drug-addicted mother and her child and charged the woman with using crack cocaine. After booking her, the police called a county child welfare worker at home. The worker, on call day and night, reached for his lap-top computer and punched in all the relevant information. When the family's complete record showed up on the screen, he drove to the woman's address and found four children, all asleep. The five youngsters ultimately were placed in a foster home. "If we didn't have the information close at hand and at night, those four could have awakened and not known what had happened to their mother or what to do," said Wes Bowerman, director of the Berrien County (Mich.) Department of Social Services. In the "old days," said Mr. Bowerman, the worker would not have had access to the information at night. Those five children avoided a scary, miserable period they could have suffered until someone figured out that their mother was gone and found the right government agency to help.

The difference between the well-remembered, but not lamented, "old days" and today is the county's installation of a computerized Child Protection System (CPS), a product of Bull HN Information Systems of Billerica, Mass. Berrien County is an urban-rural county with a population of 163,000 people in the southwestern corner of Michigan. Its size is one reason it was selected as the site of a pilot project for Bull's system, Mr. Bowerman said. The county averages 160 child cases per month, or close to 2,000 per year. An additional 253 cases per month need foster home care, about 30 for each worker, Mr. Bowerman pointed out. While not all the cases come from the lower socio-economic areas of Niles and Benton Harbor, most do. "We are measurable," Mr. Bowerman said. "We have some problems similar to Wayne County and Detroit, but we are small enough that we can measure the results."

Bull provided CPS hardware and software to 18 employees — caseworkers, supervisors and the program administrator. The equipment included a personal computer for each worker, lap-top computers and all software. The hardware comes from the Bull DP/2 family of Unix-based minicomputers, slightly larger than a personal computer and smaller than a mainframe. The lap-tops are IBM-compatible, portable personal computers. The software program creates a relational data base, with all the necessary information about families, foster homes, court forms and other information in an accessible format.

Asked what the CPS can do, Mr. Bowerman answered simply, "Almost everything. If we receive a call, the intake worker puts the information into a computer. We know if we've had previous cases. The caseworker begins with all the available information."

The CPS saves caseworkers time by eliminating the process of manually searching and updating case records, inputting and cross-referencing data, scheduling, and filling in court forms. It also frees caseworkers from tedious paperwork so they can spend more time on the human side of their jobs.

"Before, the foster home list was on paper and updated once a month," Mr. Bowerman said. "The caseworker would have to use a pay phone and keep calling around. Now, he can punch in the information on his lap-top computer and know the type of home, whether there is a vacancy and the phone number. The foster family will be awake to meet the child, ready to help."

The reason the program works so well is that it is tailored for the county. Bull representatives spent weeks in Berrien County learning what the social service workers did before creating the program, said Monty Bieber, a Bull technical adviser who helped create the program. "The most difficult issue was to make the workers understand that what they did could be automated," Mr. Bieber said, "but once they understood, they kept saying, 'I didn't think a computer could do it.' " The Bull engineers eventually tailored the program to the social services employees' — and the children's — needs.

Mr. Bowerman recalled that at least one worker did not want to participate in the staff training. "She kept saying she was over-worked, questioned why she should learn, all of that. We didn't force her. She watched the others, asked someone to show her and now she is one of our biggest supporters."

It took nine months to complete the initial study, take it back to Boston where the program was developed and return to Benton Harbor to install it, Mr. Bieber said. Since Berrien County was a pilot program, there was no immediate cost to the county government. But for others, the estimated cost is $5,000 to $6,000 per worker.

Technology enlivens government process in Vermont

Rural Vermonters cherish their self-governing tradition, but sometimes it's hard for citizens to attend town meetings and hearings where all that self-governing happens.

Enter TeleTalk, a computer forum that its creators hope will help revolutionize policy debate in Vermont government. Established by a University of Vermont staff member and a Montpelier-based lobbyist, TeleTalk tries to broaden the public dialogue by enhancing electronic access to government information. Tele-Talk made its public sector debut in 1992 by offering computer users access to drafts of the state's 10-year telecommunications plan, along with the capacity to comment electronically on the document.

Vermont is not the first state to involve computer users in policy discussions, but it may have a predisposition to success with such experiments.

"With Vermont being the country's most rural state, it's a little more difficult for people to travel to public hearings," said David Punia, an engineering specialist in the computer science department at the Burlington-based university. "If you only have to travel to your computer, you can get the information right there."

The forum, made available to users through a variety of electronic bulletin board services, included the proposed telecommunications plan because it was believed that computer users would have an innate interest in the topic, Mr. Punia said. The telecommunications plan, representing Vermont's first long-term look at the subject, involved proposals for the state's acquisition of technology and policies that would affect the private marketplace. The latter area included strategies to foster competition and keep rates affordable, said William Steinhurst, the state Department of Public Service's director for regulated utility planning.

Concurrent with public hearings on the plan, computer users were able to access drafts of the document, transcripts of completed hearings and a glossary of important terms, Mr. Punia said. Users were encouraged to leave messages with their opinions on, and suggestions for, the plan.

Mr. Steinhurst said his department received meaningful feedback from computer users on the plan, which was finalized in October 1992. "We were told about some of the opinions expressed through the bulletin board, and we were glad to have that information," he said.

Mr. Punia believes the data he collected from the project shows that dozens of users had input on the finished product, and he planned to convince policymakers that TeleTalk can be tailored to a variety of government debates. "This is absolutely applicable to other areas," he said.

It may be a while before Vermont town meetings are conducted from living room to living room, but TeleTalk should at least help Vermonters maintain their tradition of public participation in today's more complex world.

Turbo-charging information sharing with LANs, WANs

Rapidly growing numbers of state and local governments are hooking up their personal computers to one another within departments — and with larger central computers — in systems that are called local or wide area networks (LANs or WANs). The resulting systems boost personal computers by giving them more memory and more power, while giving workers more information-sharing abilities.

The difference between LANs and WANs basically is one of geographic proximity. A WAN can include an area ranging from a few contiguous buildings to an entire state. A LAN may hook up a few personal computers to an expensive laser printer, or allow access to the same software without buying multiple copies, explained Gary Samuels, executive vice president, Fourth Ware Technologies Inc., a Southfield, Mich., network systems consulting firm. "Most large government departments or agencies are tied into a mainframe computer, but they have a lot of personal computers that need to talk to one another and to the mainframe," he said. "A network among workstations is quicker for sharing information than tying each workstation into the mainframe."

Governments are installing computer networks to reduce costs and improve efficiency and productivity. "By updating their technology, governments can do what they do now but cheaper and faster, although the big savings are in productivity rather than immediate cost reductions," said Mr. Held of Ernst & Young.

Because of budget constraints, most local governments only have department-level networks, but in a few years they likely will connect all their networks to a main system. State governments with department-to-department and statewide networks are expected to take the next step, which is to hook up the networks with one another. Experts say government officials are knowledgeable about telecommunications and networking, but they remain gun-shy about setting up networks without assistance from industry consultants. Networks are the fourth generation of computer technology, after mainframes, minicomputers and personal computers.

In the early 1970s, jurisdictions bought mainframe computers for central data processing. These computers were large, expensive and inefficient. By the late 1970s, agencies wanting to develop homemade programs still had to work through the mainframe, lowering the computer's efficiency even further. In the early 1980s, governments moved into minicomputers and microcomputers. These are independent processors capable of running applications, though ultimately the information had to be stored in the mainframes. During the early 1990s, government data processing managers began appreciating the advantages of linking hundreds of isolated personal computers into networks. "Whenever you have many people working on the same task, you need some kind of network to allow them to share information," explained Mr. Chu of Andersen Consulting.

Good connections through Public Technology Inc.

Imagine a municipality that can practically read the minds of its constituents, from sending a note to forgetful Mr. Jones reminding him about his unpaid water bill to receiving information from Ms. Smith about the pothole developing in front of her house. The act of sending information instantly to people who need it and receiving messages from residents about critical service needs is the basis for the newest innovation in government information technology — the well-connected community.

New developments make the well-connected community a reality, maintains Costis Toregas, president of Washington-based Public Technology Inc. (PTI), a non-profit research and technology consulting organization supported by the National League of Cities, National Association of Counties and International City/ County Management Association. "Local governments have just begun to realize the value of the information they gather as part of their duties and the needs of their citizens as consumers of this information," Mr. Toregas said. "Information technology provides ways to unlock the value of these assets." For some local governments, that value may be measured in revenue as well as service.

PTI began in the early 1970s as a not-for-profit organization. In those days its role was to design specifications for public safety and traffic management hardware used by cities and counties. Now it is probably best known for its development with Armonk, N.Y.-based IBM Corp. of the 24-Hour City Hall/County Court House, a network of public touch-screen computers located in shopping malls and grocery stores. The system was first used in Kansas City, Mo.; Hillsborough County, Fla.; and Mercer County, Wash. The public information programs allowed citizens to access local government data (such as council agendas) and agency names, addresses, telephone numbers and procedural information through computers located in popular public areas.

"PTI has gone through a number of changes," Mr. Toregas explained. "At first, we focused on hardware technology. We designed life support systems for firefighters and we were the first organization to introduce Kevlar (bulletproof) vests for police. As technology changed and developed, we began to focus more in the area of information technology."

Decision-support software, data bases and online access projects such as the 24-Hour City Hall/County Court House were the key projects of the 1980s. As the organization evolved, so did its vision of the well-connected community that drives most of its research. During the early 1990s, PTI and its 25 staff members focused on public enterprise telecommunications — projects that can reduce local government telephone system costs and set the stage for new public information service projects involving audio and video technology, Mr. Toregas said. In 1989, PTI signed an agreement with AT&T that provided local governments with a 20% commission on long-distance service at public pay telephones in government buildings. About 3,500 jurisdictions were participating in the arrangement in 1992, according to PTI. Late in 1991, the organization announced PTS 2000, a long-distance service discount package with Washington-based MCI Communications Corp. that provided local governments with access to the telecommunications company's VNET private long-distance voice and data network. Participants in PTS 2000 received long-distance service discounts ranging from 20% to 48%, depending upon usage. In Oakland, Calif., early tests of the PTS 2000 service yielded an estimated annual savings of about $48,000. The service also featured several telephone system management options such as remote access to the network for traveling employees through a toll-free telephone number, cost allocation with telephone number accounting codes and local control over long-distance access for employees.

Many of these features were not new in the private sector. Large purchasers of telephone services, such as businesses, had discounts and the management services for years. But the discounts originally had not been available to any but the largest local governments, according to Mr. Toregas. "In the aggregate, local governments have great buying power which they have not been using effectively," he said. "Both of our telecommunications services have taken advantage of that power to negotiate discounts and service enhancements." Discounts are only the beginning, he said. PTS 2000 eventually will provide a platform onto which governments can build new services such as voice and dial-up computer bulletin boards to receive inquiries from citizens and transmit public information on their own phones.

The new services have added to both PTI's expenses and revenue. For instance, the organization's expenses jumped to $4.8 million in fiscal 1991 from about $2.5 million in fiscal 1990. Revenue grew to $6.1 million from about $2.6 million during the same period. Income from membership dues was flat at about $1.2 million, but revenue from the public enterprise projects increased to $3.7 million in fiscal 1991 from only $353,000 in fiscal 1990. PTI officials said any surplus is used to fund additional research and to aid member local governments in developing information technology applications that eventually can be shared with other jurisdictions.

Mr. Toregas believes local governments are entering a new era of public-private partnership in which governments must begin serving citizens as customers, or consumers of information. While this relationship creates many challenges for local governments, it may also provide new sources of revenue if localities can provide effective ways of delivering the information.

In particular, PTI is exploring videotext and audiotext applications that can take advantage of the flexibility of the MCI VNET, said PTI Vice President Cindy Kahan. "The telecommunications network can be used for much more than carrying long-distance calls," she said. "Applications can be developed that can help gather and distribute information to groups as well as individuals. Voice response technology can, for example, be used to help citizens locate nearest services such as recycling centers by punching their ZIP code on a telephone keypad."

Telecommunications devices developed by telemarketers also can be turned to valuable use by local governments as a means of conducting quick polls on public issues, Mr. Toregas said. It's another way to keep Everytown well-connected with Mr. Jones and Ms. Smith.

If you're in Texas, dial 1-800-COMPLAIN

When they invited citizens to air their gripes about school districts via a toll-free hot line, Texas officials realized an occasional "wacko" would respond.

"It's the people who call at 2 in the morning that I really worry about," said Susan Owens, legislative liaison in the Texas Auditor's Office, which operated the telephone line during a study of 55 public school districts.

But for every caller who used 1-800-TX-AUDIT as a personal sounding board, dozens of concerned Texans offered useful information about the need for education reform in their state. The anecdotes provided by callers reinforced several points made in the November 1992 audit report, which recommended consolidation of school districts and limits on the administrative share of local school budgets, among other reforms.

Government officials who have used toll-free telephone lines in their jobs consider them an inexpensive way to elicit public opinion, even if they don't always uncover major examples of waste or abuse in government. An investment in "1-800" technology usually runs in the hundreds of dollars, with the telephone lines typically staffed by state employees.

In Texas' case, the Auditor's Office established its hot line one month after the state's Legislative Audit Committee asked it to examine management practices in 55 of Texas' 1,053 school districts. The audit committee is chaired by the speaker of the state House of Representatives, with the lieutenant governor serving as vice chairman.

From July until September 1992, the department received 500 calls from a diverse audience of school administrators, teachers, parents and concerned citizens, Ms. Owens said. "Some school board presidents called begging for audits of their particular districts," she said. Callers could speak to an operator during business hours or leave a recorded message after hours. In some cases, operators returned calls to seek more information, while other callers chose not to give their names or telephone numbers. "Those directly involved in school districts usually wanted to stay anonymous," Ms. Owens said. "They probably felt they would lose their jobs or something." According to Ms. Owens, about 80% of the callers offered information already known to auditors, "but the other 20% were on things you couldn't even imagine," including bizarre land deals involving sitting members of one school board. After the volume of calls over the audit died down, 200 more citizens dialed 1-800-TX-AUDIT to report information about operations in state agencies and universities.

Other state offices in Texas operate their own toll-free hot lines, with the comptroller of public accounts asking citizens to report on waste and the Governor's Office seeking to help Texans who are immersed in red tape.

Privatization

Due to political ideology and financial expediency, privatization of government services is riding a wave of popularity. Government officials around the country are opening up to privatization, which has become an overused buzzword for the act of allowing businesses to operate services that are normally performed by governments.

Hundreds of municipalities have sold their garbage trucks and squeezed out public employees in favor of hiring companies to pick up, and dispose of, household trash. Small villages have turned to private contractors for fire protection and ambulance service. Large cities, including Atlanta and Los Angeles, have contemplated permitting the private sector to run, or even own, their sprawling international airports. The California state government has hired developers to build and operate toll roads. Private interests have studied construction of a magnetic-levitation train to flash back and forth from Orlando's airport to the city's tourist center. In all cases, officials contemplate the possibility that outsiders can perform public services at less cost and with more efficiency than government.

Today's drive toward privatization is a reversal of earlier trends. A seemingly endless flow of federal and state funds to municipalities, beginning with Democratic President Franklin D. Roosevelt's Depression strategy in the 1930s and continuing through Democratic President Jimmy Carter's administration in the late 1970s, encouraged government expansion into nearly all areas of service delivery. The so-called new federalism of President Ronald Reagan's Republican administration in the 1980s brought that trend to an abrupt end, and federal funds to state and local governments dried up.

A survey of 1,100 counties and cities by Deloitte & Touche, a New York-based international management consulting firm, showed that virtually every government had privatized at least one service by the end of 1987. Privatization became exceptionally popular in the economic recession of the early 1990s, when cash-strapped governments embraced virtually any idea that could save them money.

The idea that privatization is always better, cheaper and more efficient than public operations is a myth, according to the vast majority of government public works officials. They argue that municipal solid-waste operations, road maintenance and other government functions can be handled just as well by public agencies as by private contractors. Businessmen and other community leaders from the private sector, on the other hand, are quick to point out that government should be run like a business. In other words, if corporations are expected to balance their budgets and run their operations as efficiently as possible, why shouldn't governments be forced to do the same?

Privatization as an economic remedy often is prescribed merely to cure political problems, warned John D. Donahue, author of "The Privatization Decision: Public Ends, Private Means," and an assistant professor at Harvard University's John F. Kennedy School of Government, Cambridge, Mass. Privatization "often is offered by politicians as a solution to a messy problem, such as a one-time source of revenue," Mr. Donahue said.

The debate revolves around the proper role of government in delivering certain services and its accountability to the public. Is government obligated to farm out such crucial functions as public health and safety operations to private contractors just to save money? Or is government simply required to ensure that the service is available, whether through its own delivery system or through an outside private system? Each government must determine its own answers to these questions.

When officials decide to privatize, competition is the key. "There is never anything to be gained in moving from a public to a private monopoly," Mr. Donahue said. "When public officials are being pressured by business to privatize, the officials must keep in mind that no business lobbies to privatize something when there's a lively, competitive market."

Indeed, there is universal agreement that non-competitive markets are an inappropriate environment in which to privatize. In 1987, two national waste disposal giants, Browning-Ferris Industries Inc., Houston, and Waste Management Inc., Oak Brook, Ill., pleaded guilty to $10 million in price-fixing charges for garbage collection in Toledo, Ohio. The case was a prime example of a privatization effort gone awry and was cited often by privatization opponents, particularly government employee unions whose members face job losses whenever governments privatize services.

Some areas of government responsibility don't lend themselves to privatization, regardless of competition or how well the companies' operations are monitored by public officials. Switching to private from public operators at airport control towers, for instance, could undermine the confidence of the flying public and severely disrupt service. In addition, politicians often shun privatization because they fear losing control over any activity for which they have been responsible, said Irwin T. David, national director of public sector services at Deloitte & Touche.

Ultimately, the success of any privatization effort relies heavily on contract specifications. A well-drafted document can cover contingencies such as service interruptions and extraordinary charges. Most importantly, a contract should provide government officials with direct control over how the service is delivered.

Privatization cuts hauling costs . . . or does it?

Dramatic hikes in fuel costs and landfill dumping charges have increased garbage collection price tags to the point where public officials are scouting for any and all alternatives that may be cheaper. For some communities, baffled by both the complexities and costs of new environmental laws, privatization has become a realistic option. But at the same time, other jurisdictions are becoming disenchanted with the quality of their private hauling companies and are reverting to public collection.

Before officials overhaul their community's waste-disposal system, they must explore all options carefully. According to the National Solid Wastes Management Association, a Washington-based trade group, trash collection practices have not changed much since the mid-1970s, when a major study by researchers at New York's Columbia University showed that 38% of residential garbage is collected by public works departments and 62% is collected by private companies. Companies also collect 90% of the commercial waste stream. Government haulers predominate in the South, while contracts with private businesses are far more common in other parts of the country.

Harvard University's Mr. Donahue has found that private trash collectors can cost up to 40% less than the same service provided by government. But the growing popularity of private collection services doesn't necessarily mean they offer the most cost-efficient approach. Most of that cost difference is attributed to labor costs.

"The political will" in many communities keeps crew sizes larger on public garbage trucks, said Stephen Pudloski, deputy executive director of the American Public Works Association, Chicago. Until a handful of years ago, for example, Chicago's public garbage trucks carried a crew of four workers. An old joke explained this staffing arrangement: "Every city garbage truck has four people — one to drive, one to sit on the back of the truck, one to pick up the garbage and one on life support."

While even Chicago cut back to three-person garbage crews, most communities haven't reached the one-person level of private companies. Nor can some communities afford the efficient new back-loading trucks that enable companies to collect trash from hundreds of additional houses each day. Mr. Pudloski pointed out that small communities trying to collect their own trash fight even bigger expenses. "You must have a certain size to be economical," he said. "If your public workers collect garbage two days a week and maintain the streets for three days, they won't be as efficient as people who collect trash all the time."

The cost differences between government and private collection narrow when private collection is carried out on a franchise basis. Under this arrangement, companies are awarded exclusive territories where they pick up the garbage at a set rate and bill the customers directly. According to Mr. Donahue, the cost of billing customers alone can approach 15% of revenue.

In cities where public works departments and companies bid against each other for franchises, taxpayers usually are the winners. In his book, Mr. Donahue noted, "There is considerable evidence that competition, other than organizational form, is the crucial factor in efficient trash collection."

That theory is certainly well-illustrated in Phoenix. Ron Jensen, public works director of that Arizona city, said, "We began competitive bidding for the five districts here in 1978. Since then, my department has lost districts, then regained them from private companies. Now that we've become more efficient, we've won them all back." Mr. Jensen uses his observations of private contractors to make his public department more competitive. "A few years ago my department lost all the bids for special residential pickups to private firms. We had been picking up discarded appliances and furniture with a three-man or four-man crew and an open-bed truck while the companies were using two men, a small front-loader tractor and a compactor truck. The next time bids were taken, guess what we showed up with?"

Even inefficient public trash collection tends to be less expensive than an open competition system in which each homeowner contracts separately for trash pickup from a variety of companies whose trucks wind up and down the same residential streets. Open competition can cost up to one-third more than public garbage service, Mr. Donahue said. In Lansing, Mich., for example, 16 companies and the city's Public Works Department at one time competed for the same residential customers. Brent Granger, vice president of Granger Container Service Inc., in late 1990 was collecting garbage from 20% of those residents and admitted that their $12.55 monthly bill was high. "If we served 100% of the customers in Lansing, we could be more price-competitive because we could make more stops per day," Mr. Granger said.

Philip Richmond, director of sanitation for Escambia County, a

Florida Panhandle county that includes Pensacola, said the key to deciding whether your community should move from public to private collection is to pinpoint current garbage collection costs per household now. "In too many cities, there's no accountability," he explained. "The residents think garbage collection should be free, so the elected officials pay for it out of public funds or charge a low rate and subsidize the rest." To be competitive, he added, a local government must run its collection program like a business. In Escambia County, Mr. Richmond's department has served three-fourths of local residents as an enterprise system. "We pay all our own costs from revenue and have received no tax money in almost four years," he said.

If cost analyses indicate that your public collection costs more than the private collection for residents of neighboring communities, don't turn your whole community over to private collectors at once, advises Robert Peters, technical programs manager for the Governmental Refuse Collection and Disposal Association, Silver Spring, Md. "Cut your city into quarters and go out for bids on one section at a time" to see how the private contractors perform and to analyze costs before closing down the public department, he said.

Council's role: Discuss, inform on municipal services

The concept of privatization is not a new one. It has been tested and tinkered with since before the federal government contracted for pony express riders to deliver the mail. But many governments seemed to have forgotten this proven tool during the 1980s as they scrambled for solutions to their primary dilemma: meeting citizen demands for more services at a time when revenue sources were drying up.

While many governments not long ago began to tap privatization, private sector groups felt their potential to help governments was not being realized. In 1985, a group of individuals working in the fields of law, insurance, investment banking and consulting decided to play matchmaker and show both the public and private sectors why they were right for one another. They formed the Privatization Council as a forum for discussion between public and private administrators.

"Our philosophy holds that there are many problems that could be better resolved through public-private partnerships than through purely private or purely public efforts," explained Roger Feldman, Privatization Council vice chairman. "We believe that when private capital is involved in part of the solution of problems, there will be a high likelihood that efficiency of the process will be improved and benefits realized by the public will be improved." The council seeks to promote that message through research, education and debate, added Irwin T. "Ted" David, partner in the Washington office of Deloitte & Touche and a council board member.

The Washington-based council produces a number of publications, notably *Privatization Review,* a quarterly journal that profiles public-private partnership trends with in-depth case studies and essays, and a biannual compendium of state laws that affect privatization. The council acts as a clearinghouse, publishes position papers, participates in privatization-related studies, sponsors presentations with state and local governments, and offers testimony on the topic. The council also has set up subcommittees that delve into privatization concerns in the areas of health care, transportation, environment and military contracting.

Despite its commitment, the council does not engage in lobbying. "We're the pragmatic voice of privatization," said Mr. Feldman. "We just want to put the idea out for discussion."

Most members are for-profit, private enterprises serving cities, counties, state governments and public authorities. Membership in the early 1990s totaled about 150 institutions and firms, according to Marguerite Savard, director of the council's membership services. The council's growth has coincided with privatization's growing acceptance.

"Numbers indicate that privatization is enjoying wide acceptance," said William G. Reinhardt, editor and publisher of *Public Works Financing,* a monthly newsletter about public-private infrastructure projects. "While council members are not the reason for it, they've played a role in promoting the concept and winning support for it. They are an important participant."

Past speakers at Privatization Council gatherings are indicative of the kind of clout the council carries; the list includes notables like Jack Kemp, secretary of the U.S. Department of Housing and Urban Development under President George Bush; U.S. Transportation Deputy Secretary Elaine Chao; and Charles Grizzle, assistant administrator for the Environmental Protection Agency's Office of Administration and Resource Management. Indeed, now that the council's input is sought by congressional committees, requests from states, federal agencies and trade associations also are common, Mr. Feldman said.

In Michigan, privatization is slow, but it's coming

Privatization of government services often is not the fastest or easiest deficit reduction tool. Just ask Michigan Gov. John Engler, who began talking non-stop about privatization shortly after entering office in January 1991 for a four-year term.

Like a few other governors, notably Republican Gov. William F. Weld of Massachusetts, Mr. Engler is committed to allowing companies to take over public services within Michigan, even if the advantage to government isn't always dramatic. His efforts serve as an example of how difficult it is to contract out government services to businesses, especially on a large scale.

Still, privatization was looking up for Michigan in late 1992, when a commission appointed by the Republican governor unveiled the most comprehensive privatization plan ever put together by a state government. The report established Mr. Engler as a leader in the toughest and most comprehensive privatization push in the United States. Michigan's plan was designed to privatize every service or function that could be more efficiently and cost-effectively delivered by contractors.

"It's not just costs. The quality of service provided is equally important," emphasized Maureen McNulty, public information officer for the Michigan Department of Management and Budget, which oversees privatization efforts.

The commission's report offered a plethora of privatization options in nearly all departments. Virtually anything — including state parks, snow removal, lab testing of environmental samples, inspections of state facilities such as prisons, and administration of the Medicaid system — could be turned over to the private sector. There was even talk of selling off chunks of the state university system.

The report and its suggestions were left to the mercy of the Michigan Legislature in 1993. In the meantime, Mr. Engler tried to push through other privatization projects that his administration had introduced in early 1992.

Privatizing state services is just one of the many ways Mr. Engler wants to diminish the size of state government. Privatization was somewhat more popular than the elimination of general assistance to the state's poor and the cutting of aid to local governments, other ideas Mr. Engler had implemented at great political cost.

Not that privatization comes without controversy. For instance, the Democrats who control Wayne County complained that politics was behind the Republican governor's two-year contract, costing up to $6 million, to maintain a stretch of Interstate Highway 94 through the Detroit area. The contract, a pilot program for privatizing road maintenance in other areas of the state, had been held for about a half century by the county's Public Service Department, but state officials said the county had labor and overhead costs out of line with those in the Detroit area, let alone the rest of the state.

The Michigan government also was looking to negotiate with a private insurance firm to underwrite the state's worker accident fund. The workers' compensation policy was taken over by the state in the late 1980s in part because it had a large surplus the state wanted to use for other programs. In addition, Mr. Engler's administration wanted to get out of the liquor business, selling off state warehouses that distributed hard liquor to stores statewide. Michigan made money from the business, and it was not clear whether the profit from the sale and the savings in operating funds would equal the annual income.

"In areas where we can save money, the governor is looking at privatizing those services," explained John Truscott, Mr. Engler's

45

press secretary. "I think the governor has made it clear he is interested in going forward with this approach wherever it is practical."

Russell Gronevelt, director of Wayne County's Public Services Department, remarked, "I don't think there is anything wrong with privatizing some services. We have tried it here ourselves, but privatizing one stretch of interstate when we have the experience, the equipment and the plans for handling all sorts of weather emergencies is the wrong way to go about it."

John O'Doherty, chief maintenance engineer for the Michigan Department of Transportation, said, "This state is absolutely strapped for dollars to meet federal matching fund requirements for road projects. We selected Wayne County because state audits of road contracts, both in Republican and Democratic administrations, have shown over the years that the costs are substantially higher there than elsewhere in the state."

In Wayne County, benefits paid to road maintenance equipment operators equaled 77 cents for each dollar paid in salary, while state highway employees got about 60 cents in benefits, Mr. O'Doherty pointed out. The statewide average for administrative overhead for county road contracts was 8%, while it was 26% in Wayne County. In neighboring Oakland County, also urbanized and congested, the overhead ran about 15%. Wayne County officials said that efficiencies had improved in recent years, and they disputed the state's calculations of costs. Mr. Gronevelt said equipment operators in Wayne County actually earned less than their counterparts at the state level.

Heavily Republican Oakland County, the wealthiest county in the state and home to technology-rich Southfield, was put on notice that it could be the next subject of the state government's privatization movement. Patrick Nowak, director of the Michigan Department of Transportation, previously was Oakland County's deputy executive, and he personally informed County Executive Daniel T. Murphy of the plans.

"The idea is not to privatize the state highways," the state's Mr. O'Doherty explained. "We want to establish a good, healthy mixture of state and local government maintenance as well as some private contracting in areas where we see higher costs." He said the state will not know for some time how much money was saved from the projects.

So far in Michigan, saving money doesn't seem to be the point of such programs. The emphasis is more on experimenting with privatization. To that end, most state and local governments will be studying Michigan's efforts closely over the next several years.

Los Angeles County recognized as a partnership leader

One of the Privatization Council's functions is to honor governments that embrace privatization. One big winner of the council's Governmental Leadership Award in recent years has been Los

Angeles County. When it comes to privatization, Los Angeles County seems to do it better than just about everybody. During the decade of the 1980s, the county awarded 812 contracts totaling $508.3 million to companies to provide services traditionally offered by the public sector. The pacts produced estimated savings of $193.5 million, and 4,691 positions were eliminated through attrition or layoffs. "Privatization is part of public policy," said Chris Goodman, coordinator of the county's contracting program.

The county has pursued private-public partnership ever since voters passed a 1978 referendum that opened county operations to competition. That year, coincidentally, also witnessed the passage of Proposition 13, which slapped a cap on annual property tax hikes, limiting the amounts of revenue governments in the state could collect. Before 1978, the Los Angeles County Charter prevented contracting any work that county workers performed, Mr. Goodman said. The voter mandate, though, rewrote the charter to allow for privatization if the Los Angeles County Board of Supervisors showed such an arrangement could save money and result in better service.

Los Angeles County has embraced public-private partnerships with a passion. The services it has awarded run from automobile fleet maintenance and hospital meal preparation to welfare caseload management and dental care.

The county's love affair with privatization supposedly hasn't jilted employees. Although Mr. Goodman declines to be specific, he claims only a handful of the county's approximately 80,000 employees have had to be laid off due to the new service delivery approach. One reason is a policy that requires contractors to give county employees dibs on any jobs the contract may generate before offering those jobs to private sector candidates. Another reason is that the county attempts to find new employment opportunities for employees whose jobs may be eliminated by privatization.

Other contract guidelines have been created as well. Before a service is contracted out, auditors compile all costs associated with it, Mr. Goodman said. For example, if the county were to contract for security guards, it would factor in the guards' wages and benefits along with a fraction of the costs of hiring and retaining them. That figure is compared with the cost of contracting the work.

All contracts must meet detailed guidelines to prove their cost-effectiveness, Mr. Goodman said. They also must win approval from county counsel and the Board of Supervisors.

But such a detailed policy still is unable to catch all hidden costs, according to county Supervisor Ed Edelman, who was not as enthusiastic about privatization as his fellow supervisors.

Nevertheless, Los Angeles County continues to push ahead in pursuit of privatization pacts. "Los Angeles County is very creative in the area of contracting out and privatization," said Philip Fixler, director of the Local Government Center at the Reason Foundation, a Santa Monica, Calif., think-tank.

One novel approach arranged by the county involved contracted dental care. The county board arranged to buy dental services from some dentists who previously had been employed by the county. The county let the dentists step into private practice while retaining their county business and earning the option to recruit more clients. "We think that is a harbinger of the future," Mr. Fixler said.

The privatization program brought the county to the point in 1990 where it annually awarded $190.1 million in private contracts that saved an estimated $41.8 million a year, Mr. Goodman added.

New York authority wrestles with infrastructure demands

In 1984, the U.S. Army unleashed its 10th Mountain Division on eastern upstate New York, home to Fort Drum. The move was both a boom and a bomb for the picturesque, largely undeveloped region. The division's relocation transformed a tiny, 1,000-troop outpost near Watertown, N.Y., into a high-technology base of 10,000 new troops. It also added 15,000 dependents and thousands of civilians to the population of the so-called North Country. That required major infrastructure improvements for Fort Drum and the surrounding counties of Jefferson, Lewis and St. Lawrence. The Army Corps of Engineers took care of the on-base changes — a $1.2 billion effort that ranked as the Army Corps' largest post-World War II construction effort.

In addition, a special governmental district, the Development Authority of the North Country (DANC), was formed and charged with handling expanded infrastructure needs in a manner that also enhanced the region's economic well-being. The state-created DANC, which today consists of eight voting members from the three counties and five state-appointed, non-voting members, marched toward its goal at a faster clip than expected. The DANC's speedy efforts to accommodate the fort's additional sewage and water demands were saluted with a Government Leadership Award from the Privatization Council.

The authority took steps to install sewer and water pipelines by contracting the services of O'Brien & Gere Engineers Inc., Syracuse, N.Y., explained Ray Bradham, DANC director of engineering and facilities management. O'Brien & Gere designed two systems: One carries discharged wastewater from Fort Drum to Watertown on the Black River, and the other carries drinking water from Watertown's expanded water purification plant to the fort to supplement its own well supply. The sewer project, which included a pumping station near the town of Pamelia, was completed at a cost of $15.5 million, or $11.5 million less than projected costs. The system was ready to operate in April 1987, a year after the public-private contract was signed and a year ahead of schedule. The sewer line, with a daily capacity of 4.5 million gallons, is owned by the DANC and is operated and maintained by an O'Brien & Gere subsidiary, OBG Operations.

The projects predictably met opposition. As one local resident remarked, the area "hasn't seen any expansion since the War of 1812." There also were fears that the pipelines would pose future financial and environmental burdens. But the fort's expansion had to be accommodated, and a private sector partnership was deemed the cheapest and best way to accomplish it, according to Mr. Bradham.

"The strong consensus among board members was, 'Let's not create a bureaucracy here. Let's watch our taxpayers' money,' " said Mr. Bradham, one of nine authority staff members. "The board decided we could provide better services by having a small professional staff and by contracting out items that the private sector could do better."

The DANC hopes the lines will pay huge revenue dividends by ensuring development on land near the lines. "Growth is a challenge because the North Country is a rocky area," Mr. Bradham said. "Infrastructure for water and sewer is an expensive process, but once we've gotten the main transmission lines in, outside users can tap in."

Public-private pact leads to a Nevada hydroelectric plant

Truckee-Carson Irrigation District (TCID), a quasi-governmental entity, was created in 1918 by the U.S. Bureau of Land Reclamation solely to operate a dam and canal system to irrigate parched western Nevada desert into 60,000 acres of farmland. But in 1989, the TCID used the power-producing potential of its Lahontan Dam near Fallon, Nev., about 60 miles east of Reno, to branch out into the electricity business.

The TCID linked with Synergics Inc., a power projects developer based in Annapolis, Md., to build a 4.4-megawatt hydroelectric plant that began operating in June 1989. The plant is powered by Carson River water released into canals snaking across parts of Lyon and Churchill counties to 2,081 alfalfa, oat, wheat, corn and cantaloupe farms.

The TCID had pursued the idea of a power plant after congressional enactment of the 1978 Public Utilities Regulatory Policy Act, which required utilities to buy power from anyone who made it with renewable resources such as water or wind. In 1980, officials from the TCID began seeking a cost-effective way to harness the energy- and revenue-generating potential of water released from the western Nevada dam.

"They released the water every year and every year that energy was just lost down the drain," said Neal Wilkins, Synergics project manager.

Five years later, the TCID obtained a Federal Energy Regulatory Commission license allowing it to operate a power facility. The district, however, couldn't cover a plant's estimated $7 million-plus price tag, and it lacked in-house experts with the resources to build a plant or the acumen to negotiate a favorable purchase contract with a utility shopping for the lowest electric rates possible.

"We're an irrigation district. What do we know about that?" asked TCID Manager Lyman McConnell.

At the same time, some residents were growing frustrated by the district's efforts. A total of $1.3 million had been spent on studies and penstock improvements without netting tangible results.

"The district could continue to pursue a plan with full risks and full rewards, or the alternative was it could share rewards and forgo risks," said Mr. McConnell. "We decided we'd rather share the rewards to forgo risks."

Privatization, it was determined, would maximize the TCID's economic gain without requiring more investment. Minimize the TCID's liability and link it with a company that knows how to operate power plants and draw up purchase contract proposals, the district board said.

"The district felt that if it could get a partner, the partner would want to get something in his favor and it'd be to our benefit, too," Mr. McConnell said. "They'd develop the project for a certain amount and we'd share in the excess profits."

Synergics, which operates plants in several states, was selected from a field of 20 bidders to design, build and operate a power facility to harness the released water's energy potential without altering its flow to irrigation canals. Later, Synergics negotiated a power purchase contract with Sierra Pacific Power Co. of Reno, which wanted to pay the paltry sum of about 4 cents per kilowatt hour — a price that made it fiscally impossible to operate a hydro plant. With intervention from the Public Service Commission of Nevada, Synergics negotiated a 50-year, fixed-rate deal that paid 7.2 cents per kilowatt hour. It then designed a plant that operates on a schedule that doesn't influence irrigation flow. The plant generates 4,000 kilowatts of electricity in an hour, enough to supply some 2,000 households.

The revenue from the generated power reduces the TCID's operating costs in providing irrigation water. The electricity also saves the equivalent of 1 million gallons of oil, or 8,000 tons of coal, annually. The TCID-Synergics pact spans 20 years. The deal requires no more investment from the district, and it will have covered its $1.3 million investment by the year 2009.

Synergics, meanwhile, financed a plan that will make a top return on its investment. After the lenders are paid annually, both the TCID and Synergics split profits. At the end of the contract, once all debt is paid, the TCID will become the owner of the plant, which has a life expectancy of about 50 years, and the sole recipient of any revenue that the facility generates.

Obstacles clip wings of private airport drives

Despite the many success stories resulting from privatization, many efforts simply die due to insurmountable obstacles.

In an opinion piece in the *New York Times* on May 13, 1990, former New York mayoral aspirant Ronald S. Lauder proposed selling off John F. Kennedy International and LaGuardia airports to private operators. He argued that, for starters, the move would provide a huge lump of cash that could be applied to New York's budget deficit. In the long run, he claimed, the airports would generate more revenue if they were run as private businesses.

But substantial obstacles prevent such airport privatization efforts from taking off. The main one is that the Federal Aviation Administration (FAA) doesn't have a policy covering such deals. When cities receive federal funding for airport construction, they agree to follow FAA airport regulations, one of which requires any airport-generated revenue to be returned to the airport for upkeep and expansion. Therein lies the crux of the airport privatization question. If a city sells its airport, the sale proceeds would be considered airport-generated revenue, which under FAA regulations a city cannot keep.

Officials at the Port Authority of New York and New Jersey, which owns the Kennedy and LaGuardia airports (New York City merely owns the land), don't think the federal government is calling for the privatization of major airports, despite claims to the contrary in President George Bush's transportation policy of the early 1990s. "We read the transportation policy as suggesting privatization of pieces of the air transport system," said Bill Cahill, authority spokesman.

Mr. Lauder's proposal isn't the first of its kind. Cities from Atlanta to Los Angeles have considered getting out of the airport business, but so far no one has been able to find a way around the FAA. Private contractors already operate concessions at most major airports and provide janitorial and maintenance services. The Port Authority of New York and New Jersey, for example, contracts with a local building-services contractor to operate the former Eastern Airlines Inc. terminal at Kennedy International Airport, Mr. Cahill reported.

With Los Angeles' budget-balancing act growing ever more difficult, city officials are looking for ways to tap a veritable jewel box of revenue through privatization at Los Angeles International Airport (LAX). A committee of the Los Angeles City Council in April 1992 began discussing the possibility of privatizing the airport, probably by leasing the facility to a private entity. The move would allow the city to bring financial benefits from the airport into the general fund. Talk of LAX privatization became big during fiscal 1992, when the Los Angeles city general fund faced a deficit of as much as $100 million while the airport continued to turn a healthy profit of some $25 million a year. The city's charter segregates the airport account from other city funding, preventing Los Angeles officials from spending airport profits on other areas.

"Basically, we have a $2 billion property at LAX and, at the end of the year, we don't see anything from it," said Erin Egge, press deputy to Los Angeles City Council President John Ferraro, who introduced the motion that the city study privatizing LAX.

As expected, one problem confronting Los Angeles officials is the federal government's view of airport privatization. In 1989, Albany County, N.Y., attempted to lease the county's passenger airport to a partnership consisting of a developer and an airport management company. FAA officials denied the proposal, arguing they couldn't he certain that revenue generated under the lease agreement would be used for airport purposes.

"I think the obvious problem that everybody is concerned about is whether the FAA will continue to support with (federal) resources a privatized airport," said Allan Ryan, executive vice president with the investment firm of Smith Barney, Harris Upham & Co. Inc., New York. Consequently, he said, airport privatization is "a real question of the economics — what sort of savings might accrue because you are privatized vs. what you might lose."

According to Bill Mosley, spokesman for the U.S. Department of Transportation, which oversees the FAA, "The issue of privatization of airports is under review by the department and we have not yet made any policy decisions."

A federal concern with the Los Angeles idea is the issue of accountability and how to ensure that the facility is operated in a fashion which best serves the travelers who use it. In the United States, there is no real example to look to in addressing that concern. No major airport in the United States has been privately owned since the late 1970s, when Lockheed Air Terminal Inc. sold the Burbank-Pasadena Airport in Southern California to a public authority.

Outside the United States, in 1987 the British government sold the British Airport Authority, which owns and operates the three main London airports (Heathrow, Gatwick and Stansted) and four major airports in Scotland. According to Clifton A. Moore, the general manager of LAX, the British airport privatization has been wildly successful from an investor's perspective. In addition, the airports' new operators have demonstrated concern with serving their users and they pay taxes on the facilities.

Though Heathrow and Gatwick are similar to LAX in terms of scale, from a financial perspective they are different entities and comparisons are not easily made, Mr. Ryan said. "They start from a different base. They were funded by the central government to start with and didn't rely on tax-exempt debt for financing," Mr. Ryan said. Ultimately, he added, the best bet for airport privatization in the United States may be a more limited action than what occurred in Britain. "I think the privatization in the U.S. is probably going to be more effective on the operations side rather than the ownership side," he said. The biggest gains, he believes, would stem from privatizing operations such as airport and concessions management.

Mr. Moore said the LAX staff isn't taking a position on whether the facility should be privatized. Los Angeles' decision may well be something short of total privatization of LAX. Yet, with other cities facing similar budget worries, Los Angeles' solution to the problem of how to tap its airport resources may well be one applied across the country.

Privatization: A politician's promise too good to be true?

Despite the potential benefits of selling public operations to the private sector, most government officials believe that too much privatization — or, indeed, any privatization whatsoever — can harm state and local governments and the constituents they serve.

Richard C. Leone, chairman of the Port Authority of New York and New Jersey, hammered home that point during an interview in the fall of 1990. His comments came in response to the calls by certain New York City politicians — including Mr. Lauder — to privatize major airports and the city's subways.

"When a politician's promises sound too good to be true, they usually are," Mr. Leone said. "Certainly that's the case with the scheme recently endorsed by some political figures to sell New York City's airports to the private sector. That privatization idea was followed by a second one to peddle the city's flagging subway system. No doubt the Brooklyn Bridge goes next.

"Selling the subways is an idea too fatuous to discuss, but the general notion of privatizing large pieces of indispensable public infrastructure bears examination. It is the natural, if illogical, outgrowth of the past decade's deregulation mania. What is really being proposed is nothing but an immense leveraged buy-out that attempts to lure the city and metropolitan region into cashing out some of their most valuable public assets in exchange for a quick revenue fix.

"If the 1980s taught us anything, it is that taking on debt does not necessarily solve problems. Rather, it often defers and enlarges them. For example, how would this debt-laden airport buyer come up with additional capital equal to one or 1½ times the purchase price to invest in the airports' modernization and expansion? This deal quickly wilts in light of the $3.5 billion in capital investment the Port Authority of New York & New Jersey plans for John F. Kennedy International and LaGuardia airports during the decade. Instead of investing, the over-leveraged private owners likely would take the airports down the familiar leveraged-buy-out road of reckless cost-cutting. In this business, that amounts to cannibalizing operations and services such as security, traveler assistance and environmental programs.

"Even the promised tax windfalls to the city and state would evaporate thanks to the debt-related write-offs. The most optimistic property tax estimate would not equal the $82 million rent the Port Authority of New York & New Jersey paid the city in 1989. No evidence supports the claims that private ownership would improve efficiency or increase revenue at a level remotely close to what would be needed to cover the purchase debt. The privatizers blithely presume that airport fees and rents can be raised indiscriminately and readily accepted by the airlines, travelers, and other tenants and patrons. These self-proclaimed free-market proponents apparently don't know that the airport market is fiercely competitive. A business strategy based on bleeding cash from the 'business' is a dead end that would only lead to a negative spiral of declining traffic, declining revenue and declining regional prosperity.

"Government intervention in the market had its modern origins in the efforts during the Progressive Era to break up the great trusts that were devouring all competition. Some of the deregulation of the recent past yielded public benefits precisely because it sparked a new wave of competition. But as the savings and loans, cable television and other examples remind us, deregulation is not magic. In a deregulated economy, we need a renewed toughness to prevent the return of the cartels and monopolies by vigorously enforcing antitrust laws and principles. We must maintain an effective public presence in aviation to ensure public safety, responsible environmental practices and adequate service to all the traveling public, not merely the select insiders who are positioned to exploit their private advantage. Privatization has its virtues, but only where competition and fairness are assured."

Garbage disposal

What should we do with all this garbage? That's the question local governments around the country are trying to answer.

Recycling programs for household trash like bottles, metal cans and plastic milk cartons are growing in popularity, but contemporary technology enables governments and private businesses to recycle only a small percentage of the waste stream. Incineration, especially in waste-to-energy facilities that convert heat from burning garbage into steam power and electricity, can destroy non-recyclable trash but contributes to air pollution and produces toxic ash. Garbage dumps, more pleasingly called "landfills," always have been popular final destinations for waste, but they're beginning to overflow, especially in urban areas where land is expensive.

Officials are coming to the realization that the best waste-management programs include all three of these tiers: recycling, incineration and landfilling. None of the three can stand alone.

The word recycling usually is misused when talking about the average solid-waste program. Governments focus too often on how to collect material, not how to ensure it is turned into new products. The United States has become very good at collecting cans, newspapers and plastic, but only isolated steps have been taken to address the problem of markets. What good does it do to collect newspapers when no company is willing to purchase that paper and convert it into new products? As a result, a portion — nobody knows what portion — of the material so carefully separated into recycling bins at the curbside actually winds up in landfills. Phillip B. Rooney, president and chief operating officer of Waste Management Inc., Oak Brook, Ill., challenged governments in the early 1990s to come up with incentives for research and development to help private industry handle the glut of material pouring in from mandated recycling programs. "Emphasis has been on recovery and collection, but there has not been much of an effort made on reprocessing or developing markets for these materials," he said.

Trash incinerators have met great amounts of opposition, especially from environmentalists and residents who simply do not want to live near garbage-burning plants. But waste-to-energy incinerators are becoming the preferred method of disposing of any waste that remains after recycling has been implemented. State-of-the-art landfills are used for disposal of the incinerators' ash residue.

The U.S. Environmental Protection Agency (EPA) predicts that by the year 2000 about 49% of the 216 tons of waste produced in the United States each year will be buried in landfills. Another 25% will be recycled, 25.5% will be burned in waste-to-energy facilities and less than 0.1% will be burned in incinerators that do not produce energy. In contrast, the EPA reported that in 1988 about 72.7% of the 179.5 tons of waste went to landfills, 13.6% was burned in waste-to-energy plants, 13.1% was recycled and 0.6% was burned in non-energy-producing incinerators. The year 1960 presents a striking contrast, when 62.5% of the 87.8 tons of waste went to landfills, 30.8% was burned (the technology for waste-to-energy facilities had not been perfected yet) and 6.7% was recycled.

"Ultimately, recycling will actually help encourage support for incineration as a technology because as people find out about the high costs of collecting and processing certain kinds of recyclables, they will learn that many of these materials can be combusted and turned into energy without any impact on public health," said H. Lanier Hickman, executive director of the pro-incineration Solid Waste Association of North America, Silver Spring, Md.

The true costs of collecting, processing and disposing of solid waste are rising astronomically throughout most of the country, and most citizens are still blissfully unaware of the facts. Determining who pays for waste services and figuring out how much they pay are among the most critical financial issues facing towns, cities, counties, villages, special districts and other local governments. The fact is that, for most U.S. residents, at least a part of the true cost of solid-waste disposal is hidden. Most municipalities do not assess the full costs of collection, processing and disposal. Even recycling, a growing ethic in most communities, rarely pays its own way. Some municipalities have been forced to complete assessments of their costs. The result? Dramatically higher garbage-collection charges for constituents.

Governments turn to volume and weight pricing

As if shopping for a car or selecting a long-distance telephone company weren't difficult enough, Portland, Ore., residents have to choose from among five different sizes of garbage cans. But you won't hear many complaints. After the city expanded its variable-rate system for garbage collection, recycling picked up so much that Portland's best recyclers received breaks on their garbage rates. City Council members reduced monthly rates for homeowners who used a 20-gallon "mini-can" or a standard 32-gallon container to dispose of waste. Users of the two smallest containers in Portland's variable-rate system paid less than the actual cost of their garbage service, said Councilman Earl Blumenauer, who also has served as the city's public works commissioner. "We decided our best course was to give a price reduction to the majority of our residential customers to highlight the program's pay-back to the community," said Mr. Blumenauer, who was a 1992 mayoral candidate.

As recently as the turn of the decade, it was hard to find examples of communities that had discarded their uniform rates for trash collection in favor of variable-rate pricing. Today, Portland finds itself in good company. Communities are discovering that variable rates are a more equitable way of financing waste disposal, requiring homeowners to pay for only what they generate. According to the EPA, more than 200 communities in 19 states have adopted variable-rate collection. Portland and Seattle embraced variable rates years ago, but few large cities in the Eastern United States have considered such a system, said Lisa Skumatz, director of Synergic Resources Corp., a Seattle-based waste consulting company.

Giving a price break to those who generate less waste can encourage households to throw away less and recycle more. Portland homeowners threw away about 25% less garbage after the city's variable-rate system was enhanced in February 1992. That was when the city's newspaper, glass and metal recycling program was expanded to include plastic containers and magazines. Meanwhile, nearly 70% of Portland households participated in curbside recycling, about twice as many recyclers as there were in 1991. Because less waste was being sent to landfills, Mr. Blumenauer said, the city was able to absorb a $7-per-ton increase in landfill tipping fees and still reduce garbage rates for most Portland citizens. Each household that disposed of its weekly garbage in a 20-gallon can paid $13 a month for service, down from $13.15 at the program's outset. Each user of the 32-gallon can paid $17.30, down from $17.50. These two groups represented nearly 70% of the city's households. Monthly rates were $19.70 for users of the 35-gallon to 40-gallon roll carts, $24.20 for the 60-gallon carts and $27.25 for the 90-gallon carts. All three rates were increased slightly in July 1992, and users of the two largest containers paid more than the actual cost of their garbage service.

As more communities see the wisdom of variable-rate collection systems, questions remain over the best way to encourage the most recycling. Variable-rate systems can involve the use of different-sized cans, special garbage bags purchased at local retail outlets or stickers attached to any garbage bag.

The central New York counties of Oneida and Herkimer, with a combined population of 320,000 people, serve as a laboratory of sorts for variable-rate collection. Every possible collection system is at work somewhere in the counties, with some cities operating their own systems, some under the direction of private haulers, some using variable-can systems and others using per-bag fees. Momentum toward variable-rate collection started in 1985 when a local hauler experimented with a per-bag system for customers in several towns, said Kevin Manion, director of recycling for the two counties' regional solid waste authority. The first major city in the area to turn to variable rates was Utica, population 68,000, which initiated a per-bag fee in 1989. About two-thirds of the counties' households were on some type of variable-rate system in late 1992, but differences of opinion remained over which method was most effective.

"People often will say that a per-bag system encourages recycling more than the cans, but I haven't seen that," Mr. Manion said. "Some of the highest recycling rates in our area are with carts, and the carts seem to be a lot more convenient to residents than bags."

Ms. Skumatz points out several advantages to charging homeowners by the number of bags they place on the curb. Such a system does not require communities to supply cans of different sizes, and it rewards households that dispose of less garbage in a given week. Under a can system, homeowners pay the same monthly fee no matter how full their garbage can is each week, or even if they are away from home for several weeks.

But now there is another alternative that is beginning to gain attention. With the help of a federal grant, Ms. Skumatz conducted a field test of a weight-based pricing system. A three-month experiment in 1992 involving 1,500 Seattle households tried to determine whether it was feasible to weigh garbage cans on the back of haulers' trucks and charge customers accordingly. Residents in the Seattle experiment were billed every two weeks and commented positively on the program, said Ms. Skumatz, who added that manufacturers are trying to develop the technology that would make weight-based pricing possible on a widespread basis. "In a weight-based system, a community could vary its charges in finer increments than it could with the others," Ms. Skumatz said.

Whatever way a community chooses to implement variable-rate collection, any method is preferable to sending no garbage bill and simply hiding garbage costs in property taxes, Ms. Skumatz insists.

Florida's purchasing policy closes the recycling loop

For any government to be truly involved in recycling, that government must make a commitment to purchase products made from recycled material.

The Florida governor's office has come up with a recycling plan that would sign up the state to purchase recycled products made from the waste being hauled away from state offices. If successful, the plan would be a major step toward solving the problem of weak markets for recyclable goods.

Florida's effort to recycle and buy recycled products is a continuation of moves in most state governments to stimulate markets by buying recycled products. In 1992, more than 40 states had regulations mandating procurement of recycled products or establishing purchasing preferences for such goods.

Democratic Gov. Lawton Chiles of Florida wanted to create substantial business ventures in the recycling industry for various commodities such as glass, paper and plastic. The state would close the recycling loop by guaranteeing to the joint ventures that haul away the government's recyclable material that the state would purchase what is made to its specifications from its discarded items.

"This one takes on the problem of the stagnant markets," said former state legislator Robert W. McKnight, executive staff policy coordinator in the governor's office. The state planned to enter into contracts with companies dealing in paper, glass, spent fuel and other ventures. The added bonus was the potential for these dual hauling and purchasing contracts to stimulate economic development, Mr. McKnight said. "It raises an obvious benefit," he said. If the state could offer a group of companies enough waste and promise enough procurement of the recycled products, the companies might move to the area or expand their operations to reap the benefits of a tidy, concentrated business opportunity. "It doesn't make sense to haul waste away from Gainesville, bring it to Michigan and then bring (products) back to Florida," Mr. McKnight added. "We think the result very clearly will be economic development."

There were no subsidies for the program. Mr. McKnight estimated the value to companies would be $200 million to $300 million in the first year and expected Florida municipalities to join in and save from 25% to 40% on hauling costs. The state also would insist on quality products and offer a state designation indicating a product was made from Florida waste.

The proposal has "tremendous merit," said Ken Small, director of economic research for the Florida League of Cities, based in Tallahassee. "Cities have been keen on how to save money. They're in tight budget times." The program was just getting under way in 1992. Interested companies were negotiating with state officials, so most cities were not aware of the potential savings, Mr. Small added. "I suspect a tremendous number of cities will jump at this," he said. But the idea makes the most sense for larger urban areas. "It's got to be convenient and cost-effective for the city to use it," Mr. Small said.

The program was not designed to be mandatory. Cities that had successful recycling and procurement programs could choose to stick with them. Cities were under a state mandate to reduce solid waste by 30% by 1994, and they could get credits toward that goal under the governor's program, Mr. McKnight said. The state's first venture would be recycling spent fuel, a contract worth about $18 million, he said. Florida would recycle its fuel and buy back recycled antifreeze and re-refined oil. The state also was doing a paper inventory for its next venture to see how much paper it could offer to a joint venture for recycling.

Outside of Florida, a consortium of corporations, state legislatures, mayors and county officials called during the spring of 1992 for private and public entities to significantly increase their purchases of products made from recycled paper. "They developed a strategy calling for a voluntary market approach rather than more laws. These are not mandatory," said Brian A. Day, director of the National Office Paper Recycling Project, Washington. The group targeted the 1,000 largest corporations, counties and cities, as well as all 50 governors, inviting them to accept the challenge to establish a "buy recycled" program, set up a collection program and go even further with their own ideas for "harnessing the entrepreneurial and creative spirit," Mr. Day said. "If people think they're recycling by separating waste, they're not. They're sorting. They must purchase" recycled goods, he said.

Debris converted into building blocks for new products

Construction and demolition debris — the waste generated as buildings are built and torn down — make up better than 20% of the solid-waste stream, yet the recycling of such debris frequently is overlooked. So state and local governments are stepping up programs to recycle construction and demolition material to save precious landfill space, cut dumping costs, create jobs, provide useful products and even reduce housing costs.

Construction debris is "easy to identify, it's easy to transport and now it's easy to recycle about two-thirds of it," said John Kraft, director of corporate development for ReClaim Inc., Tampa, Fla., a firm that turns discarded asphalt building material into recycled asphalt and paving products. Wood and concrete also can be recycled easily. Concrete can become aggregate for roadbeds or new concrete, while wood is converted into pellets that can be used for fuel or mulch.

With 500-odd buildings being demolished in Los Angeles as part of a Rebuild LA effort following riots in late April 1992, the city government tried moving toward increased recycling of construction debris. City officials encouraged contractors to recycle demolition waste. There was no recycling requirement, but the city provided contractors with a guide to recycling construction and demolition material.

"We were doing kind of a public education outreach and technical assistance for contractors," said Kelly Ingalls, senior management analyst for the Los Angeles Integrated Solid Waste Management Office.

The city also began a pilot program aimed at construction companies that won city contracts for street improvements and other public works projects. Under the program, those contractors were required to report to the city's Board of Public Works to explain how they disposed of solid waste generated on the job. What the city hoped to develop, Mr. Ingalls said, was "a data base of what kind of solid-waste practices our contractors are into." That information could form the basis for setting construction and demolition debris recycling requirements.

At its Upper Marlboro, Md., National Research Home Park, the National Association of Home Builders has worked on the issue of construction-debris recycling from several perspectives. The group's Resource Conservation Research House is a demonstration project built with material not typically seen in home construction, such as steel framing and hardboard siding. The framing is made primarily of recycled scrap from demolished buildings and bridges and from automobile and industrial plants. The siding comes from wood fiber and sawmill scraps.

Back in the late 1970s, the National Association of Home Builders' Cost Buster House project aimed at developing building processes that minimized the amount of scrap generated in construction. Since fees paid to dump scrap construction material ultimately make their way into a home's cost, minimizing the amount of scrap sent to landfills would help keep housing price tags down, the organization's officials reasoned.

"What we're doing now is a continuation of what was done with the Cost Buster House, to look at minimizing scrap and waste because they add to the cost," said Larry Zarker, director of marketing for the National Association of Home Builders' research center. "What we're trying to do is that plus reuse and recycle."

As homes are built at the research park, scrap and waste material are segregated to give the association's researchers "a clear idea of the volume of all that material, and then we try to come up with creative uses for it."

Meanwhile, ReClaim Inc. has developed successful techniques for recycling asphalt roofing scraps into asphalt and paving products. Asphalt roofing debris represents about 38% of construction and demolition debris, according to Mr. Kraft. While in many cases recycling programs stall for a lack of markets for recycled material, the products ReClaim Inc. produces from recycled asphalt building material have been well-received in the marketplace. Those products include RePave, a cold-asphalt patching material for fixing potholes, and ReActs-HMA, a hot-mix asphalt paving additive. RePave has been sold on a retail basis in the Northeast.

Solon, Ohio: Waste not, compost all

The dictionary defines Solon as a wise and skillful lawgiver. In that case, Edmund R. Butler should feel right at home as the architect of the composting and curbside recycling programs in Solon, Ohio. Using a combination of scientific expertise and homespun wisdom, Mr. Butler has helped turn the community of 20,000 people near Cleveland into a virtual test market for the latest in composting and recycling technology. He might not even mind if you referred to Solon as one giant compost heap.

"We decided it was easiest to get the yard waste out of the waste stream first," said Mr. Butler, a retired science teacher who is Solon's solid-waste program manager. "We started in 1988 by shredding Christmas trees. The next year we started shredding leaves for composting. Then, in 1991, we ran a pilot program for composting grass clippings, and now we do that for the whole city."

In many communities around the country, curbside recycling takes priority in the effort to divert material from the land-filled waste stream. But in Solon, composting has taken off as fast as the city's recycling collection. City officials are painfully aware that about one-quarter of the area's waste stream is made up of yard waste, and half of the odor problems associated with land-fills are attributable to food waste, most of which can be com-posted. Officials can't help knowing the percentages — Solon houses the landfill that serves the city and more than a dozen of its neighboring communities.

"Even though the landfill is in an industrial area away from homes, our people know it's there," said Solon Mayor Robert A. Paulson. "They are well aware of the landfill space problem."

Composting, involving the decomposition of organic waste into a usable product, takes many forms in Solon. The city's own composting operation received a boost in 1992 when grass clip-pings were added to a program that includes leaves, trees and cer-tain types of construction debris. Homeowners place their lawn clippings into paper bags, which are shredded and deposited in compost rows. Residents also are encouraged to set up their own backyard composting operations, which can include anything from yard trimmings to food waste. If homeowners do not want to bag their lawn clippings, they are urged to throw them in their compost bins, or simply leave them on the lawn to renourish it.

"We felt we were not going to burden residents with one op-tion," Mr. Butler said. "It's to our advantage to have multiple choices."

Homeowners become familiar with the range of possibilities be-cause they are literally bombarded with written notices — printed on recycled paper, of course — from Mr. Butler's department. Homeowners are shown how to build their own composting bins, or how to maintain an orderly compost pile in their back yards. They are taught how 200 red-worms in a composting box will eat three to four pounds of food waste every week. Particularly effective meals for the worms are apple cores, vegetables and bread, which eventually become high-quality compost for the garden. Meat, bones and dairy products are discouraged. Residents learn the kind of composting trivia that would make a "Jeopardy" game show contestant envious. For example, newspapers can be added to the mix if shredded, but magazines should not be added because of their ink. Manure from horses, cows and even elephants is usable (though elephants aren't known to roam the Ohio suburbs), but waste from dogs and cats is not because it often contains disease organisms. Homeowners also are taught how to ward off composting problems, with instructions that resemble a television owner's manual. Instead of learning what to do when the picture is fuzzy, residents are told how to combat odors (turn the compost pile) or heat up the bin (mix in nitrogen-rich fertilizer).

More than 1,000 Solon homes participate in backyard composting, with at least 100 using worm composting bins for food waste. In addition, Mr. Butler said, the city collects 20,000 cubic yards of leaves each year, which is converted to 5,000 cubic yards of usable humus. The city expects to collect about the same amount of grass clippings, though the grass will generate only 1,000 more cubic yards of humus.

Mr. Butler has no problem finding customers for the end product. City residents line up for the humus, eager to turn the remnants of last summer into next spring's soil conditioner. In fact, finding markets for recyclables hardly has been an issue in Solon. Recycling and composting still have to be subsidized with city funds, but Solon harbors no tales of newspapers and glass bottles gathering dust in warehouses.

Through recycling and composting, Solon has been able to reduce its waste stream headed to the landfill by 50%. Its goal for the 21st century is an eye-popping 90% reduction.

The pace of Solon's efforts has caught the eye of its neighbors. Officials from many nearby cities, including Cleveland, have visited Solon to gather hints for their own composting operations.

The city was one of Ohio's first to react to a state environmental law adopted in 1988. The law warned that as of Dec. 1, 1993, communities no longer would be allowed to deposit grass, leaves or brush in municipal landfills.

Solon's fascination with composting has filtered to the business community. Stouffer Foods Corp., the city's largest employer, is working with a local contractor to plan for food-waste composting. Solon is one of three Stouffer sites for the processing and packaging of frozen foods. The company is testing a composting technique on 200 yards of pasta, said Dale Shalashnow, senior industrial engineer with the company.

With all of the city's outreach efforts, it would be difficult to find a Solon resident who is not recycling-literate.

"I know people who tell me they're glad they're saving trees from Minnesota and Wisconsin when they use recycled paper," said Dick Evans, owner of a local printing company and former president of the Solon Chamber of Commerce. "If we're successful here, other people will think they can make a difference."

That's the kind of wisdom with which no one can argue.

Davis, Calif.: Reduce, reuse, recycle, rebuy

Recycling, energy conservation and wetlands creation all go together in 50,000-resident Davis, Calif., said City Manager John Meyer. "Everyone is an environmentalist."

Davis, home of the University of California at Davis, has a long history of recycling, Mr. Meyer explained. The city has worked its way up to one of the most comprehensive programs a government can have, linking the four Rs: reduce, reuse, recycle and rebuy. Davis, just west of Sacramento in Northern California, operates five recycling programs: drop-off, buy-back, curbside, multifamily dwellings and commercial. All are offered citywide, according to Diane Makley, recycling coordinator.

Recycling and an increased awareness of the environment began in Davis with the first Earth Day in the early 1970s, Ms. Makley recounted. The small university community and the city population have since worked together to create a place where citizens can "live appropriately with their environment." Over the past 20 years, the five major programs have been instituted incrementally until the city has in place the comprehensive programs of today.

Ms. Makley admitted that after Davis instituted curbside service, it was more difficult to add the programs for multifamily (apartment and condominium) recycling and commercial recycling. Yet Davis now is one of the few cities in the United States with universal multifamily recycling programs. Buildings with 10 or more units provide communal recycling bins at convenient locations, while locations with nine or fewer units put their recyclable material in bins for weekly pickup at curbside. Building permits for apartment units must be accompanied by recycling enclosure retrofit plans, according to a 1989 city ordinance. Residences of 10 or more units are required to make recycling carts available for tenants.

A wide range of material can be recycled in Davis, which boasts a diversion rate of more than 40%:

■ Beverage and food containers made of aluminum, glass, steel, tin and two types of plastic — the common polyethylene terephthlate (PET) and high-density polyethylene (HDPE, which is used for milk jugs and the rigid bottoms of soda-pop bottles).

■ Mixed paper, including newsprint, magazines, and white and colored office paper.

■ Corrugated cardboard.

■ Used motor oil.

The city emphasizes waste reduction, reuse and purchase of recycled goods. A 1990 ordinance includes a purchasing preference for recycled goods and requires that all consultant contract work submitted on paper be on recycled paper.

The city has as a key target recycled office paper. Although some envelopes in city offices probably are not made of recycled material, all other paper is, Ms. Makley said, as are all janitorial products. Copy-machine toner cartridges are refilled rather than replaced.

Davis contracts with Davis Waste Removal, a part of EBA Waste Technology, Santa Rosa, for garbage collection. The fee is negotiated with each contract and is funded by the city from sanitation fees. On so-called "garbage day," three different trucks run the trash collection routes, one each for non-recyclable household garbage, yard waste and recyclables, Mr. Meyer said. Ms. Makley calls the relationship between Davis Waste Removal and the city a successful joint effort. "It's an outstanding example of what can be accomplished when public and private entities work together on education and promotion of recycling, waste reduction and buying recycled," she said.

Educating the public about the four Rs is a major responsibility of the city, Ms. Makley noted. That is particularly important in a college town with large numbers of transients. Flyers are sent to residents at least once a year regarding curbside recycling, twice a year for apartment recycling. Of the two multifamily recycling flyers, one is a multilanguage form. For commercial recycling, much cooperative work is done with the Davis Chamber of Commerce, Ms. Makley added. Flyers targeting office recycling and newsletter announcements are sent out annually. No one curriculum exists for the education system, but the city targets information to different grades, Ms. Makley said. The state government of California also has provided a curriculum.

Within the city's own departments, in-house training is held regarding waste reduction and recycling. Ms. Makley and Solid Waste/Recycling Manager Robert Weis, assistant public works director, work hard on keeping city workers up-to-date on new recycling techniques and technologies.

In addition, Ms. Makley has written or edited weekly columns in a local newspaper since the fall of 1990. Multimedia displays of information on the four Rs are presented at various locations in the city and at special events, and a 30-minute video has been produced in cooperation with the Yolo County Environmental Resource Center and Davis Community Television (the local cable access channel) for local TV showings.

The city is immersed in environmentalism, Mr. Meyer said. In addition to recycling, residential standards for energy conservation have been set up and the city is working to create a recreational wetland using wastewater treatment. "Recycling has been embraced by the community, it's a matter of habit," said the city manager. "It's an ethic here. You don't throw cans out. When new residents come, the city sends them literature and puts them online. It's expected."

Tacoma, Wash.: TRASH preserves natural habitat

If the idea of a link between recycling garbage and saving endangered species sounds confusing, just ask any elementary school student in Tacoma, Wash., to spell it out for you.

In the spring of 1988, one of the United States' most innovative public education campaigns for recycling was launched in Tacoma elementary schools, though its impact went far beyond young children.

Almost every city that recycles has a school recycling curriculum, but in Tacoma there is a real-world link between the lessons and the reality of recycling. The city's drop-off recycling program, which until 1990 was the primary method of recycling, is based in school parking lots. The drop-off boxes still are the main way newspapers and aluminum cans are recycled in Tacoma, a city of 177,500 people 32 miles south of Seattle along the Puget Sound.

"When we went to curbside collection, we thought the kids had been so successful with the TRASH program, we didn't want to just take the drop boxes away from them," explained David Frutiger, the recycling supervisor for the city's refuse utility. TRASH stands for Tacoma Recycles and Saves Habitat, a program developed by the city and the Point Defiance Zoo and Aquarium in Tacoma.

In addition to a 45-minute, multimedia assembly program, students design a classroom recycling project, participate in five follow-up sessions, take home recycling kits to encourage parents to get involved, and visit the zoo. The link between animals and habitat, made clear in the curriculum and accented at the zoo, is that use of raw materials in foreign-made products causes the loss of habitat in those countries through deforestation, strip mining and energy production. For every aluminum can buried in the Tacoma landfill, more bauxite must be mined in Australia and Brazil, where some endangered species live.

A Tacoma curriculum guide reads, "When we throw away a cardboard box from a new Japanese television, the label on the box doesn't say, 'Made of trees from tropical forests in a factory using electricity generated by burning oil from Indonesia. Orangutans lived in this forest and other animals lived where the oil was drilled.' " The lessons also note that the Pacific Northwest is home to old-growth forests and the endangered spotted owl, so throwing away newsprint and packaging can have a direct local impact.

City officials have learned their own lessons about recycling. The city's landfill has been a Superfund toxic waste site for years. In 1990, the city had made an agreement with the EPA to line and cap the landfill, but a federal judge declared the agreement illegal, a violation of the EPA's own standards. Running on a platform of cleaning up the landfill and starting curbside recycling, mayoral candidate Karen L.R. Vialle defeated the incumbent mayor. One of her first actions was to move ahead with a full-scale, $25 million cleanup of the dump.

"Recycling is obviously of importance for us, but we link it to the whole issue of the environment, which plays a central role in this administration," Ms. Vialle said.

A past administration was responsible for the start of a small-scale recycling program at the landfill in 1986, but from there things stagnated. Ms. Vialle's administration turned the program into one of the most comprehensive in the country. In April 1988, the landfill began accepting a full range of waste for processing into recycling markets. The center still accepts almost every kind of material that can be reused or recycled, including appliances, car batteries and motor oil. In 1989, an office recycling service for every city office was added. In early 1990, a dedicated Recycling Hotline was established for anyone in the residential or commercial sector who needed information about specialized recycling. Later that year, residential yard and garden waste collection services, residential curbside recycling, multifamily curbside collection for buildings up to 50 units, commercial curbside pickup and plate glass recycling were added. A household hazardous-waste collection facility at the landfill was established in 1990, along with mobile neighborhood collection. Of the household hazardous waste, motor oil, solvents, antifreeze and automotive batteries are recycled. In 1991, numerous other materials were added to the recycling program, including motor oil, telephone books, cardboard, tires, polyurethane foam and magazines. Added in 1992 was a program to recycle ash from the local incinerator, which produces steam for electricity generation; the ash is blended with other material into Portland Cement.

"We have come so far so quickly. A lot of that has to do with our residents, who have responded to every change in our program positively," Ms. Vialle said.

The scope of the city program can best be seen in the composting operation, owned by a private firm in the city. City refuse trucks pick up yard and garden waste every other week from homes at the curbside. Landscaping companies drop off their waste for a fee at the landfill. The city solicits grocery produce waste. Sludge from the city's sewage treatment plant also is composted. The material is compacted and trucked to the compost company and used as a soil additive.

Unlike many recycling officials, those in Tacoma refuse to cite inflated recycling percentage figures that often include items not routinely found in the municipal solid-waste stream, including so-called white goods like stoves and refrigerators. Thus, the city acknowledges a 12% recycling rate, reflecting only the ma-

terial actually weighed at the processing facility prior to ship-
ment to recycling markets. Adding commercial material picked
up at curbside, the rate is estimated at 32%.

Like other recycling programs, Tacoma's is looking harder at
reducing hazardous waste and packaging used by industry. The
city performs waste audits of companies to show them how
to reduce waste and reuse material.

Hennepin County, Minn.: Disposing of hazardous waste

If you had to describe the Hennepin County, Minn., recycling
program in a single phrase, it would be "ahead of its time." Before Minnesota adopted a statewide recycling law in 1988,
987,000-resident Hennepin County, which includes Minneapolis,
was already well under way with a comprehensive curbside collection program in several communities. The authors of the
county recycling ordinance were consultants to the state on
drafting the statewide law.

Today, all 47 cities within the county have programs that
are further advanced than typical programs in other areas of the
country. The county recycles or composts 46% of its total waste
stream, processing 52% in a waste-to-energy facility. Only 2% is
sent to landfills.

"There is nothing less glamorous or more important than
solid-waste management, especially recycling," said John Derus,
chairman of the Hennepin County Board of Commissioners. "We
have had some problems in the area of marketing plastics and
paper, like many others have had, but overall this program has
developed beautifully."

Like other areas, Hennepin County leaped before it looked into
plastic recycling with one of the country's most ambitious programs, picking up the entire range of recyclable plastic. But a
drop in world oil prices in 1990 made recycled fibers difficult to
market because virgin fiber became cheaper to produce. Local
recyclers had stockpiles of plastic bottles and other containers
that no one would buy. The market for newsprint fell off completely. Today, through a combination of market development
and sales work, localities are having more luck marketing the material, though the situation remains fluid.

The county reviewed all of its options for achieving a high
recycling rate when it looked to adopting a countywide law in the
mid-1980s. "When we started, we talked about a typical mandatory recycling program that would have forced county residents
to recycle," said Dan Huschke, the first county recycling coordinator who later took a job with a private firm that markets some
of the county's recyclables. "But I was against that. It would have
left a bad taste in the mouths of residents to start out by forcing
them to participate. So we opted to mandate that cities offer
residents the chance to recycle." Mr. Huschke believes cities

within the county have made great strides toward marketing their material. "They share the same problems everyone does. There has been more attention made to collections than marketing. They seem to have turned that situation around."

The county has been able to meet its high recycling numbers with a program that includes single-family and multifamily curbside pickup; commercial, industrial and institutional recycling programs; an in-house county office recycling program; a successful education and promotion campaign; and strong efforts to develop markets.

Before integrated solid-waste management became a recycling buzzword, Hennepin County officials looked at a way to reduce landfill dependency in a variety of ways. After recycling separates the material that can be reused or turned into new products, the county's refuse-derived fuel plant makes pellets of unrecyclable waste, which is burned in the county incinerator in Minneapolis. The county also operates several material recovery facilities (MRFs), waste transfer stations, yard-waste composting sites and a landfill.

The focus of the recycling program has shifted to the handling of hazardous waste and of special waste that is hard to recycle. "Televisions, computers and fluorescent light tubes all have a lot of materials that are actually recyclable but would be hazardous if put in a landfill or burned," said Janet Lieck, director of the county's Department of Environmental Management.

Each year, Hennepin County spends about $10 million on recycling programs, a lot of it through a funding assistance policy that encourages municipalities to hit high recycling rates. The higher the rate, the higher the reimbursement. To be eligible for funding under the county policy, municipalities must collect newspapers, cardboard, metal cans, glass containers and plastic bottles. In county offices, workers must recycle all of that material, plus scrap metal, telephone books, laser printer cartridges, batteries and polystyrene packaging "peanuts."

The county permits municipalities to obtain reimbursement for providing curbside collection at buildings with eight or fewer units. In addition, the county ordered several styles and sizes of recycling containers and recycling signs to meet the needs of the various kinds of buildings. Property owners buy the containers directly from the county. The county has published a recycling guidebook for multifamily units.

In 1987, before most other metropolitan areas had begun to think about industrial recycling and waste reduction, Hennepin County had published its first industrial recycling guide. The book, updated annually, provides step-by-step instructions for beginning an industrial recycling program. The guide also details where each kind of industrial waste can be recycled, such as grease, batteries, pallets, tires and plate glass.

New York City (finally) moves to limit garbage volume

In 1991, New York City Mayor David N. Dinkins warned there might not be enough money to continue curbside recycling. But one year later, city officials were talking about shrinking the waste stream through recycling and source reduction by 50% in eight years.

Same city, wildly different outcomes.

To some degree, New York state should take credit for the turnaround. A 1988 state law requiring communities to adopt guidelines for separation of recyclable material finally got the city to make long-range planning decisions.

The city's mandated waste plan, adopted in August 1992 after months of debate, set ambitious recycling goals and called for construction of a waste-to-energy plant in Brooklyn to begin in 1996. Government officials and the city's building lobby hailed the plan as an integrated approach to waste management, including the three major options of landfilling, recycling and incinerating. In that regard, the plan was a far cry from one advanced around the same time by Rhode Island legislators, who became the country's first to enact a statewide ban on waste incineration.

Criticism of New York City's blueprint came from two sources: those who opposed incineration at all costs, and those who doubted the plan went far enough to meet the disposal needs of the populous city. The first group was heard primarily during heated public hearings; the second claimed the plan was inadequate because it projected that the city would export 15% of its waste and would landfill 20% in the year 2000. Landfilling and exports in 1992 took care of a staggering 81% of the city's waste stream, but it was believed that the city's Fresh Kills landfill would be at capacity by the year 2012.

"To assume we will still be able to export 15% of our waste, in view of the likelihood of federal law on exports, puts us at the mercy of other governments," said Sheldon Leffler, a City Council member from Queens. Mr. Leffler believed the city should accelerate construction of the planned Brooklyn incinerator and perhaps build two or three more plants. But, he said, Mr. Dinkins believed he would have trouble winning public support for more than one plant. "The waste plan is a political arrangement, heavily influenced by what is politically acceptable," Mr. Leffler said.

The planned trash-to-energy facility at the Brooklyn Navy Yard was expected to burn at least 3,000 tons of an estimated 27,000 tons per day of city garbage by the turn of the century. The waste plan called for closing smaller incinerators in Queens and Brooklyn. City officials insisted their plan was realistic and said incinerator construction should not start until a comprehensive recycling program was fully developed.

In early 1993, a total of 38 of the city's 59 sanitation districts were on curbside recycling, with all of Manhattan, the Bronx and Staten Island covered. Every sanitation district in Brooklyn was scheduled to be on board by June 1993, and all of Queens by the end of that year, said Kathy Dawkins, spokeswoman for the city Sanitation Department. From then on, the city would have to devise methods to improve collection of newspapers, magazines, glass, metal, plastic and corrugated cardboard, especially in densely populated areas. In 1992, New York was recycling about 12% of its waste stream. Also, the city would have to pick up the pace of commercial recycling, which, according to Ms. Dawkins, was lagging.

By 2000, city officials expected to divert 42% of the residential, commercial and institutional waste streams through recycling, and another 9% would be eliminated by convincing businesses to phase out unnecessary packaging, Ms. Dawkins said. To increase recycling participation, New York was trying to provide residents with more than one disposal option. Most of the households that had been separating recyclables for a while deposited the items in plastic bins for pickup. But because the popular bins tended to "walk away" in New York, as Ms. Dawkins put it, residents also would be allowed to deposit recyclables in plastic "blue bags," separate from the bags that contained their regular trash.

Despite the challenges a large city can face in implementing recycling, most New Yorkers embraced the idea of a comprehensive program. A March 1992 survey of 752 registered voters, conducted for the New York Building Congress, indicated overwhelming support for recycling. The poll also showed support for a balanced strategy involving landfilling, recycling and incineration. Some 54% of respondents favored a three-pronged approach, while only 23% preferred a strategy without waste-to-energy burning. The Building Congress, a non-partisan group representing labor and management interests in the construction industry, used the poll to persuade City Council members to embrace Mr. Dinkins' waste plan. In the end, council members approved the plan 36-15, despite environmentalists' opposition to incineration.

"Two weeks before the vote, a majority of council members said the plan was dead," said Building Congress President Louis J. Coletti. "There was outstanding political leadership by the mayor and council in recognizing that the issue had to be dealt with."

Local builder groups estimated the incinerator would create 1,000 jobs during the peak construction period in the mid-1990s.

The city's waste planning had moved a long way since fiscal 1992 budget hearings in the spring of 1991, when Mr. Dinkins suggested that curbside recycling might cease because of fiscal constraints. Reactions to his comments were highly negative, with people worrying that once recycling stopped it would never resume. The city put that near-crisis behind it. What remained to be seen, however, was whether New York's long-range planning went far enough to avert future crises.

Police & public safety

From small towns to large cities, law enforcement officers and municipal officials are struggling to keep crime down. Crime prevention has become a priority, especially in major urban areas such as Chicago, Los Angeles, New York and Washington, D.C. — cities where a fierce trade in illegal drugs exacerbates matters.

When local governments are unable to come up with money to hire additional police officers, they turn to extraordinary programs to try to stem rising crime rates. In St. Louis, for example, officials in October 1991 announced they would pay $50 for each firearm that residents turned in to police. The city government prepared to collect 2,000 guns in the monthlong program, but they received that number in just two days. "We weren't so naive to think that drug dealers would come to turn in their weapons, but we discovered a lot of people who don't want or need their guns," said Christine Nelson, public information assistant with the St. Louis Police Department. "They feel threatened to have the guns in their homes, or they may fear the guns could be stolen in a robbery." In a growing number of cities, police have concluded that fewer guns on the streets and in homes mean safer neighborhoods. Several police departments have instituted temporary gun buy-back programs in which residents exchange their firearms for cash — with no questions asked.

Other jurisdictions, however, prefer to stick with traditional methods of police work while incorporating new technology to help them better preserve law and order.

Municipalities take diverse paths to community policing

Ask 100 city officials about community policing, and most will say their police departments either are doing it or are thinking about it. Ask the same 100 to define community policing, and you might get 100 different answers. Therein lies the dilemma facing cities that are riding the new wave in law enforcement. Because people don't always agree on what community policing means, there is little consensus over whether it is working — or even how to make it work.

Community- or neighborhood-oriented policing seeks to reduce the physical and psychological distance between police and citizens. It is a strategy designed to involve residents in crime prevention and welcome their help in investigating incidents and attacking social problems.

All neighborhood-oriented policing efforts have crime reduction as their ultimate goal through dealing with the root causes of crime in declining communities. But there is no Bible on how to achieve community policing, so cities have taken widely divergent paths.

Community policing in Elgin, Ill., involves moving several police officers and their families to high-crime housing projects. In Seattle, it means officers giving up their cars and bicycling their ways around their beats. In Springfield, Ohio, it means giving police flexible hours so they can tailor their schedules to neighborhood needs.

"The philosophy behind community-oriented policing is that the police need to start thinking service," said E. Roberta Lesh, director of police programs for the International City/County Management Association, Washington, which conducts training sessions for mayors and police chiefs interested in the concept. "This is as opposed to the young person seeking adventure in the police department, or what I call the 'John Wayne syndrome.' "

According to the National Center for Community Policing at Michigan State University, East Lansing, 65% of cities with at least 50,000 residents say they either have implemented community policing or are about to do so. Robert Trojanowicz, the center's director, said smaller cities probably have been into community policing all along because their officers are more familiar with the community's key personalities. In recent years, city officials have been compelled to consider a new policing strategy because of a growing sense that neighborhoods are declining. "It might just be that rowdy kids are terrorizing the elderly, or there might already be open drug deals," Mr. Trojanowicz said. "But people come to realize that, if they don't deal with it now, it'll be much worse in 10 years."

One community that reached that conclusion is Aurora, Colo., once a quiet suburb of Denver but now a city with 225,000 low- to middle-income residents and a host of urban problems. Facing a rise in street-gang activity and drug trafficking, the Police Department in 1983 assigned officers to act as community ombudsmen in five pilot areas. Community policing now encompasses all of Aurora, division chief Ron Sloan said. Police at first dismissed the effort as liberal window-dressing, something that resembled social work more than police work. But the department has succeeded in selling community policing as a more effective way of doing business — preferable to sitting in a squad car waiting for the next call. "I would say I'm a convert to community policing," Mr. Sloan said. "I can look back at things I did as a patrolman that were more oriented toward the community side. They were much more satisfying than the typical reactive approach."

A more recent convert is Springfield, Ohio, a city of 70,000 located west of Columbus. After city voters in 1990 authorized a tax increase to add 24 officers to a 100-member Police Department, city officials decided they would not place all of the new officers in traditional roles. Officials selected two neighborhoods in transition as pilot areas for community policing, City Manager Matt Kridler said. In June 1992, three officers were assigned to each area to serve as neighborhood liaisons, working closely with families and community groups and recommending intervention by social service agencies on specific problems. Unlike police officers in most cities, who are routinely transferred from beat to beat, these Springfield officers will spend more time in their assigned neighborhoods to build relationships with community leaders and problem youths. Mr. Kridler and other city officials meet monthly to assess community policing's progress.

But how can cities measure the success of these efforts? That is a question which puzzles officials in New York City, where Police Commissioner Lee P. Brown preached community policing almost from the first day of his 1990 arrival. City Councilman Sheldon Leffler, representing the borough of Queens, wants a group of academics to evaluate the city's effort.

"It's not sufficient to say this person or that is working more with the community now," Mr. Leffler said. "Are you also preventing crime? Are you uprooting patterns of crime? Is there a sense among members of the community that the police are being more responsive?"

Mr. Trojanowicz is not surprised by such concerns. But he warns against measuring the success of community policing in the same way traditional police work is evaluated. Community policing is a long-term strategy too often subjected to short-term reviews, Mr. Trojanowicz said. In the short term, community policing might cause crime rates to increase because citizens with a closer relationship to police feel less reluctant to report crime than they did before. Community policing also can mean slower response times for non-emergency calls. Crime rate increases should subside in the long term under community policing, Mr. Trojanowicz said, but elected officials often do not want to look past the next election.

Then there are those who simply dismiss community policing as being soft on crime. Cities like Richmond, Va., fight that notion by stressing that community policing and a tough approach to law enforcement are not mutually exclusive. The hallmark of Richmond's community policing effort, which began in 1989, is a program designed to enlist residents in helping bring drug criminals to justice. In the city's "Drug-Free Blocks" program, at least 80% of a neighborhood's residents pledge in writing not to be involved in drugs and to report suspected drug activity. In the seven Richmond neighborhoods designated as drug-free, residents agree they will testify in court against accused drug dealers, City Manager Robert Bobb said. That not only helps achieve convictions, but reduces a community's fear of crime, he said. "Community policing may appear to be soft, but we have an aggressive law enforcement effort coupled with it," Mr. Bobb said. He reports that crime has virtually disappeared from the seven areas, which are marked with street signs. He says improvement was noticeable almost from the start. As is the case in many cities, Richmond police have decentralized their management structure under community policing. Precinct captains have more authority to involve officers in specific community-oriented programs. Some officers are working out of apartment buildings in low-income neighborhoods, and one police substation is being relocated to a drug-infested area.

A community-policing philosophy can generate unlimited innovation, but the strategy might not be for everyone. Flint, Mich., one of the first cities to embrace the concept, has retreated from a community-oriented approach because its police force has been overwhelmed with incident calls since the local economy collapsed, Mr. Trojanowicz said. A department must have time to allow officers to work with citizens or it must hire additional officers for those duties, experts say.

Aside from such considerations, politics still looms as the greatest threat to community policing's potential success. Elected officials who treat community policing as a program instead of a philosophy, expecting it to produce overnight results, are bound to be disappointed. And if that feeling becomes widespread around the country, community policing could become a short-lived approach to municipal law enforcement.

Pressure forces police chiefs to escape from their jobs

The trend toward a more community-oriented approach to law enforcement, however, has opened police chiefs to more criticism.

If police administrators in the past simply had to be tough on crime and strong managers, now they are expected to have good community-relations skills on top of that, said Sam Nuchia, Houston's police chief. "You now have to deal with more diverse groups that have political power, including your own employees," said Mr. Nuchia, who is openly critical of any tendency to over-emphasize neighborhood-oriented policing. "I thought I had a good idea of what the job entailed, but it's been significantly more demanding." A former assistant chief in Houston, Mr. Nuchia took over in March 1992 for Elizabeth Watson, who was replaced after the 1991 mayoral election of Bob Lanier. Ms. Watson, appointed by previous Houston Mayor Kathryn J. Whitmire, later was named Austin's police chief.

Neighborhood-oriented policing, focused on involving the community more in crime prevention and investigation, often presents a dilemma for police chiefs. It fulfills the demand that chiefs be innovative in fighting crime, but it also exposes them to heavy criticism if the newfangled ideas don't reduce crime right away — and they usually don't. "Chiefs are expected to be innovative and creative, but they are being judged on the traditional criteria of crime statistics," Mr. Trojanowicz said.

Police chiefs who advocate community policing are boxed into a corner when asked to support civilian review boards for cases of police misconduct. Such boards are anathema to rank-and-file police officers. In New York in 1992, Mayor David N. Dinkins' push for an all-civilian review board hurt his relations with police officers.

Several other problems also face police chiefs around the country, making the job one of the least stable in local government — especially in areas where crime is on the rise.

1992 was a tumultuous year at the helm of the country's police departments. Major cities that replaced or began the process of replacing police chiefs that year included New York, Chicago, Los Angeles, Philadelphia, Houston, San Francisco, Denver, Washington and Austin. The heavy turnover followed a 1991 that saw new police chiefs take charge in several large communities, including Dallas, St. Louis, Phoenix and San Jose, Calif.

Certainly not all of the departures could be blamed on the growing frustration associated with fighting urban crime in a highly politicized setting. In New York, for instance, Mr. Brown resigned during the summer of 1992 because his wife was seriously ill. Those close to Mr. Brown believe that, despite internal conflicts within his department, he would have stayed on absent his family problem. In Denver, Police Chief Jim Collier stepped down because he would not force his family to abide by a city residency requirement; Mr. Collier returned to the rank of captain, allowing his family to stay in the suburbs.

But a former Newark, N.J., police chief, without citing specific examples, remains skeptical regarding the use of "personal reasons" to explain resignations. "Whether the issue is chiefs who are retiring because they've put their time in, or those who have pressing obligations with the family, I would question whether many would leave if their job satisfaction were higher," said Hubert Williams, president of the Washington-based Police Foundation, a law-enforcement research group. A universe of reasons exists to explain why the job of police chief has gotten harder — and could become harder still. Topping the list are the unrealistic expectations that political leaders and citizens place on police chiefs throughout their careers. From the day a new chief is brought in, there is an expectation that the crime rate and the fear of crime will fall. Of course, both of those goals are affected by many other governmental and societal factors besides law enforcement.

Gerald Williams did not become a police chief to be popular. Nonetheless, 10 years of complaints from every imaginable interest group in the two Colorado cities he served took its toll. "I was tired," Mr. Williams said in explaining his unexpected decision in March 1992 to leave the Police Department in 225,000-resident Aurora, Colo. "You don't get a lot of positive strokes as a police chief. It doesn't happen from the city manager, the council, the mayor or your own employees." Mr. Williams, who now directs a training program for mid-level police managers at North Carolina State University, Raleigh, added, "You can't hold the police to unrealistic levels of accountability and let everyone else off the hook. Blaming chiefs all the time will reduce their willingness to take risks."

Dispassionate observers would say a problem as serious as violent crime has many causes, some rooted in the family and many beyond the reach of one government official. But often the police chief becomes the undeserving focal point because no one else is willing or able to bear that burden. Take the case of Washington, D.C., where Police Chief Isaac Fulwood left his position in October 1992 after more than three years in charge. At an emotional resignation announcement, Mr. Fulwood expressed deep disappointment over not being able to put a dent in Washington's high homicide rate. Mr. Fulwood moved over to Mayor Sharon Pratt Kelly's office, where he began directing the mayor's anti-violence program.

Other problems that have worsened for police chiefs include breakdowns in the rest of the criminal-justice system — which put offenders back on the streets too soon — and racial conflicts both within and outside police departments.

All of these factors bring experts to the most obvious conclusion: police chiefs simply can't be expected to do it all.

"As a chief you don't have time to do quality research or quality thinking," said Gerald Williams, who after serving as chief in the Colorado cities of Aurora and Arvada now has time to study key public policy questions at North Carolina State.

As the problems facing police chiefs are many, so too are the diverse symptoms they produce in the officeholders. The average tenure of a city police chief increased to about 5.5 years in the early 1980s but, a decade later, dropped to about 4 years, said Sheldon Greenberg, associate director of the Police Executive Research Forum, Washington, a non-profit research organization of the largest state and local police agencies. Mr. Greenberg attributes some of 1992's turnovers to the retirements of those who entered police service during a high-growth period in the late

1960s and early 1970s. He also acknowledges that police chiefs are taking more heat than they used to because they are relied upon to be problem-solvers.

It seems every police official knows at least one story of a colleague who stayed in the job too long and was overcome by stress. Sometimes the wounds are more than psychological.

Just like their officers, police chiefs can be targets for violence. Yonkers, N.Y., Police Commissioner Robert K. Olson was injured Nov. 3, 1992, when a bomb planted near his car exploded as he was backing away from the vehicle. Mr. Olson had been assisting a mayoral investigation into public corruption in Yonkers.

What can be done to reduce the stresses affecting chiefs? Some say chiefs need to be encouraged to be innovative, and one way to do that is to offer them employment contracts that eliminate the possibility of arbitrary dismissal. Mr. Greenberg said contracts are becoming more common for police chiefs, who in most large cities have served at the pleasure of the mayor or city manager. The contracts, generally running three to five years, can protect the city by setting clear policy goals and criteria for termination, Mr. Greenberg added.

Cities are trying to avoid the situation experienced by Los Angeles, where former Police Chief Daryl F. Gates benefited from an organizational structure that shielded him from any reasonable threat of dismissal. Mr. Gates retired in June 1992 in the wake of the police beating of motorist Rodney King and the related Los Angeles riots. Mr. Gates' successor was former Philadelphia Police Commissioner Willie L. Williams.

With police chiefs playing musical chairs or leaving police work altogether, many mayors are having to seek replacements. Hubert Williams of the Police Foundation does not envy their task, but he advises them to look for experienced managers. "My advice to them would be to take a chief from another city," he said. "If I were a mayor, I'd be looking for a person who could exercise good judgment under stress, someone who had already shown that."

Gerald Williams insists stress never got the better of him in his 10 years as a police chief. But even the most thick-skinned person needs a break from all the bad news. In his mid-40s, he is not closing the door to becoming a police chief again someday. But for now, he enjoys being closer to the classroom than the squad room.

Computerized fingerprint files lead to more arrests

In December 1990, a Los Angeles Police Department crime lab technician fed fingerprints found at the scene of an unsolved 1963 murder of a Hollywood waitress into a computer. In a matter of minutes, the computer, known as the Automated Fingerprint Identification System (AFIS), scanned more than 1 million images of fingerprints stored on a data base. It stopped on a set of prints belonging to Vernon Robinson, who used to live in the Los Angeles region but had long since departed for the Minneapolis-St.

Paul area, where he was living a comfortable middle-class life. Mr. Robinson now is awaiting trial in the murder of the waitress, Thora Rose.

It was far from the first time AFIS had been the key snoop in solving a big crime in California. The Los Angeles Police Department system is linked to the statewide Cal-ID AFIS computer, which is run by the state Department of Justice. That system, which has almost 7 million prints stored in its data base, helped convict "Night Stalker" Richard Ramirez and matched more than 30,000 fingerprints taken from evidence at crime scenes or directly from the fingers of suspects between 1985 and 1991. In fact, around the country AFIS has become such a popular tool that several states, including California and Illinois, have had to consider expanding systems purchased just a handful of years ago at a cost averaging around $18 million to $20 million.

Computerized fingerprint data storage and retrieval systems are the fastest-growing — and perhaps the most important — law enforcement technology on the market, police officials say. Although AFIS has some drawbacks, the technology keeps improving. Chicago pioneered a system in 1990 to render the old ink-and-paper fingerprinting process obsolete. The "live-scan" system makes a high-quality laser print of a suspect's hand held over glass, much like a photocopy machine.

AFIS actually is a generic term describing a technology developed by four companies: Identification and Security Systems Inc., Albany, N.Y.; North American Morpho Systems Inc., Tacoma, Wash.; NEC Information Systems Inc., Washington, D.C.; and De La Rue Printak Inc., Anaheim, Calif.

In an October 1990 survey, the Illinois Criminal Justice Information Authority, based in Chicago, found that 29 state police or state crime laboratories either already had AFIS or were in the procurement phase. Almost every other state was beginning to look at buying AFIS systems. In addition, many big-city police departments have AFIS but, because of its high costs, mid-size and smaller cities and county sheriff's offices to not have it. Instead, they must mail or send a facsimile transmission of prints to state crime labs — if they can gain access. Still, many cities are looking at accessing state systems through remote terminals or buying scaled-down systems with smaller memories than the huge state mainframes.

Under federal law, fingerprint evidence from solved and unsolved felonies and from misdemeanors punishable by jail terms must be sent to the states for filing. In states without AFIS, the prints are stored in file cabinets and must be laboriously checked by hand, a process so time-consuming that only in the most serious cases can a blind search be performed.

AFIS works but, like any other large-scale computer application, it has its flaws. Chief among the drawbacks are the time it takes to input the prints in the first place (something the live-scan technology is designed to reduce), the time it takes to verify that two prints match and, most importantly, the overly heightened expectations for solving crimes.

Examining how AFIS works helps to illustrate both its potential and its drawbacks. Once a print has been lifted from a piece of evidence, a highly trained crime lab technician must blow up the image and trace it to remove temporary imperfections such as cuts. Using a scanner, the prints are transferred into the computer. Once a match has been made with a print already on file, the two prints still must be analyzed to ensure they really are the same. Altogether, the process can take up to half an hour. With an extremely important case such as a mass murder, 30 minutes is no problem. But when investigators from dozens of local departments begin trying to clear up not only current cases but major backlogs of unsolved cases, officials begin to realize they have bitten off more of a problem than they envisioned. "I don't think anybody thought AFIS would get the kind of (system use) it has gotten," said John Loverude, assistant chief of the Illinois State Police Bureau of Identification in Joliet, Ill.

Joseph P. Bonino, commanding officer of the Los Angeles Police Department's records and identification, said his department is prioritizing which unsolved cases to feed into the local AFIS system. "It isn't enough to just get a (print) match. You have to have witnesses and other evidence to build a case. How much time do you devote to cases that go back 30, 40 years? Do you (use AFIS) for every crime?"

In 1991, the Florida Department of Law Enforcement announced its $21.7 million AFIS system was able to handle less than half the workload originally anticipated. The problem stemmed not from system malfunctions but from an all-too-common problem of expecting too much from a computer. "We had too much of a Cadillac version (of AFIS) in mind," said James T. Moore, commissioner of the department. "Our vision was ahead of where the industry had gotten to. We wanted the largest, the best customized system in America, but we expected too much from it." Part of the trouble included what Mr. Loverude called the "logistical nightmare" of scanning millions of prints on file. "You want the system to start working right away," he said, "but you have to work out the bugs and have staff go through a staggering amount of work. You don't just start solving cases." But it is still better than the old system. Until the automated system was put in place in Florida, detectives often spent hundreds of hours questioning witnesses in the field in efforts to identify suspects. Then they would ask fingerprint technicians to compare the prints of suspects to prints from the crime scene.

Police working on California's Thora Rose case in 1963 reviewed more than 30,000 sets of prints by hand in Sacramento. When the state system went online, officials ran prints from 400 unsolved Northern California homicides and matched prints with suspects in 75 of those cases, leading to 39 arrests. Andy Kojita, manager of the identification section of the California Department of Justice, said that AFIS allowed him to cut the personnel in his section by half, to 125 workers from 250. But productivity increased threefold. "Viewed from that perspective, there really isn't a downside to the system," Mr. Kojita said.

California was the first state to go into what is known as a "full-use access" AFIS system. Under the program, local AFIS systems in some 46 communities also can access the state data base. In addition, California is linked via the Western Identification Network, with data bases in Oregon, Washington and Alaska. Also in the network are Idaho, New Mexico, Utah and Wyoming, states that don't have their own AFIS systems but, for just a few hundred thousand dollars each, bought access terminals.

Jails & prisons

Law-and-order proponents point to every community's teeming jails and insist crime is out of control. Yet, from the inside, what often appears chaotic are governments' attempts to deal with the burgeoning numbers of inmates at the federal, state and county levels.

Public officials are caught in the grip of a jail and prison crowding crisis that has enveloped all levels of government. No longer can maximum-security prison crowding be called "the state's problem." No longer can the lack of local jail space merely be dismissed as a local issue. And while the citizens' sentiment for locking up people manifests itself in rigid sentencing guidelines and fewer paroles, governments are finding that they are unable to pour money into new prison beds fast enough. In fiscal 1991, states were trying to build their ways out of the crowding quagmire to the tune of $4 billion, said Robert B. Levinson, special projects manager for the 25,000-member American Correctional Association in Laurel, Md.

"If the courts keep committing people, the corrections people have no alternative," Mr. Levinson said.

Prison populations, which declined slightly during the 1970s, have climbed steadily since the end of that decade. While in 1972 about 275,000 inmates in federal, state and county facilities were serving sentences of one year or more, that number shot up to 670,000 by 1989, according to data cited by Charles Wellford, director of the Institute of Criminal Justice and Criminology at the University of Maryland, College Park. Add offenders serving short jail sentences and those on probation or under home confinement and the total number of people swirling through the

83

correctional system comes to 3 million to 4 million.

The San Francisco-based National Council on Crime and Delinquency projected a 68.4% increase in inmate populations over a five-year period ending in 1994 — further evidence that building plans alone will not solve the problem. Even without that expected growth, at least 40 states and the municipal government of Washington, D.C., recently were under federal court orders to improve conditions or reduce crowding — or do both — at some or all of their correctional facilities. Systems as large as the ones in Texas and Florida virtually have been run from the federal bench, although pronouncements made by the U.S. Supreme Court and U.S. Justice Department in 1992 could dilute federal control.

According to data from the Criminal Justice Institute Inc., South Salem, N.Y., the 10 most burdened state prison systems (based on the number of inmates over capacity) at the end of the decade of the 1980s were California (29,892 inmates over capacity/total annual operating costs of $1.48 billion), Ohio (7,379 inmates over capacity/operating costs of $387.2 million), Michigan (5,582 inmates/$627.3 million), Pennsylvania (4,957 inmates/$306.1 million), New York (4,465 inmates/$1.12 billion), Massachusetts (3,037 inmates/$207.7 million), Maryland (2,902 inmates/$251.9 million), North Carolina (2,527 inmates/$317.2 million), Oklahoma (1,840 inmates/$145.5 million) and New Jersey (1,593 inmates/$417.7 million).

California's experience serves as an accentuated version of a national malady. In fiscal 1992, the state prison system was ushering in between 200 and 400 new inmates a week. The total prison population had grown to 91,500 in April 1990 from 22,500 in 1979. Although little of the state system has been placed under federal court orders related to crowding, several California counties are under such mandates, said Christine May, information officer for the California Department of Corrections. That means the state can no longer house inmates in county facilities whenever the state system becomes overburdened, Ms. May said. Before 1980, many state parole violators awaiting hearings were held in county jails in California. Those individuals now go back to state prisons even before a judge decides whether they should return permanently.

"Most of the local jails have restrictions on the length of time a state inmate can spend there, anywhere from 24 hours to five days," Ms. May said.

Such factors have led to a non-stop building program that produced 26,000 new prison beds in California from 1983 to 1990. But the state will need to generate 51,000 more beds through 1995 at a cost of $2.7 billion just to operate at 130% of capacity.

Criminologists and other experts cite several reasons for the United States' crowding epidemic:

■ The most basic reason is demographics. The profile of the

habitual criminal is overwhelmingly young and male, a subgroup of 18-year-olds to 34-year-olds whose numbers have soared during the baby boom generation.

■ Offenders are receiving longer sentences. Almost 25% of California's prison population never turns over because more people are serving life sentences or mandatory sentences of at least 20 years, Mr. Wellford said.

■ Sentencing guidelines, once seen as a way to achieve equity in the criminal-justice system, have served mostly to increase the average sentences served by everyone, according to the majority of experts.

■ Once criminals are sentenced, they serve higher percentages of their sentences. More inmates in Maryland's state system serve out their sentences instead of being paroled, Mr. Wellford noted. Traditionally, about 60% of the state's inmate population had been paroled.

■ Growing problems of substance abuse and firearms use have led to mandatory prison sentences for drug-related and weapons-related offenses. In some cases, convicted drunken drivers now serve time in state prisons instead of in county jails.

Such issues have provoked interjurisdictional conflicts that exacerbate the general problem.

Unlike California, where court-ordered population caps at county jails are hurting state facilities, most states have witnessed the dumping of state-level inmates into county jails. New York allowed a backlog of 1,200 state-level inmates into county jails before starting to double-up in March 1990 on the number of prisoners in some state facilities. Double-bunking applies only to prisoners classified as medium-security risks who are two to four years away from being eligible for parole. New York correctional officials resist any thoughts that double-bunking could become a permanent fixture in their system. Meanwhile, Gov. Mario M. Cuomo opposes the idea of fighting crowding by releasing inmates shortly before their parole dates.

"The governor feels we have a compact with the people in the state," said Jim Flateau, Mr. Cuomo's chief spokesman on criminal-justice issues, referring to the length of time a convict is expected to serve.

In many cases, counties have had to resort to extreme measures to halt states' inmate dumping and to solve their own problems. Because of the difficulty of finding appropriate sites for federal prisons (especially in convincing local communities to welcome a facility that will house criminal outsiders), the U.S. government traditionally has housed its inmate overflow in local jails. With federal prison populations climbing, states are finding it harder to get the federal government to take in state inmates.

In 1990's most publicized case of a system gone haywire, Sheriff Michael Ashe of Hampden County in south-central Massachusetts made waves when he commandeered a National Guard armory to avoid having to release convicts into the community. After weeks of posturing among all players in the drama, the state agreed to let Mr. Ashe use space in another armory until a new county jail was completed.

Some communities have begun to see that not all jail plans are subject to the NIMBY — not in my back yard — syndrome, as small towns like Horton, Kan., bank on prisons to revive their sagging economies.

Yet, in urban Los Angeles County, the former home of 40% of the state's inmate population, not one state prison has been sited.

"We have to have people start taking the responsibility for their problems," Ms. May said. "This is not just the state's problem. They are community problems. These inmates will be paroled back into that community."

Intermediate sanctions can ease county jail crowding

County jails have come to resemble the great melting pot of the criminal justice system. For that reason, jail administration ranks among a county's most troubling challenges.

Jail officials, who often oversee only one facility per county, must house a variety of people: misdemeanor offenders serving sentences of a year or less, accused felons awaiting trial, state inmates from overcrowded prison systems, and growing numbers of women and juveniles.

"The whole correctional population is under one roof," said Wayne Huggins, director of the Washington-based National Institute of Corrections and a former sheriff in Fairfax County, Va. "And because counties generally don't receive the same level of funding as a state, jail people are paid less and quality employees can be hard to find."

For county officials seeking to curb growing jail populations, the catch phrase for innovation is "intermediate sanctions," or the search for a middle ground between harsh jail sentences and largely unsupervised probation.

Corrections represented about 5% of county spending, or a total of $5.7 billion, in fiscal 1989, according to the U.S. Census Bureau. The U.S. Department of Justice's Bureau of Justice Statistics reported that local jails as of July 1, 1990, held 405,000 inmates, or 104% of total capacity. In the 50 jurisdictions with 100 inmates or more, 87% held prisoners for state governments, the federal government or other municipalities, and 28% were under court orders to reduce their jail populations.

"The backlog of state inmates in county jails is only symptomatic of a deeper pathology — a lack of cooperation between states and counties," said Donald Murray, associate legislative director with the National Association of Counties, Washington.

Added Mr. Huggins, "States with a backlog of inmates can use county jails as a pressure relief valve, but jails have no relief valve."

Harris County, Texas, has experienced the double whammy of being under a court order to improve jail conditions and being located in a state with severe prison crowding of its own. Harris County has led a drive among Texas counties to end the wholesale dumping of state-ready inmates in county jails. Harris County law enforcers have found themselves stymied by a system offering little compromise between incarceration and probation, said Mark Kellar, director of the county's Criminal Justice Command, which administers county detention facilities. Officials would prefer a continuum in which probation and jail would be only the two most extreme of several sentencing options, including work release, home confinement, restitution and substance-abuse treatment.

To lend credence to the county's point of view, officials established a 384-bed, military-style "boot camp," primarily for nonviolent offenders who might be on the road to more serious offenses. The camp offers a heavy dose of military discipline and hard labor, combined with education, vocational training, and drug and alcohol treatment. Opened in May 1991, the facility is designed to be a sentenced inmate's home for three months, after which the offender's case is reviewed before a decision on the balance of the sentence is made. The government of Harris County, which covers the Houston metropolitan area, used part of its share of $50 million in Texas state money for innovative jail programs to construct the $3.5 million boot camp, located in a remote area near the town of Humble. Mr. Kellar suspects the program will appeal to conservative, lock-'em-up judges because of its disciplinary element and to liberal judges due to its accent on education. Most importantly, a program that instills discipline and teaches skills should help reduce recidivism, Mr. Kellar believes. Nearly all of Harris County's 6,000 jail inmates are repeat offenders; most received probation or were fined for prior offenses before committing the crimes that landed them in jail.

In Minnesota, a community corrections program run by the state offers subsidies to counties that design and receive state approval for creative projects. Tom Larson, director of the community services support unit at the Minnesota Department of Corrections, said 30 of 87 counties in the state have participated. Those counties received a total of $19 million for the state fiscal year that ended June 30, 1991; the state budget boosted that amount to about $22.5 million for fiscal 1992.

Counties haven't stopped building bigger jails when confronted with growing inmate populations, but once those facilities are completed smart officials continue adopting programs that will keep their populations low.

"Most counties on the day they open a new jail disband all their criminal justice committees," said Michael Mahoney, executive director of the John Howard Association, Chicago, a prison watchdog group. "A year later, they're scurrying around asking what they did wrong."

Counties that explore innovative ways to combat crowding should know from the beginning that most options are not cheap, experts warn. Harris County built its boot camp for one-third the price of a conventional jail, but the savings will be lost in the costs of staffing and treatment programs. Still, if a financial commitment today means fewer habitual offenders tomorrow, counties like Harris will have gone a long way toward simplifying one of their most unwieldy functions.

Home confinement faces risks and public opposition

A man serving a home-confinement sentence in 1989 for burglary and drug possession found a way to remove an electronic device attached to his ankle and leave his Polk County, Fla., home several times to commit a number of rapes. The debacle, which became the state of Florida's version of the Willie Horton case that haunted Democrat Michael S. Dukakis' 1988 presidential campaign, showed how a devious offender could outfox the state's high-technology alternative to traditional imprisonment. The man was arrested and later died during a prison escape attempt.

Corrections officials say such incidents, however rare, should erase the public misconception that home confinement is a foolproof system of incarceration. Those same officials, however, hope the bold headlines won't blur home confinement's potential as an alternative to a prison sentence.

"We do not turn a bedroom into a jail cell," said Harry Dodd, director of the Florida Department of Corrections' probation and parole services unit. "There is a perception that electronic monitoring really forces somebody to stay at home all the time."

In reality, electronic monitoring — instituted to alleviate jail and prison overcrowding, and seen by some as middle ground between probation (viewed in some cases as too lenient) and imprisonment (viewed as too harsh) — can involve simple or complex technology, periodic or constant monitoring, and relative freedom or tight restrictions on an offender's whereabouts.

Home confinement programs, used to some degree in at least 47 states, are divided into continuous and non-continuous monitoring. In continuous monitoring, an offender wears a wrist or ankle bracelet that transmits a signal to a receiver placed in the home. Workers at a 24-hour monitoring center can detect when an offender roams a certain distance from the receiver or tampers with the equipment. In a non-continuous system, offenders receive calls from a monitoring center at random intervals ranging from five minutes to several hours. The monitoring centers usually are operated by companies that enter into contracts with state or local corrections officials.

"The risk associated with the random-calling system is high," explained Gary Schlatter, vice president for sales and marketing at Cincinnati-based Guardian Technologies, which develops and markets home monitoring equipment.

In continuous and non-continuous systems, offenders often are allowed to leave their homes at certain hours to go to work, attend school, receive medical treatment, run errands or attend religious services.

Few corrections officials consider home confinement a panacea for the pervasive prison and jail crowding problem. Mr. Dodd said crowding is best addressed through sentencing guidelines that produce a manageable number of inmates.

Mark Renzema, associate professor of criminal justice at Kutztown University in Kutztown, Pa., said about 12,000 offenders in mid-1990 were enrolled in electronic monitoring programs nationally — twice the number enrolled a year earlier.

Still, many states have fallen short of their participation goals. Some have been hamstrung with legal restrictions that make few offenders eligible for home confinement. Others have found that judges are reluctant to substitute home confinement for a traditional prison sentence.

"Judges want to see people do time," said Dennis Wagner, research associate with the National Council on Crime and Delinquency, Madison, Wis. "The issue of punishment and just desserts is an element."

Rhode Island's home confinement program, launched in early 1989, was doomed because of legal constraints. Concerned about public safety, state legislators excluded several categories of offenders. The program was prohibited from admitting most repeat offenders who had prior convictions over the previous five years, nor could it include anyone guilty of a capital crime, a felony involving the use of force, a break-in and most drug offenses.

Joseph DiNitto, assistant to the director of the Rhode Island Department of Corrections, said the program's intent was to decrease overcrowding, but that did not happen.

Despite the doubts, many corrections officials across the country believe home confinement will become a more significant element of criminal justice. The concept still is relatively young, having been piloted for the first time by a New Mexico judge in 1983.

Fortress mentality straps privately operated facilities

Even those who do not support large-scale privatization of prisons acknowledge some early successes with the concept. Most privately operated facilities that have been around for any length of time have become cost-savers, or at least not drains on government budgets. Inmates even seem to prefer them. So why do so many people predict a limited role for private prisons in an atmosphere of soaring corrections costs and swelling inmate populations?

Peggy Wilson sums up the answer in one word: turf. Ms. Wilson, vice president with a leading management firm dealing with private correctional facilities, sees territorial state officials and public employee unions as the hurdles her industry must overcome.

"Quite honestly, there are times when people in the departments of corrections resent that the private sector will be considered," said Ms. Wilson, who works for Corrections Corp. of America, Nashville, Tenn.

The firm and its competitors have been able to make their presence felt. In 1990, they were overseeing about 1% of the United States' total inmate population. Ms. Wilson's firm managed 5,000 prison beds in five states, including such facilities as a women's state penitentiary in New Mexico, two 500-bed state prisons in Texas and a 610-bed, medium-security prison in Winnfield, La.

If privatization ever reaches household-word status, it will more likely be preceded by "garbage" or "airport" than "prison," said John D. Donahue, assistant professor at Harvard University's John F. Kennedy School of Government, Cambridge, Mass.

"If you were to put together a list of all the candidates for privatization, I think supporters and opponents of privatization would pretty much agree that prisons would be at the bottom of the list," said Mr. Donahue, who also is author of a book, "The Privatization Decision," on privatization options.

Mr. Donahue has few hopes for large-scale private prisons for two reasons. What government wants out of corrections is less easily defined than other services, and it is difficult to envision a truly competitive corrections market that would allow governments to change contractors.

"It's difficult to write a contract (with a company) that gets the public purpose accomplished," Mr. Donahue said, "and it's pretty hard to imagine a jurisdiction replacing its prison contractor."

Mr. Donahue acknowledges that the limited emergence of private prisons has provided good ammunition for those who think their use should grow. In Hamilton County, Tenn., for example, Corrections Corp. of America has operated a men's work camp at a lower daily cost than when the county was running the facility more than five years earlier. Combined with the women's jail that the company also has run, Corrections Corp. of America was responsible for 437 inmates in the county. In mid-1990, the company's contract with Hamilton County, which covers the Chattanooga area, included a county payment of $22.66 per inmate per day to the private manager. Before the work camp and jail were privatized, the county spent about $24.60 per person per day. The difference amounted to an annual savings of nearly $310,000.

Such numbers are hard to ignore in states like Louisiana, where legislators have searched desperately for cost-cutting measures. In 1989, Louisiana lawmakers passed an enabling bill to allow private prison ventures. According to Martha Jumonville, public information officer for the Louisiana Department of Corrections, the state envisioned a time when the private sector would do everything from acquiring the land for a new facility to building and operating it.

Liability and security issues have stalled the private sector's progress in entering the prison business. Some jurisdictions have been surprised to learn that they cannot automatically pass on their insurance liability to contractors when prison operations are privatized. Contractors often pledge in their contract agreements to absorb government costs whenever there is a claim, but Mr. Donahue said that could be a problem because he believes leading firms might be underinsured.

Public sector unions also have been persuasive in insisting that contractors will hire less-qualified employees at correctional facilities to cut costs. The American Federation of State, County and Municipal Employees "fights us tooth and nail," Ms. Wilson said. "They love to throw up red flags wherever they can."

Correctional facilities lock into private health-care services

While private management of prisons remains one of the most controversial applications of privatization, a microcosm of the idea has taken hold in the operation of correctional health services. More state and local governments are designating national companies, regional outfits and even local hospitals or doctors to take on the provision of medical services to inmates. In 32% of the country's prisons or jails, the government does not run the in-house health service, said Steve Collier, director of marketing for Correctional Medical Systems, St. Louis, a division of ARA Services Inc. Mr. Collier's company operates inmate health services at 102 sites in 16 states. Some states, including Delaware and New Mexico, have turned over their entire correctional health services to private companies.

Yet the same concerns that hinder growth in the number of fully privatized prisons also color the debate on privatizing prison medical services. Governments continue to worry that the profit motive will compel private contractors to skimp on such services.

In the cases of Delaware and Alabama, the Washington-based National Prison Project, an inmate advocacy group affiliated with the American Civil Liberties Union, sued state governments to challenge the quality of inmate health care provided by private groups. In an out-of-court settlement, Delaware agreed to require its vendor to upgrade overall medical services. Alabama withstood a court challenge over its contractor's handling of inmates who tested positive for the acquired immune deficiency syndrome (AIDS) virus, but the state switched contractors after the lawsuit was filed, said Elizabeth Alexander, staff counsel for the National Prison Project.

Governments also have discovered that, as in the case of full prison privatization, they do not relinquish their own liability by placing medical care in a private contractor's hands. In 1988, the

U.S. Supreme Court ruled that governments and private entities can be sued in federal court for privatized health care that does not meet constitutional guidelines.

The privatization of inmate medical services still outpaces the privatization of the jail and prison cells themselves, at least partly because health care traditionally has been a problematic area for corrections professionals. Governments do not choose to contract out inmate medical services simply to cut costs.

"The savings depend on what kind of care a community is providing," Mr. Collier said. "Some aren't spending a lot to begin with, but they are running a (liability) risk (due to poor care). They may come to us because they're getting sued." Governments that privatize their inmate health services today can expect to spend about $1,500 to $2,500 each year per inmate, Mr. Collier said.

In New Mexico's case, state officials wanted to render their prison health-care costs more predictable, explained Steven Spencer, a physician and medical director for the state prison system. A contract with a private vendor can be more reliable in department budgeting, as a contract easily separates out the cost of inmate health care, Mr. Spencer said. He believes the state has saved money since privatizing the prison health system, though he could not provide specific figures. A private company also is better able to monitor and control costs for inmates who are transferred from prison to a hospital for advanced care. According to Mr. Spencer, the state generally has been satisfied with the quality of care inmates are receiving. New Mexico's contract with Correctional Medical Systems began in October 1989.

Governments that choose to privatize generally pay the contractor a flat fee based on the jail or prison system's average daily census, with provisions for additional payments if the facility is crowded. Private vendors operate everything from one-room infirmaries in small county jails to large clinic-like settings with a staff of several physicians and equipment to handle diagnostic and trauma care. Government officials considering privatization should realize they will lose at least some of their control over daily operations.

Cookie-cutter design adopted as blueprint for savings

If Tennessee prison officials have to mass-produce prison cells to keep the federal courts happy, they figure they might as well cut them from the same mold. Adopting a practice that has gained national acceptance, state officials have issued uniform design standards for all new state prisons — cookie-cutter correctional facilities, if you will.

Tennessee officials believe the state will save millions of dollars per facility by issuing precise drawings to design teams and asking contractors on separate projects to share information. More importantly, a set of predictable standards will save construction time as the state plays catch-up with court-ordered capacity limits.

"We're saving construction time because we're producing a clearer set of documents for the contractor to work from," said Thomas Giese, director of engineering for the Tennessee Department of Correction. "Most of your state agencies have drifted toward uniformity."

Not only are many states adopting uniform design standards for prisons and other government buildings, but states are sharing design information with their neighbors, said Sharon A. Williams, corrections specialist with the National Criminal Justice Reference Service of Rockville, Md. The reference service's parent organization, the National Institute of Justice, has created a construction information exchange for the sharing of ideas on innovative design and cost-cutting techniques.

In South Carolina, officials have visited other states to borrow concepts, said Francis X. Archibald, director of public affairs for the state Department of Corrections. As part of the planning effort for a 1,200-bed prison in rural Lee County to replace the 124-year-old Central Correctional Institution in Columbia, officials visited a federal prison in Marion, Ill., Mr. Archibald said. In addition, South Carolina has established its own design prototype for future facilities.

"Like any other profession, there's a kind of networking that goes on here," Mr. Archibald said. "When someone re-invents the wheel, an article will go in the American Correctional Association's newsletter."

What all this uniform design boils down to, say Tennessee prison officials, is there are only so many ways to lock up offenders. Since 1983, Tennessee has been under a federal court order to bring its prison system to constitutional standards. That forced the state in the early 1990s to reduce the population at the Tennessee State Penitentiary in Nashville, which at its peak housed 2,100 inmates but worked its way to well under the court-mandated capacity of 1,068. To reduce the burden on the old Nashville facility, the state built two maximum-security prisons — one at Fort Pillow, near a Civil War site in western Tennessee, and the other in Nashville. Two design teams worked on the projects, one concentrating on inmate housing areas and the other on support buildings. When the two were finished, they swapped information, Mr. Giese said. Though furniture and equipment in some Tennessee prison buildings may differ, officials want exterior and interior layouts at each complex to be the same. Officials expect to test the procedure again at several facilities planned for construction to ease the burden on county jails, many of which are housing inmates awaiting transfer to the state system.

Uniform design improves operating efficiency, Mr. Giese believes. Similar building layouts will ease the transition for correctional officers who are transferred from one facility to another, he added.

With the state's construction drawings wearing out from being passed around so much, officials are transferring their design data onto a computer.

Federal pronouncements ease governments' burdens

Two 1992 federal actions — one from the Justice Department and the other from the Supreme Court — should help states free themselves from burdensome corrections requirements that have put them in a bind over how best to fund fast-growing needs, allocate prison dollars, house prisoners and comply with consent decrees that in some cases are more than a decade old.

U.S. Attorney Gen. William P. Barr in January opened the way for state officials to avoid huge construction costs by allowing state governments to increase capacity beyond court-imposed prison population caps at some institutions. Population caps on state prisons have wrought havoc with states' abilities to lock up criminals, Mr. Barr said.

State officials certainly won't argue. In Florida, for instance, population limits under a consent decree have forced the state to release inmates early, said Kimberly Tucker, deputy general counsel of the Florida Department of Legal Affairs. "We've got to let one (inmate) out to let one in," she said.

Mr. Barr proposed allowing state prisons to operate at the level of federal prisons, which were filled to 165% of capacity in January 1991. There is "enormous potential in terms of additional bed space that may be available if states are left to manage their own affairs," Mr. Barr said. "If the states could operate at the level of the federal prison system, that would mean an additional 286,000 inmate beds, which translates into a savings of $13 billion in construction costs."

At the Supreme Court, the justices opened the door a crack to allow state and local officials to challenge consent decrees, which usually dictate prison population limits, cell sizes, inmate treatment and other conditions. In the wake of the high court's decision, Texas Attorney Gen. Dan Morales asked a federal district judge to end the federal court system's 18-year control of the Texas prison system. The state was "well on the way to having this resolved anyway," but the Supreme Court decision "can only help," said Ron Dusek, spokesman in the Texas Attorney General's Office. Texas is an example of the massive burden that corrections costs place on state budgets. Since 1974, Texas has spent $1.3 billion on construction of new prisons and support facilities.

Spending on corrections by all states increased 8% in fiscal 1992, following a year in which expenditures rose 16%, reported the National Conference of State Legislatures, Denver. For state governments to keep to the lower 8% growth level, they will have to shorten sentences and lower incarceration rates, state legislators say. Corrections spending is the third fastest growing appropriations category for state governments.

Prisoner rights groups have criticized the U.S. Justice Department's policy change. Allowing states to crowd more inmates into prisons is shortsighted and can lead to explosive situations, argued Mark J. Lopez, staff attorney with the New York-based American Civil Liberties Union Foundation's National Prison Project. Mr. Lopez pointed out that a state prisoner in a Maine facility for violent offenders tortured and killed a cell-mate who was double-bunked with him; Maine officials now double-bunk inmates only in minimum-security or medium-security facilities. The federal prison system can operate over capacity because it is able to increase staff size and shift prisoners around to deal with crowding, but state systems get most of the violent criminals, Mr. Lopez contended. States also do not have the resources to increase staff sizes adequately to handle extra prisoners, the civil liberties advocate said. He added that the attorney general's policy pronouncement was a political decision pegged to the November 1992 congressional and presidential elections.

While at least 40 states and Washington, D.C., are under court orders or consent decrees to limit prison populations and-or improve conditions in one or more facilities, only five states have never been challenged on prison conditions.

States enter into consent decrees to avoid lengthy, expensive trials over lawsuits brought by inmates seeking improved prison conditions. The state ends up agreeing to certain conditions and pays for any federal monitors assigned to enforce the agreements. The state also covers the costs of the plaintiffs' attorneys. Many states are finding it difficult to get out of consent decrees, even if officials meet all the conditions under the original agreements, Florida's Ms. Tucker said. States "are not intended to be easily extricated from consent decrees," she added. "If they didn't think to put an expiration date in the contract — and very few states did that — they could last forever."

Attorneys representing state governments say the Supreme Court's ruling offers some hope that governments can successfully challenge court settlements which dictate improvements at public facilities. A divided court in *Rufo vs. Inmates of Suffolk County (Mass.) Jail* ruled that federal courts must apply a "flexible standard" when considering modifying the requirements of consent decrees. The case involved a jail that settled a case with inmates unhappy with facility conditions. Local officials agreed to stop doubling up inmates in single cells, but later they asked a federal judge to let them out from under the requirement due to a large increase in the jail population. The Supreme Court ruled that consent decrees can be altered when conditions have changed to a degree that compliance with them is too difficult, impractical or against the public interest.

The high court's decision "provides some openings for states and localities to seek changes based on changed circumstances," said Paul M. Smith, partner in the Washington law firm of Klein, Farr, Smith & Taranto, which filed a brief for several states in the *Rufo* case. Still, the decision doesn't go as far as states would like because the justices emphasized that a state must be able to point to a specific change that altered the circumstances of the original consent decree, Mr. Smith pointed out. "If all you did was sign an overly broad decree, that can go on forever," he said.

A consent decree has forced Michigan to spend six years and more than $90 million remodeling prisons, enlarging cells, and improving sprinkler systems, safety doors and the treatment of mentally ill inmates, said Gail Light, spokeswoman for the state's Corrections Department. Michigan officials complain that the federal courts keep modifying the decree and expanding the original requirements. Michigan officials are hopeful that the Supreme Court decision will end the federal courts' burdensome oversight.

Even with the high court's decision, if a state sues to change things, it is responsible for heavy litigation costs.

"It's not a self-executing decision," Ms. Tucker said. A state would have to pay "something like $160 an hour to go through a trial to litigate, whether you win or not. It's an open-ended penalty (and) it has a chilling effect on states."

Many state officials will find it easier to keep doing what the consent decrees require, she said.

Health care

With the federal government failing to address the rising costs of medical treatment and the plight of uninsured Americans, health care has become a major burden on state and local governments. Much of the U.S. population is receiving inadequate care from the federal government's two main health-care programs: Medicaid, a federal-state program that helps pay for health care for the needy, the aged, the disabled and low-income families with children, and Medicare, the federal health-care insurance program for the disabled and people aged 65 and older (eligibility is based mainly on eligibility for Social Security).

Meanwhile, hospitals run by public hospital authorities and city and county governments struggle to survive, and state governments fight to keep up with Medicaid payments and to pass comprehensive legislation that would supply medical insurance coverage to all residents.

Aging, needy and in deteriorating physical condition, government-run hospitals are more and more resembling the clients they most often serve. These facilities suffer the most from inadequate Medicare and Medicaid reimbursements because they are the main local treatment centers for elderly and low-income citizens in many regions of the country. As the only recourse for the penniless — many of whom are turned away by private and for-profit facilities — government-operated, non-specialized community hospitals, also known as acute-care centers, bear the greatest burden for treating the United States' 34 million uninsured people.

Inconsistent government support compounds the hospitals' financial woes. Limited tax dollars mean city and county governments often are hard-pressed to maintain health-care services, especially when faced with reduced funds from shrinking federal and state revenue-sharing programs. And when a mayor, county executive, councilman or other local official must choose between greater funding for a hospital or for public services such as police protection and road repairs, health care often loses the battle, health industry experts contend.

Financial losses and other burdens have spread like a virus across most municipalities that support government-owned hospitals:

- Thirty-eight public hospitals provided 75% of California's care for the indigent in 1990.
- The New York City Health and Hospitals Corp., which runs the city's health-care system with a $2.7 billion budget, lost more than $500 million in 1988.
- Twenty of the 105 Texas hospitals that closed between 1980 and 1990 were tax-supported; at city-owned hospitals in 1989, the dollar value of care provided free to poor, uninsured patients amounted to 28% of the hospitals' gross revenue.

"Public facilities find themselves hamstrung because of a non-sophisticated staff," explained George Pillari, president of Health Care Investment Analysts Inc., a Baltimore group that tracks industry trends. "Often their staff is just an extension of the county bureaucracy, with a lot of turnover . . . They're just not managing as well as private hospitals."

Statistics compiled by Mr. Pillari's organization show that non-government hospitals also are in worsening financial shape because of low Medicare and Medicaid reimbursements, skyrocketing costs of medical treatment and other concerns. But the numbers point to significant differences between the two groups.

In general, government-run hospitals are smaller and less-utilized, offer less-specialized care and wait longer for their patients to pay medical bills. The typical government hospital in 1989 had 50 beds and was 29.6% occupied, compared with the 136-bed, 51% occupied non-government facility. A large number of government-owned rural hospitals — viewed by the health-care industry as terminally ill facilities because of the decline of rural economies — account for the surprisingly small number of available beds. "You're talking about 15 people in your hospital at any one time on the average," Mr. Pillari said.

The least optimistic outlook is that many governments will be forced to close their underutilized, revenue-sapping facilities. The American Hospital Association noted that 85 community hospitals — generally defined as government and non-government facilities offering short-term care — closed in 1988. That's the highest number of closings ever recorded by the Chicago-based association. The National Association for Hospital Development, a Falls Church, Va., organization representing fund-raising executives at non-profit hospitals, predicts that about 2,700 of the country's 6,800 acute-care hospitals and specialized facilities for drug treatment, psychiatric care and other disciplines will close between 1990 and the year 2000. Government hospitals will be hit the hardest, according to an association report.

Analysts are armed with statistics to explain why government-run hospitals are on the critical list. Bond rating agencies generally point to inadequate reimbursement from medical insurance coverage. According to the U.S. Department of Health and Human Services, 43% of all hospitals lost money treating Medicare recipients in 1987. The American Hospital Association estimated that in fiscal 1990 the figure rose to 66%. The National Association for Hospital Development points to losses of up to $11.5 billion a year for public and non-profit hospitals in uncompensated care.

Officials in the business of public health care point to one basic problem: Government agencies have never received enough money to invest needed capital in hospitals. While some states prohibit agencies from accumulating revenue for capital expansion, others simply have never taken capital needs into account when distributing dollars.

So while government-run hospitals use every available dollar for salaries and basic services, private hospitals are rebuilding facilities and investing in new technology, making themselves more attractive to consumers, officials say.

"Even when the state had money, the Legislature never appropriated enough for capital improvements," repined Mary Ann Hart, spokeswoman for the Massachusetts Department of Public Health. Severe budget constraints forced the Massachusetts state government to eliminate 700 of the department's 3,800 employees and to slash $20 million from the agency's $233 million budget in fiscal 1990.

Some state governments are trying to head off an epidemic of government hospital closures by assisting facilities that take in a disproportionate share of non-paying patients. Creating indigent-care pools is one approach. In Florida, where legislators in 1984 agreed to expand the state's Medicaid program through an annual assessment on every hospital, the state collected $538.7 million in less than six years by assessing each facility for 1.5% of its net operating revenue. The state used the money to expand Medicaid eligibility, making it more likely that normally uninsured patients would be insured and would be able to pay their bills.

'Centers of excellence' generate life-saving revenue

While some people consider the public hospital the care-giver of last resort, more and more big-city facilities are earning accolades for establishing specialized services to attract paying patients.

Suddenly, a hot phrase in public health care is "center of excellence," as government-affiliated facilities rush to create units for hard-to-find services like high-level trauma care, burn treatment, diagnostic testing and organ transplants. Hospital officials recognize that these centers are potential revenue-raisers, but they also serve a greater purpose.

"A lot of government-owned hospitals are affiliated with medical schools and, if they are, there's a strong research component to all of this," said Richard Klass, administrator of planning at Jackson Memorial Hospital, Miami, which receives about $100 million of its $457 million operating budget from the Dade County, Fla., government. "This also adds status to your facility."

Added Christine Burch, executive vice president of the National Association of Public Hospitals, Washington, "For some hospitals, the reason for creating centers of excellence is to be competitive. Every time there's local recognition of a hospital service, it helps."

For hospitals whose primary mission is to care for a community's poor residents, there is a clear need to offer services appealing to a wider range of clients, especially insured and paying clients. Members of the National Association of Public Hospitals, which represents 100 primarily government-owned hospitals in urban areas, in 1988 reported an average of $76.9 million in charity care or bad debt — a figure representing 42% of their overall patient charges. The American Hospital Association reports that uncompensated care, which totaled $3 billion nationally in 1980, had nearly tripled to $8.3 billion by 1988.

No wonder so many administrators at government-run hospitals have hit the luncheon circuit to promote their centers of excellence.

In Dade County, you would be hard-pressed to find someone unaware of Jackson Memorial Hospital's regional centers for trauma, burn treatment and organ transplants. "Trauma care is certainly the most well-known feature in the community," Mr. Klass said. "You hear about it nightly on the news." While most of the trauma victims Dade County residents hear about are from lower-income neighborhoods, it is not only the indigent who realize they will be taken to Jackson Memorial if they are involved in serious accidents. "Some people think it's the hospital of last resort, but sometimes it's also the hospital of only resort" in providing superior care to accident victims, Mr. Klass said.

In southeastern Wisconsin, literature distributed by the Milwaukee County Medical Complex lists the facility's first priority as caring for all county residents regardless of financial status. The complex's secondary goal involves offering highly specialized services in areas such as cancer treatment, bone marrow transplants and ophthalmology.

A similar mission exists at Harborview Medical Center in Seattle, a 330-bed facility that receives state funds and is owned and operated by the University of Washington. Not only has Harborview traditionally cared for King County's indigent population, it has specialized in procedures not available at other facilities, including advanced neurosurgery and burn treatment. "We look at our role as treating those for whom other hospitals either are unwilling or unable to care, whether for social reasons or because of the complexity of the illness," said James LoGerfo, medical director at Harborview. The hospital serves as a regional burn center for four states: Alaska, Idaho, Montana and Washington. "That's not a large volume of patients but they are desperately ill people and, in the public's mind, this function has huge importance," Mr. LoGerfo said.

When a public hospital like Harborview begins to provide a specialized service, it enhances its reputation in the region. Soon, more and more paying patients are referred to the facility, and other facilities may stop providing the service.

In fact, patients from any part of the country who need complex diagnoses or intensive medical treatment likely will receive it at a big-city hospital, and usually one owned or partially funded by local government. According to a January 1991 National Association of Public Hospitals report, "America's Safety Net Hospitals: The Foundation of Our Nation's Health System," urban hospitals that are members of the association far outpace other public and private hospitals in the availability of services like trauma care and magnetic resonance imaging.

If there is a downside to public hospitals touting centers of excellence, it is the tendency of some facilities to use the centers as ways to stray from their original missions of serving the needy.

Dr. Ron Anderson, president and chief executive officer of Parkland Memorial Hospital in Dallas, considers centers of excellence critical if government-related hospitals are to receive broader public support. But he remains suspicious of officials who create treatment options for paying patients at the expense of services for the poor.

"Some public hospitals are trying to become less public through these centers of excellence," Mr. Anderson claimed. "Many public hospitals want not to change direction but to change their mission."

At government-affiliated hospitals that have struck a balance between fulfilling their original goals and enhancing their community standings, centers of excellence have meant better care options for both payers and non-payers alike. That's a winning situation that health-care providers seldom encounter these days.

Creating an epilepsy center for severely afflicted patients came naturally to Parkland Memorial. The teaching hospital's neurologists had studied the plight of those with uncontrolled seizures, and no other medical facility nearby seemed willing, or able, to meet such patients' needs. Though the center holds only a handful of the public hospital's 850 beds, it has contributed immeasurably toward improving the hospital's image among Dallas County residents, whose taxes support the indigent care that Parkland Memorial was created to provide.

101

"The goal is for our taxpayers not to have a sense of separateness about the hospital, a feeling that they're paying into a bottomless pit," explained Kathy Matney, Parkland Memorial's vice president for medicine.

By supplementing its primary function with specialized centers for epilepsy, kidney disorders, trauma, burn treatment and other services, Parkland Memorial is considered a precious community resource for paying and non-paying patients alike — not simply a drain on public coffers. By diversifying its patient mix, Parkland Memorial also has lessened its reliance on tax revenue, Mr. Anderson said. The tax-supported share of the facility's expenses shrank to 51% in 1992 from 63% in 1982, Mr. Anderson reported. Parkland Memorial is governed by a Dallas County Hospital District board, but elected county commissioners adopt the hospital's tax rate.

The epilepsy center illustrates how specialized services can fiscally strengthen a public hospital that serves mainly the indigent. While 70% of Parkland Memorial's patient revenue is written off as charity care or bad debt, half of those treated at the epilepsy center are paying patients, Ms. Matney said. At the center, which started as a two-bed unit in the early 1980s, patients are monitored on videotape and with the help of electroencephalograph technicians. The constant monitoring allows physicians to chart a suitable course of treatment for each severely afflicted patient. For some patients, electrode implants allow the doctor to pinpoint the area of the brain causing the seizures. Surgical removal of those sections often produces startling results, Ms. Matney said. About eight patients at a time undergo treatment at the center.

Parkland Memorial officials say they fare better financially with their specialized centers than with general hospital operations. But Mr. Anderson insists the hospital would not create a so-called "center of excellence" unless it could be made available to both paying and non-paying clients. "We don't do heart transplants here because we can't serve non-paying patients in that way," Mr. Anderson said. "We're not going to interfere with our primary mission, which is to take care of the indigent sick in Dallas County."

Another success story is Tampa General Hospital. The Florida facility had, to put it mildly, a bad year in 1983. The public hospital had launched a $160 million, 500-bed expansion at a time the U.S. health-care market was shrinking because of a growing emphasis on outpatient treatment. Diagnosis-related groups — the federal government's reimbursement method for holding down Medicare costs — contributed to an accumulated $12 million budget shortfall. About 300 employees were laid off. In April 1984, Standard & Poor's Corp. of New York lowered the hospital's bond rating to a weak BBB from A-.

"We were in danger of defaulting on bonds and going bankrupt," said Charles Butler, Tampa General Hospital's vice president for marketing. "It was a disaster."

Today, the situation couldn't be healthier. Tampa General, operated by a public hospital district, banked on a comprehensive, aggressive marketing campaign to save an institution near death. Tampa General has focused marketing efforts on its centers of excellence, identifying specific services the hospital can deliver well and, as one health-care expert put it, "promoting the heck out of them." Besides advertising its programs through the media, Tampa General promotes itself to large employers and to outside physicians who can refer insured patients to the hospital.

By all accounts, the strategy paid off. Between 1983 and 1989, Tampa General's annual net income more than doubled to $225,058 from $92,949. The hospital's market share — measured by the number of commercially insured patient days — jumped by 74%, while its nearest competitor, St. Joseph's Hospital, a church-operated, non-profit facility, fell by 24% and overall commercial patient days declined by 12%. Commercially insured patients in 1990 accounted for 34.3% of Tampa General's patients, up from 25.8% in 1983. In addition, the hospital added a new source of revenue — bringing in $33,500 in 1990, its first full year — by contracting for patients with health maintenance organizations (HMOs) and other managed-care companies.

"There were a lot of people who didn't believe health-care marketing worked, particularly not in a public hospital setting," said Mr. Butler. "Some people thought it was a shame to be spending money on this, but we felt it was a question of survival."

Marketing has become a buzzword among public hospital officials across the country, said Robert Katzfey, director of the American Hospital Association's section for metropolitan hospitals. While some tend to equate marketing and advertising, many understand marketing involves more than billboards and television commercials.

"Public hospitals are trying to change their image," Mr. Katzfey said.

That image is one of overcrowded emergency rooms, poorly managed programs and substandard health care — all under the umbrella of a cumbersome governmental bureaucracy. In fact, added Mr. Katzfey, "some of the best medical care around is provided at public hospitals, but most people don't know that and would never dream of going there if they have a choice." For most public hospitals to survive, he said, they have to persuade private-pay patients to seek care there. "The way things stand now, privately insured patients are just about the only ones on which you can have any hope recovering anywhere near your costs."

Financing, public support give new hope to capital projects

Heartened by successes in Dade County, Fla., and Boston, officials who oversee government-run hospitals are more aggressively seeking ways to keep their aging facilities from losing ground to non-government competitors.

Voters in Dade County, which covers the Miami metropolitan area, on Sept. 3, 1991, approved a half-cent sales tax on every dollar of retail sales to generate $60 million a year for Jackson Memorial Hospital. In a county where voters agreed to tax themselves only once before (for school construction), the vote was interpreted as a strong sign of community support for better public health care.

"People can relate to Jackson Memorial," said Ronald Ruppel, the hospital's chief financial officer. "It's not like they were being asked just to put the money in a big pot."

In Boston, officials in 1990 launched a four-year schedule for the complete reconstruction of Boston City Hospital, which serves about half of the city's indigent population. Reconstruction of the 19th-century facility was made possible through a ground-breaking, federally insured revenue bond issue. By purchasing Federal Housing Administration (FHA) mortgage insurance for the $170 million in borrowed money, the city secured a solid debt rating of double-A (the best rating is triple-A), ensured a market for the bonds and preserved the Boston city government's long-term ability to borrow for other capital projects.

"We demonstrated that the hospital and the city are well-managed," said Lee F. Jackson, city treasurer. "The feds originally thought the city's involvement would be detrimental, but we argued the opposite."

When it comes to funding major capital improvements for hospitals, government success stories are rare. The National Association of Public Hospitals reports that capital financing remains a thorny issue for most of those hospitals, with 10-year capital needs totaling $15 billion. Capital investment for public facilities pales in comparison to private hospitals. With the average age of government facilities at 26 years, as opposed to seven years for private hospitals, public hospitals are spending $12,600 per bed on capital, or about half of what private facilities spend.

"The image of the hospital with the newest technology is not what you usually find in the public sector," said Lynne Fagnani, the association's director of finance and reimbursement.

Government officials are rallying around the association, which often briefs congressional staff members on the need for a capital financing mechanism for its members. Several possible funding mechanisms have been identified, including federal loan guarantees or interest subsidies to reduce the costs of borrowing, or direct grants for smaller rehabilitation projects. Yet hoping for a bill to be introduced in Congress may be wishful thinking.

That forces government officials to continue studying successful programs like the ones in Dade County and Boston.

In Jackson Memorial's case, inadequate operating rooms and overburdened diagnostic centers have meant fewer paying patients. While the Dade County hospital has no problem attracting non-paying patients or those who need specialized care they cannot find elsewhere, it receives few insured patients for routine procedures like outpatient surgery or obstetrics.

Having seen their budget allocation from the county remain the same for four years, hospital officials needed another revenue source to improve their facility, Mr. Ruppel said. Debate centered on creating an independent health-care district, to be financed with a countywide property tax assessment, or pushing for a sales tax hike. Officials opted for the 0.5% sales tax, in part because they could show voters that about 40% of the revenue generated from the tax would be paid by tourists and other outsiders. The ballot measure passed with 58% of the vote, raising the county's overall sales tax to 6.5%. Starting Jan. 1, 1992, the tax began generating about $83 million a year, with a net of only $60 million going to the hospital because Dade County will be decreasing its annual allocation to Jackson Memorial. Mr. Ruppel said the hospital's initial aims are to expand operating rooms and acquire new equipment, particularly in radiology. It is hoped that as the hospital begins to identify long-term capital needs the sales tax revenue could back a future construction bond issue.

"We can't rely solely on Dade County to issue debt on our behalf; the county has debt limits of its own," Mr. Ruppel said.

In Boston, officials were concerned about more than upkeep of Boston City Hospital. Some advisers told Mayor Raymond L. Flynn that the city should get out of the costly hospital business altogether. Since the hospital has been an annual money-loser, bond investors would not have been interested in a traditional revenue bond issue to rebuild. So the city, committed to the services Boston City Hospital provides, pursued an unprecedented application for FHA mortgage insurance to enhance the potential bond rating. The $170 million deal closed in December 1990 after about six years of work, Mr. Jackson said. There were several delays in gaining approval because it was the first time a publicly owned and operated hospital had pursued FHA insurance.

"I think the feds had problems with the commingling of hospital and city revenues," Mr. Jackson said. "They were used to looking at a stand-alone facility."

While Ms. Fagnani believes that the city of Boston's lengthy process might dissuade other communities — and the federal government — from following suit, Mr. Jackson said other governments are studying the model with the hope that they, too, can address their pressing capital needs.

Privatization: An antidote for ailing facilities?

In the late 1970s, the Shelby County (Tenn.) Board of Commissioners launched a $60 million project to replace the county's aging, overcrowded public hospital, paradoxically called the City of Memphis Hospital. But while construction promised a new look, it quickly became clear that bricks and mortar couldn't disguise the hospital's negative public image or shaky financial standing.

"We found out that the big problems were not really the physical plant but the people and programs and how they were managed," said Jim Rout, a county commissioner since 1978. "We could have built forever, but we couldn't change the image or the financial drain on the hospital unless we did something drastic."

After studying the problem for 14 months and talking to a wide range of hospital management experts, Mr. Rout went to the county board in early 1981 with a "drastic" proposal: Get out of the hospital business. By spring, the county had done just that, winning state legislative approval to abolish the hospital district and create a private, non-profit corporation to lease and manage the hospital. After two years of transition management by an outside firm, the hospital began operating in 1983 as the Regional Medical Center at Memphis, known locally as The Med.

While most elected officials avoid the term "privatization," the concept of adopting private management seems to be gaining attention as public hospitals struggle to survive in a fiercely competitive marketplace. No definitive numbers are available, but the American Hospital Association and the National Association of Public Hospitals report that at least a half-dozen large urban public hospitals are undergoing or, more commonly, studying some form of privatization. That number could be much higher when smaller government-operated facilities are thrown into the equation.

All hospitals are coping with shrinking health-care reimbursements and the escalating costs of providing care, but hospitals run by local governments carry the added burden of providing uncompensated care for a growing number of uninsured patients. What's more, the ability of public hospitals to manage effectively often is hampered because they are public enterprises. There are civil service requirements for employees, purchasing rules that often are burdensome, restrictive open-meetings laws that effectively mean the hospital's competitors are privy to planning sessions, and governing boards composed of public officials who may have no expertise or interest in running a public hospital.

"The governance stinks, to put it bluntly, in most public hospitals," said Larry Gage, president of the National Association of Public Hospitals and a Washington, D.C., attorney specializing in hospital restructuring. "If you don't have a board with a broad range of expertise in finance, real estate and management, you're way behind the pack."

Mr. Gage by no means recommends privatization for all troubled public hospitals. In many locales such a switch would be politically infeasible, he said. Less dramatic restructuring, such as converting a hospital into its own independent governmental district, can help financially struggling institutions operate more efficiently and compete with the private sector.

While some public hospitals have experimented or are operating with private contract management, such arrangements typically don't solve the core problems facing public hospitals, said Mr. Katzfey of the American Hospital Association. "You still have restrictions on what can be done with revenues, and all your management decisions are open to the public and the press," Mr. Katzfey said.

Mr. Gage added that many successful hospital restructurings don't involve privatization at all. "They address some specific problem areas that prevent the hospital from having adequate governance or from competing effectively or getting adequate financing," he said. Louisiana, for example, recently addressed the chronic difficulty in raising capital for state-owned public hospitals by transferring governance to separate hospital districts with the authority to levy taxes and set policies. Mr. Gage credited a similar governing structure in Texas for the relative good health of that state's two largest public hospitals, Harris County Hospital in Houston and Parkland Memorial Hospital in Dallas. "They are great success stories because they have hospital-focused boards that don't get kicked out every time there's an election. They have developed their own personnel and procurement policies, they have revenue-generating capacity and a great deal of flexibility," Mr. Gage said. Still, he noted, hospital districts can fall prey to the same political and bureaucratic problems of any governmental body. In some cases, the solution may be shedding the government structure altogether.

The transition wasn't easy in Shelby County, Mr. Rout said. But as the issue was debated, one thing became clear: "We did not know how to run a hospital." While The Med now is legally a non-profit corporation, the hospital walks a fine line between its new rights as a private entity and its historic role as a government-run facility. The Med remains the hospital of last resort for the county's poor, who take priority over patients with private insurance. Maintaining that commitment was key to winning the county board's approval for the new hospital structure, Mr. Rout said. Proponents of the restructured hospital made other political concessions, too. The county guaranteed that workers covered by the American Federation of State, County and Municipal Employees (AFSCME) union would not lose pension benefits. And even though The Med isn't legally subject to Tennessee's Open Meetings Act, the hospital board's monthly meetings are open to the public. (Other meetings, however, are closed).

The benefits of privatization far outweigh the complications, said Charlotte Collins, vice president for corporate affairs and general counsel for The Med. The hospital no longer must solicit bids and win county board approval for every purchase, Ms. Collins said. Instead, the hospital negotiates price discounts with vendors and participates in group buying arrangements with other public hospitals nationally. In addition, she said, the privately run hospital now can retain revenue or borrow money for capital projects instead of lobbying county commissioners for more money. And while 1,100 of the hospital's 2,700 employees still were represented by AFSCME at the start of the 1990s, many professional workers have been "unbundled" from civil service requirements.

Under privatization, The Med also took advantage of its new name to work on altering a longstanding public image as a facility catering only to indigent patients. To attract paying patients, The Med developed four special centers — the region's only burn unit, a high-risk obstetrics program, a newborn-prenatal center and a trauma center — and began aggressively promoting the centers and what administrators see as another competitive edge: an affiliation with the University of Tennessee-Memphis Medical School.

States try assuming leadership on health-care reform

While Washington, D.C., says, "Call me in the morning," to a country aching for health-care reform, state governments are preparing their own emergency treatments to control medical costs and reduce the ranks of the uninsured.

While some observers and lawmakers question whether it is the states' job to help finance coverage for the working poor and other uninsured people — especially when states are sagging under the pressure of funding Medicaid for their lowest-income citizens — one policy expert says a high number of uninsured residents can have several adverse effects on state budgets. "Having more uninsured citizens could eventually increase a state's Medicaid rolls as uninsured people become eligible," said Daniel M. Campion, an associate with the Washington-based Alpha Center, a non-profit health policy group. States also bear some of the costs of treating the uninsured at government-owned hospitals, Mr. Campion explained, though in many areas that problem is felt more severely at the local level. While spiraling health-care costs and the growing uninsured population adversely affect all levels of government, states seem most poised to deal with the issues.

The Minnesota Legislature on April 16, 1992, jumped ahead of the states that consider government intervention the best prescription for the ailing health-care system by adopting a so-called HealthRight plan, which offers state-subsidized insurance to the working poor, the unemployed and other uninsured citizens. The plan, under which Minnesota sought to become the first state with universal health-care coverage, is being paid for with a 5-cent-a-pack increase in the state cigarette tax, a 2% tax on hospital and physician revenue, and a 1% tax on the revenue of HMOs. The amount of a resident's subsidy fluctuates based on a client's income level and, to reduce costs, participants are limited in their choices of health-care providers. Republican Gov. Arne Carlson and a bipartisan coalition of legislators supported the idea.

But in other states, officials favor an approach that places the responsibility to insure citizens on employers. Florida's Democratic Gov. Lawton Chiles signed a law in March 1992 requiring all employers to provide affordable coverage to workers by Dec. 31, 1994. Some critics contend, however, that the Florida measure lacks a specific strategy for covering the state's 2.4 million uninsured people, or nearly one in five residents.

In the state of Washington, Democratic Gov. Booth Gardner had backed a pay-or-play system requiring employers to insure workers or pay into a state pool to cover the uninsured. But Republican legislators wouldn't even consider the smaller step of creating a health-care commission to consider a variety of benefit structures and financing options, said Sheryl Hutchison, the governor's deputy press secretary.

In Oregon, state health officials have designed a comprehensive insurance reform effort that has drawn fire for the controversial feature of rationing health services in the state Medicaid program.

Whether a state opts for a government-run system or a pay-or-play model, the same goal of universal access predominates. So far, no state has found the key to creating true universal coverage. Virtually all employers in Hawaii already are required to insure their workers, but about 7% of the state's population still lacks insurance. In Massachusetts, where a pay-or-play system was supposed to take effect in 1992, government budget concerns and resistance from GOP Gov. William F. Weld placed the program on hold.

Reform-minded states also are finding it difficult to loosen themselves from the tentacles of federal regulation. States whose plans include expansions of Medicaid to incorporate more uninsured citizens need federal waivers of Medicaid regulations.

Not all states are opting for government-intensive approaches. Thanks partly to the efforts of the conservative American Legislative Exchange Council (ALEC), Washington, some states are exploring market-oriented reforms that would maintain the employer-based health insurance system with some modifications. Prodded by conservative lawmakers around the country, ALEC has issued 31 model bills that address a free-market approach to health-care reform. Measures include tax credits for the purchase of private insurance and Medicaid vouchers that would give the poor cash incentives to manage their own care. ALEC's national chairman on health issues, GOP state Rep. Tom Wilder of Georgia, introduced most of the organization's package into his Legislature in 1992, but only one bill, directed at insurance company practices, passed.

Economic redevelopment

To strengthen — or revive — their local economies, city governments are promoting redevelopment of their downtowns and waterfronts to attract tourists, shoppers, theater-goers and other visitors with money to spend.

Such redevelopment is especially needed in larger, established municipalities. Across the country over the past 20 years, cities have watched their downtowns deteriorate from essential elements in the urban fabric to office districts or, worse, stretches of gutted storefronts. Only now are city leaders beginning to realize that answers are not financial but come with the articulation of strong policy positions. City leaders with limited financial resources still can reshape their downtowns significantly if they take appropriate policy actions.

Without a clear idea of policy and its concomitant planning, and unless officials get all the players in the process — including citizens, the business community and state government — to buy in, all the money in the world won't lead to successful downtown revitalization.

Cities try to save their downtowns for obvious aesthetic reasons: Vacant storefronts aren't pretty. But a sizable financial motive exists, too: The tax base withers as shoppers pay sales taxes on purchases at suburban malls instead of at downtown stores. In addition, as downtown businesses die, retail jobs disappear.

"Downtowns are basically office and retail centers, and they need to function overall for that purpose," explained Hunter Morrison, Cleveland's director of city planning.

A typical downtown district is located at the center of a city or, for larger cities, the center of a region.

While they have much in common, downtowns are so diverse that it is impossible to fashion a template for revitalization that can simply be plopped down from city to city.

When Denver Mayor Wellington Webb entered office in 1991, he took over a city faced with the usual litany of urban problems, not the least of which was the future viability of the downtown. Local leaders faced a growing concern that this Western city would follow the lead of other American cities whose downtowns turn into ghost towns once the sun sets. Making the concern of particular importance in Denver was the city's reliance on the sales tax, which is the primary general fund revenue source.

Efforts to prevent the erosion of Denver's downtown go back to the administration of Mr. Webb's predecessor, Federico Pena. For years, government and business representatives had offered many good programs aimed at saving Denver's downtown, but those efforts suffered for lack of coordination. Concerns continued that downtown department stores would leave, prompting other retail outlets to follow.

The early 1990s, though, helped set the stage for downtown Denver to thrive throughout the rest of the decade. Many of the pieces that will make that happen already are in place. The 16th Street Mall stitches the downtown together, and the 130,000-square-foot retail mall of the mixed-use Tabor Center is a popular attraction. The downtown boasts an active retail scene (though in 1992 one department store was leaving and concerns for the other two lingered) and a popular performing arts complex.

What offers new hope is that city officials recognized what was lacking previously: a coordinated program with broad-based support and a plan for making that program a reality.

It began in October 1991, when, fulfilling a campaign promise, Mr. Webb convened a Downtown Summit. From that summit came a Downtown Denver Agenda that recognized the need for a unified strategy supported by a cross-section of the community. The next step was creation of seven public-private task forces that drew up plans for implementing the agenda, identifying problems, and spelling out solutions and timetables for implementation and financing. The plans covered business development; cultural arts, entertainment and tourism; housing; image; planning, preservation, zoning and design; retail; and transportation and parking.

The downtown agenda was based on three points — recognition of the downtown's identity, playing off the strengths of that identity and putting local leaders in a position to take advantage of opportunities as they occurred — and included the new home for the expansion Colorado Rockies Major League Baseball club and a downtown amusement park, both of which were considered centers of attraction that would draw people from throughout the region.

A key distinction of any city's downtown is character, the city's personality and the elements that contribute to its unique sense of place. In Boston it's the sense of history, the harbor, and a population both intellectual and blue-collar. In Cincinnati it's the Ohio River, a love affair with baseball and a German immigrant heritage. In Denver it's the city's Western heritage, the surrounding mountains and residents' love of the outdoors.

"If the people making policy don't have a vision of the sort of character of their population, then opportunities don't happen," said Lee Benish, principal with Daniel P. Coffey & Associates Ltd., a Chicago architectural firm specializing in downtown revitalization. "If each place had the same character there would be no difference between places, except maybe the weather."

Recognizing a city's character is critical in maximizing the chances for success. As Denver puts the other factors in place, local officials are cognizant of the city's Western heritage and are making the most of what's left of the historic architecture. That could be a difficult task, considering that most of the architecture disappeared during the 1960s, a period when well-intentioned local leaders across the country leveled entire blocks of older structures in the name of urban renewal. They acted unilaterally and without clear plans for the future. Only a handful of Denver's older structures were saved, like the buildings in Larimer Square, a block of Victorian structures restored into a fashionable shopping and people-watching district. In the early 1960s, urban renewal destroyed about 20 blocks of older residences, lamented Charles H. Woolley, a real-estate broker with Fuller & Co., Denver.

Denver grew during the 1970s and early 1980s. As the oil market boomed, so did the city's downtown office market.

"Our downtown grew phenomenally. It was one of the hottest real-estate markets in the country," Mr. Woolley recalled. "But we overbuilt."

The overbuilding became obvious with the oil crisis of 1985 and 1986. The high office vacancy rate caused by the overbuilding and the resulting low lease rates created opportunities to convert office space to residential use. Officials in some cities downplay the importance of a residential component downtown, but Denver officials see it as essential. Since the end of Mr. Pena's mayoral administration, the city government has been working hard to create new downtown residential units, aiming for 100 to 200 a year, and some exciting things are being done in converting older downtown buildings into residential lofts.

"We try to treat downtown as a neighborhood," said David Gaon, Mr. Webb's assistant for business affairs and coordinator of the city's downtown plan. "We think that every neighborhood has to have a housing component in it. It's tougher downtown, but we're just trying to do it either through rehabbing or new construction."

Added John Carney, principal with the Urban Design Group,

a Denver architecture firm active in many of the city's downtown projects, "As recently as 20 years ago Denver had more residents downtown. I think there is a notion, whether it's supportable or not, that people living downtown will enliven it for more hours than the typical work group" that returns home to the suburbs at the end of each business day.

Dana Crawford, president of Urban Neighborhoods Inc., a Denver development firm involved in many of the downtown rehabilitation projects, said, "I don't think a city can have an 18-hour or 24-hour sense of somebody being home unless somebody is home. It gives your city a heart. If you've got a lot of people living down here and a lot of people working down here it's pretty obvious what's going to happen with your retail."

There are myriad ways cities can leverage their resources to encourage a private sector role in downtown revitalization, maintains Daniel P. Coffey, another principal at Daniel P. Coffey & Associates Ltd. in Chicago. He points to the work that the city of Boston did in the late 1980s. Officials there were adept at recognizing the market, developing an appropriate set of zoning changes to create a downtown cultural district and highlighting a statistical argument to convince developers that their participation was in their best economic interest. In other cases, city governments that need space for their workers can offer to lease space in newly built or renovated structures as inducements to developers, Mr. Coffey pointed out.

Mr. Coffey indicated that Cleveland is a good example of a city that has accomplished a lot downtown with little in the way of financial resources.

"I think it's interesting that a city that was pretty broke was able with the private sector — basically by stepping out of the way — to create Playhouse Square," Mr. Coffey said. Playhouse Square involved the renovation of aging downtown Cleveland theaters into a performing arts center.

Cleveland also has used federal Urban Development Action Grant (UDAG) funds to get the private sector to foot the bill for development. "We were very successful in the '80s with UDAG money used for pump-priming," the city's Mr. Morrison said. "More important, we established a history of public-private partnerships. The major purpose of Playhouse Square was not only to restore these wonderful vaudeville houses but to create in downtown a major entertainment center."

The Cleveland city government worked throughout most of the 1980s to promote its downtown as the primary regional office center, a strong retail center, a crowd draw with museums and a baseball stadium, and a meeting place for conventions. On the retail side, "we've been pretty lucky," Mr. Morrison said. "We've retained two of our department stores." Cleveland had three downtown department stores in the early 1980s and five such stores in the late 1960s. The two that remain, locally based May

Co. and Higbee Co., have put significant investments into their downtown property, and their investments have been bolstered by the development of two downtown retail malls.

Elsewhere downtown, Cleveland in the early 1990s became involved in construction of a new baseball stadium and a new basketball arena. A planned North Coast Harbor will "create an attractive setting for museum developments," Mr. Morrison said. The Rock and Roll Hall of Fame will be located there, along with an aquarium and other museums. Cleveland's convention district adjoins those developments with a clustering of downtown hotels around the convention center and near retail and entertainment outlets. Finally, the city has gone after downtown residential development.

A key to Cleveland's success clearly is involving all the affected parties in the process. When the city updated its downtown and citywide plans, it took a similar approach to the Playhouse Square project, doing so "with a significant contribution from the corporate and foundation communities, important because it became a game plan that is a public-private plan," Mr. Morrison said. The plan was written with an eye toward minimizing investment risk for both the city and private investors. "That's really the take-home lesson of all this. It's got to be a joint effort."

Downtown Charleston sports a new look

In the mid-1980s, downtown Charleston, W.Va., faced a situation common to many downtowns across the country — retail business had relocated to a mall, leaving vacant storefronts behind. Unlike other cities, however, downtown retail operations didn't leave the city of 57,000 people for the suburbs. Instead, stores moved to a new downtown mall that opened in 1984, just a few blocks from the old central business district.

That fact didn't lessen the concern of city officials, who worried about a two-block-by-three-block area of storefronts suddenly left vacant, or, worse, "they'd be occupied by undesirable tenants, sleazy bars, that sort of thing," remarked Pat Brown, executive director of the Charleston Urban Renewal Authority.

Anticipating the problem, a non-profit group called the Charleston Renaissance Corp. formed to focus on revitalizing the old downtown shopping area. Working together, the city's Urban Renewal Authority, the Renaissance Corp. and the city government in 1985 began to encourage investment in the old shopping area. The area was designated the Downtown Village District, and the city invested in streetscape improvements.

Next, the groups established architectural guidelines for the restoration of the old buildings, many of which had seen their old stone facades covered with siding during the 1960s. Working with local banks, the Urban Renewal Authority developed a low-income loan program to help owners finance improvements in the

Downtown Village District. Ultimately, the Urban Renewal Authority was able to offer facade restoration loans at 4 percentage points under the prime rate.

The overall approach, Mr. Brown said, was to promote investor confidence in the Downtown Village District, and little by little buildings have been restored and occupied. About half the buildings in the designated area had been restored by the end of 1992.

"It isn't something that's happened overnight, but it has been moving steadily," Mr. Brown said. "There are still some vacancies. We are finding that these buildings for the most part are not being occupied by retail but by professionals. A lot of people wanted it to return to a retail section, but that's not going to happen when you've got retail two blocks away."

Some specialty shops have located in the restored area of downtown, but the newly renovated buildings basically house professional offices top to bottom. With a walkway and a bus line linking the new office area with the downtown mall, downtown vitality has been maintained and even has increased, Mr. Brown added.

Boston is a tough act to follow

In the late 1980s, the real-estate boom that caught Boston saw development in the city's financial district poised to spread into what had once been the city's theater district.

"It was an underutilized area comprised of a retail area and the heart of what was the theater district in Boston," said Brian DeLorey, director of midtown for the Boston Redevelopment Authority. "It had suffered from years of blight. Some buildings were used for so-called adult entertainment."

City residents had long dubbed the spot "The Combat Zone." With development set to move into the area, however, Boston officials recognized a chance to let that development carry the weight of refurbishing the old theater district. A two-year planning and zoning process that ended in 1989 established a 27-acre cultural district, with the requirement that any theater torn down in the district had to be replaced with another theater.

"There were planning principles involved and a number of historic structures were to be preserved," Mr. DeLorey said.

The threat of new high-rise construction spreading from the financial district forced Boston officials' hand in creating the district. Their action provided a case study in both growth management and bootstrap redevelopment. Looking to continue the financial district office boom, developers initially resisted the move to the theater district. But Boston officials came back with hard numbers to make the case that if people came in from outside Boston to go to the theater, they also would buy at the shops, eat at the restaurants and stay at the hotels.

116

"Boston has historically been the city where plays are tried out before going to Broadway, and we have many small, non-profit theater companies as well," Mr. DeLorey said.

By making a market argument, Boston officials won the private sector over to the cultural district concept. The theater groups, private developers and other institutions all became part of the planning process for the district. While the city completed infrastructure improvements, developers and various institutions contributed to the new performing arts spaces.

Cincinnati serves as a historic model of consensus

When they studied the results of the city's 1960 quadrennial assessment, Cincinnati officials came to a grim realization: The assessed value of the city's downtown had dropped significantly. The numbers offered proof of what already was painfully obvious to many in Cincinnati: The city's downtown was deteriorating.

To reverse that trend, the city formed a panel representing a cross-section of interests to meet with consultants and develop a plan. In 1964, the panel released an outline for saving the city's downtown. The overriding aim was simple: Make downtown important. The plan didn't include any unique proposals but had something more significant — consensus.

When work began, Cincinnati's Fountain Square was nothing more than "an island in the middle of downtown with a fountain in the middle of it," as one former city official described it. But the redevelopment plan placed the fountain at the hub of the improvements, making the square the most important spot in downtown and, in fact, the focus of the entire region.

Using federal economic development tools of the time — the power of eminent domain and the sale of property — the city accumulated a 12-block core around the fountain and found developers for it. Private development expanded around that core, making Fountain Square Plaza the city's focus. At the same time, city officials launched construction of a second-story skywalk system. A third, and hugely successful, factor in downtown Cincinnati's revitalization was an unusual decision to locate Riverfront Stadium there. The stadium brings people downtown to watch Major League Baseball's Reds and the National Football League's Bengals; those who attend the games are left with a sense that downtown is the place to be, even when the two teams aren't playing.

The success of the city's plan is evidenced by the downtown's vitality. A number of people remain on the streets and in the plaza long after weekday 9-to-5 business hours are over. Downtown amenities include three department stores, museums and top restaurants that might surprise those otherwise unfamiliar with Cincinnati.

"Without those three elements we certainly would have a more difficult task than we have right now," said Mark McKillip, development officer in the Cincinnati Department of Economic Development. "We're building off of strength rather than facing impossible battles."

In the early 1990s, the city was moving into the next phase of downtown development — battling suburban malls by further concentrating Cincinnati's retail core and trying to locate another downtown anchor store.

Interest runs deep in waterfront projects

There's gold in them thar' waterways. As if local rivers were medicinal baths, economic development officials everywhere are immersing themselves in the possibilities a rejuvenated waterfront holds for their communities.

Interest in riverfront development cuts across lines of population, geography and demographics. For every San Antonio or Baltimore whose effort has received national publicity, there is a Shreveport, La., or Davenport, Iowa, working less conspicuously to make its waterfront a showplace. The list of those with active projects numbers in the hundreds, with New Orleans, Minneapolis and Fort Lauderdale, Fla., as prime examples.

"The interest in this issue is well-established, well-known and well-emulated," said Richard Rigby, co-director of The Waterfront Center, a Washington-based, non-profit advisory group.

For many city officials, the temptation to model efforts after a successful program elsewhere is great. San Antonio, with its riverfront mall and other attractions proving a magnet for tourists and residents alike, gets as much attention as anyone these days. But rather than trying to copy exemplary waterfront projects, Mr. Rigby recommends that cities analyze both the need to refurbish a waterfront and the method for doing it on a case-by-case basis.

"Some people recite seven steps to creating a successful waterfront. This is utter nonsense," he said.

Still, cities embarking on waterfront projects generally must address two major issues: how to maximize public access to the waterway while stimulating private investment, and how to tailor amenities to residents of the community, whose support can be crucial.

In New Orleans, those issues have created an attempt at a difficult balancing act. As the city prepares the portion of its citywide master plan that affects land fronting the Mississippi River, stake-holders worry about how New Orleans will improve on its piecemeal planning of the past. Public access to the river always has been an issue in the city because of an unusual configuration of land masses at the riverfront, said John Wilson, executive director of the City Planning Commission. On one occasion, transportation engineers suggested a riverfront expressway running parallel to the Mississippi, but residents concerned about access shouted down the idea.

The concept of building highways to facilitate movement

around waterfronts held much support in the 1970s, but most cities that took the plunge, like Louisville, Ky., and Boston, have been trying to overcome their mistakes in the 1990s, Mr. Rigby insisted. "It resulted in a severance of the waterfront from the rest of the city," he said.

New Orleans' waterfront development, which in 1992 took on a new sense of urgency because vessels used for riverboat gambling were expected to dock there one day, is littered with potential mine fields. Residents around the nearby French Quarter fear that commercial development along the river will be geared to tourists and offer nothing to them, Mr. Wilson said. Others warn of traffic problems that could arise from a proposed 400,000-square-foot expansion of a riverfront convention center.

Not every city struggles as much as New Orleans to define its waterfront. Fort Lauderdale officials are crowing about a river-walk development that they say already is breathing new life into a downtown that languished in the 1980s. City officials have been able to maintain control over their designs for the New River area because they own most of the surrounding land, making public access less of an issue. The centerpieces of their plan are a 1.5-mile linear park complete with walkways and a tropical motif, a science museum and a performing arts center. Completion of the entire project was slated for 1994. A $44 million bond issue approved by city voters in 1986 has financed some of the improvements, but private donations also have contributed.

William Johnson, Fort Lauderdale's economic development director, said the city has tried to use public money as a catalyst for commercial development. Also, the city has clearly identified the beneficiaries of its riverfront efforts — local residents. While the city's renowned beachfront Strip and a new convention center serve as tourist magnets, the riverwalk is for the local community, Mr. Johnson indicated.

"We're trying to create an around-the-clock downtown," he said. "Right now, people jump in their cars at 5 p.m. and head west. We'd also like to make downtown a residential community."

Though it is difficult to pinpoint trends among literally hundreds of ongoing waterfront projects, it is clear that the obsession in the 1980s with waterfront festival marketplaces like Baltimore's pioneering Harborplace has waned considerably. Mr. Rigby believes that festival marketplaces offered a sexy topic for the media but that officials mistakenly assumed the projects would rejuvenate any dying industrial riverfront. While Baltimore's turnaround involved a great deal more than Harborplace, too many people attributed it to the retail complex alone. As a result, cities like Toledo, Ohio, and Flint, Mich., ventured into festival marketplaces with disastrous results, Mr. Rigby said.

Today, many communities have scrapped the giant marketplace in favor of mixed-use developments emphasizing retail, housing, and some offices or research-and-development facilities.

Minneapolis officials are trying to refurbish two riverfront areas, on the downtown and east sides of the Mississippi River. They envision projects combining residential, commercial, research-and-development and historic uses, and they have created three tax increment financing (TIF) districts in an attempt to stimulate development. In a TIF district, a government borrows money to pay for capital needs, with the bonds repaid from tax revenue generated by new development in the district. Progress in the three Minneapolis districts at first was slow because of a sluggish economy and a delay-ridden process of removing abandoned railroad tracks from the riverfront, said James Moore, the city's director of downtown and riverfront development.

"Our redevelopment of the river is meant to bring people there to live and do business and to rebuild our tax base," Mr. Moore said. "We're hoping a couple of developments will gel and create some momentum."

Even in a less-than-stellar economy, cities push forward with ambitious waterfront visions. Arlington, Texas, officials, for example, in the recession of the early 1990s spent as much time talking about plans for a so-called riverwalk surrounding a planned new baseball stadium for the Texas Rangers as they spent discussing the ballpark. Mayor Richard Greene considered land adjacent to a creek traversing the stadium property a fertile ground for such possibilities as baseball-related shops and a 2,000-seat amphitheater, with amenities geared for year-round use.

"When people heard about this, their eyes lit up. They thought of San Antonio's riverwalk," Mr. Greene said. "Ours would be considerably smaller than that, but we still like the idea."

Technology parks energize economies, government budgets

Economic development officials often do their best to lure research parks to their areas. But while research parks often are mainstays of revitalized, mixed-use downtowns and waterfronts in large cities, the parks also can boost the economies of smaller communities.

Outside Pullman, Wash., a one-story, modernistic structure pokes up from the rolling wheat fields. In this rural setting near the Idaho border, about 75 miles south of Spokane, the Washington State University Research Park is home to a bevy of small, emerging companies. Most were founded by entrepreneurial university engineers and scientists wanting to bridge the gap between their laboratories and the marketplace.

This research park typifies an economic development strategy being tried by state and local officials in a variety of settings — from the Stanford Research Park in Palo Alto, Calif., to the Research Triangle Park near Raleigh, N.C. The parks, private real-estate ventures sweetened with government incentives, gen-

120

erally are attached to major research universities. For the states and communities in which they are located, the parks provide high-quality jobs, prestige and expanded tax revenue. In colder climates, the parks might keep some graduates from fleeing to high-technology meccas in warmer climates. Most encouraging, research parks remain relatively unscathed by economic downslides, including the national recession of the early 1990s.

"Research parks are continuing to be quite active," said Chris Boettcher, executive director of the Association of University Related Research Parks, Tempe, Ariz. The early 1990s economic pinch was "the first recession since research parks have had a major presence," and the parks "held their own quite well."

In early 1991, about 130 university research parks existed or were under development in the United States, compared to only 14 before 1980.

Stanford Research Park in Palo Alto, the grand dame of technology parks, was established in 1951. It laid the groundwork for what eventually became known as Silicon Valley, the legendary 30-mile corridor in the Palo Alto-San Jose area with the greatest concentration of high-technology companies in the world, said Zera Murphy, director of Lands Management, Stanford University. The 660-acre Stanford Research Park, which contains 150 buildings, is the only one of its kind that is fully developed.

The park generates 20% of the Palo Alto government's annual sales tax revenue ($2.3 million in fiscal 1991). Property tax payments also are "fairly significant," though solid figures are not available, said Emily Harrison, city finance director. The city must provide the roads, sewers and other infrastructure leading to the research park, but the financial burden is worth it, Ms. Harrison said. The park is a "major corporate citizen. The problem more than pays for itself." But the government of Palo Alto is beginning to look over its shoulder at competition from other research parks — particularly since living costs are high and traffic congestion is a problem. "We don't think we can be complacent," Ms. Harrison continued. "We have to work hard to make sure the park stays competitive."

Planning for the Stanford Research Park began shortly after World War II, during a fast-growth period, but without financial incentives from state and local governments. When the park was being developed, Palo Alto had no planning department, and surrounding Santa Clara County had only one planner. Palo Alto officials moved quickly with zoning, annexed the park and agreed to provide municipal services with the property taxes from development. Marketing was done by "the seat of one's pants" at cocktail parties and luncheons, Ms. Murphy recalled.

The budding electronics industry helped Stanford lure government and private research funds, in addition to top students and faculty. Among the first tenants at the park were two computer engineers who later founded Hewlett-Packard Co. As the research park attracted more entrepreneurs, researchers and business people, it rapidly achieved a critical mass that nurtured its growth.

Late-night visions of Silicon Valley II light up the eyes of university and municipal officials in other parts of the country. In most cases, however, these ventures are not a quick fix — or any kind of a fix — for creaky local economies.

"Research parks are not the answer to all city and state ills," Mr. Boettcher cautioned. "A research park can enhance technology and economic development, but you need an all-encompassing plan to make it work. It's a very long-term development. It takes time to attract the kind of companies you want to see located there."

The parks can take decades to get warmed up and fully leased, while local governments must invest up-front in infrastructure improvements and repairs.

"One of the problems is everyone thinks this is the panacea, the solution for economic development problems," said Michael H. Wacholder, director of the Rensselaer Technology Park in east-central New York. "If there isn't a strong intellectual base and institutional base, it's hard to suggest university-based research parks will be successful."

The 1,300-acre Rensselaer Technology Park infused economic vigor into the Albany suburban area. Financial benefits from the park — which is owned, operated and funded by Rensselaer Polytechnic Institute in Troy — have spread over surrounding localities. North Greenbush and its school district, for instance, received $300,000 in tax revenue in fiscal 1991. That figure was expected to increase each year as tax abatements gradually expired. North Greenbush played a part in sustaining the research park by injecting $2 million in venture capital into 16 companies in the technology park. For the money it invested, town officials expect each $5,000 to create one job. Other incentives are provided for companies to hire people laid off from businesses in the area or people going through retraining. About 1,100 jobs were created by 40 tenant companies about six years after the park opened up in 1985. North Greenbush developed a master plan for the park and completed an environmental impact statement for the site. When companies want to move in, the town can offer a speedy process.

Most technology parks will never come close to evolving into a Stanford-Silicon Valley bonanza, nor will they attract major companies. In addition, parks usually shun heavy industry and allow no more than light manufacturing. Most parks end up with a theme that attracts like firms; for example, in and around the Central Florida Research Park in Orlando is housed the third-largest concentration of firms — about 300 — involved in laser research.

122

Cable television

As the popularity of cable television grew during the early 1980s, each municipal government exercised its power to choose the single communications company that would supply cable TV's many channels — from the network affiliates that households normally picked up by TV antenna to the popular Home Box Office (HBO) movie station — to local residents. Once a city, county, town or other local government entered into a franchise agreement with a cable company, that company became the monopoly cable TV provider for the area.

At first, government officials controlled some aspects of company operations, but much of their regulatory power was taken away with the federal Cable Communications Policy Act of 1984. Once the act took effect, cable viewers' monthly bills began to rise because local governments no longer could force companies to keep their rates down. Franchise contracts between the average government and company covered three to seven years, but once that contract expired, the 1984 act prohibited local officials from switching to a new company unless they could prove that the current company committed egregious wrongs and refused to remedy them. Local governments eventually joined with consumer groups to lobby Congress for greater control over cable franchises.

On Oct. 5, 1992, with a national election just one month away, the Democrat-controlled Congress managed its first override of a veto by Republican President George Bush, and cable television again came under a form of rate regulation — albeit a weak form. City and county government officials immediately complained that they did not receive the kind of strong local control of rates and services that they wanted. Nor did the law ensure lower rates for their constituents. Still, Mr. Bush had opposed re-regulation, so local officials were content that at least they had received *something*.

The 1992 law, which reversed some provisions of the deregulatory 1984 act, contained elements allowing for greater checks on cable companies — most of them imposed by Washington, D.C., not municipal governments. The bill also left much up to the Federal Communications Commission (FCC) of Chairman Alfred C. Sikes, who was known to favor the free market over rate regulation. Left out in large part were the cities, counties, towns and other governments that act as the local franchising authorities. Local governments that wished to play a role in rate regulation would have to petition the FCC for that authority and show that the national rates the FCC was expected to establish should not apply to their areas.

"Would we have liked to have strong local control over cable rates and services? Of course we would have," said David C. Olson, president of the National Association of Telecommunications Officers and Advisors (NATOA) and cable director of Portland, Ore. "But after years of deregulation and rate increases three to four times the rate of inflation, of course we support this bill."

A 1991 report from the General Accounting Office, *Survey of Cable Television Rates and Services,* found that rates paid by cable customers rose faster than the rate of inflation. About 66% of subscribers for the lowest-priced basic service faced rate increases of more than 10% between December 1989 and April 1991. Average rates for the lowest-priced basic service increased by 9%, to $17.34 from $15.95 per subscriber, with an average decrease of one channel. The average monthly rate for the most popular basic cable services rose by 15%, to $18.84 from $16.33, with an increase of two channels. The General Accounting Office, a nonpartisan agency of the U.S. Congress that audits government-related programs, also found that the number of systems offering only one tier, or level, of service fell by about 25 percentage points. The number of systems offering two or more tiers increased to 41.4% from 16.6%. On the revenue side, overall monthly revenue to cable operators climbed an average of 4.2% between December 1989 and December 1990 and 4.7% between December 1990 and March 1991.

The 1992 cable legislation imposed government controls on rates for cable equipment as well as basic service. It also let broadcast TV stations seek compensation when cable operators air their signals. It entitled rival services, such as home satellite dish operators, to buy cable programming at prices similar to those charged cable franchises.

The FCC on April 1, 1993, ordered all cable television companies, which distribute shows to 57 million U.S. homes, to freeze rate increases for 120 days and to roll back consumer prices to levels of Sept. 30, 1992. The exact rates that cable customers could expect to pay in future years were not immediately known because the FCC was developing a formula establishing a cost per channel.

The FCC before the end of 1993 was scheduled to write rules for rates and customer service standards, including signal quality and response time to customer needs. Some elements of the bill were more favorable to localities, opening up the prospect that, down the road a year or two, cities could begin influencing rates and service quality, according to Mr. Olson of NATOA, an organization that is affiliated with the Washington-based National League of Cities. Most importantly, the law contained a provision that NATOA worked hard to include in the House-Senate conference committee report on the bill: A municipal damage immunity provision that would stop cable companies from suing cities for exceeding their regulatory authority. Up until the 1992 act, courts had been awarding the companies large monetary damages.

"With so many cable franchises up for renewal, the threat of the cable operators suing for damages was very real, which is why this was such a critical provision of the bill," Mr. Olson said.

But will viewers' TV bills ever come down?

Backers of the bill warned against expectations that it would automatically bring down rates for cable subscribers.

"Cable prices are going to rise less rapidly than they have in the past," but they will still continue to go up, said David Londoner, a cable industry analyst with the New York investment firm of Wertheim Schroder & Co. Inc. Mr. Londoner made his comments shortly after Congress' override of Mr. Bush's veto. "It is basically the end of what has been one of the very few unregulated monopolies of any size in the United States, if not the only one, and it's going to result in more of a free market."

Lynnea Dalton of the Washington-based U.S. Independent Microwave Television Association, the cable industry's chief competitors, agreed that consumers "will see lower prices in the long run, once competition comes in."

In contrast, Peggy Laramie, a spokeswoman for the Washington-based National Cable Television Association, said, "Subscribers are likely to see no immediate change. After that, it's anybody's guess. Our view is that consumer advocates are misleading people when they suggest massive rollbacks. It may never happen."

Consumer advocates felt the law "will bring down rates up to 30%, depending on the individual cable system," said Bradley Steelman, a spokesman for the Consumer Federation of America, Washington.

U.S. Rep. John Dingell, D-Mich., added, "It doesn't mean that rates are going to go down or that rates aren't going to go up. What it means is that rates aren't going to go up as much as they would without the bill."

The rates targeted in the law were for basic service, the lowest tier of service that typically includes the broadcast channels, local access channels and some satellite services, such as C-SPAN and Cable News Network. At the beginning of 1993, this basic service cost an average of $20 a month. Once the FCC decided on its formula, local authorities would be allowed to force cable companies to reduce any rates exceeding the ceiling. Premium channels, such as HBO, were not regulated, according to an analysis by the U.S. House Subcommittee on Telecommunications.

The second tier of cable service, which may include such offerings as channels featuring country music, home shopping, sports, movies, comedy, programs for children, religious programs and news, were not immediately regulated under the 1992 legislation. However, the FCC could intervene and limit rate increases for this tier if local governments and consumers one day complained that cable companies were raising rates rapidly to compensate for any rollbacks in the charge for basic service.

Congressional sponsors of the measure said it would ultimately save consumers $6 billion annually. The cable industry countered that a retransmission consent provision, which allowed broadcasters to negotiate for compensation from cable operators that carry local broadcasts, would result in $1 billion to $2 billion in increased costs that the industry would be forced to pass on to consumers each year.

The legislation gave the FCC latitude to define unreasonable rates for basic service. Among other criteria, the measure allowed the FCC to compare one operator's rates against rates charged by a "similarly situated" cable system. Mr. Sikes, who had opposed the bill, said the day after Congress' veto override that the FCC would do its best to implement the law, and he hoped Congress would supply the money for the additional work that would follow.

"The Congressional Budget Office estimated the cost of implementing the act at more than $20 million a year for the next six years. That is one-sixth of the FCC's budget, but Congress has not yet provided any additional resources," Mr. Sikes said.

Robert Pepper, chief of planning and policy for the FCC, predicted that sections of the law requiring cable companies to carry certain programs would be challenged in the courts, but he said the court cases would not delay implementation of the legislation as a whole. Indeed, one of the largest providers of cable television programs sued the day after passage of the legislation. Atlanta-based Turner Broadcasting System Inc. claimed a requirement that cable companies carry local affiliates of ABC, CBS, NBC,

Fox and other over-the-air broadcasters was unconstitutional. The suit was filed in federal court in Washington, D.C. Courts have ruled twice before that the so-called "must carry" provision violates the First Amendment of the U.S. Constitution by giving broadcast stations and broadcast networks unfair advantages over cable networks, said Bert Carp, Turner Broadcasting System vice president for government affairs.

How officials can deny renewals of cable TV franchises

It was a shocking moment in cable television history that, at least for cable executives, was more frightening than a horror film on HBO. The New York Board of Estimate in May 1990 decided to turn down requests by Manhattan Cable TV and Paragon Cable Manhattan to renew their franchises serving the New York City borough of Manhattan. Both franchises were worth about $1 billion to the parent company of both operations, New York-based Time Warner Inc. Among the thousands of franchises that had come up for renewal in the United States, only a small handful had ever been turned down, and none had been anywhere near the size of the two Manhattan franchises covering some 400,000 subscribers. It would have been every cable executive's worst nightmare come true if the city had stuck to its guns. But just a month later, the soon-to-be-defunct Board of Estimate overturned its own decision, granting new franchises to Paragon and Manhattan Cable. During that month, the cable companies quickly came to terms with the city on a detailed plan to upgrade service and expand the capital investment in the service area.

The situation was an example of how a municipal government can have a meaningful impact on a local cable company — keep detailed records of cable problems, then threaten to break off relations when the franchise contract expires. The Cable Communications Policy Act of 1984 took away the most compelling power of local franchising authorities over cable companies — the power to set rules — and made it far more difficult to deny renewal of a franchise, meaning jurisdictions had to begin carefully documenting cable operators' performance problems.

As cable franchise agreements expire — most of the 10,000-plus franchises came up for renewal in 1991 and 1992 — more and more jurisdictions have studied their options in the wake of subscribers complaining about spiraling rate increases, problems with TV signal quality and the failure of cable companies to respond to complaints.

Before the 1992 cable law, the restrictions in the 1984 act prompted most cities to simply grant outright franchise renewals. Cities were unprepared to face lawsuits or to challenge the companies to do better, said Gary D. Michaels, an attorney who has done cable TV legal work with the Washington law firm of Krivit & Krivit. The 1992 cable law will help make things easier, but local officials also can continue using the pressure tactics they learned during the years leading up to that legislation.

In addition, court decisions in the early 1990s made the job of defeating franchise renewals a little easier. U.S. District Judge Edward Filippine ruled April 16, 1991, that the city of Rolla, Mo., could deny the renewal of a cable franchise to Omega Communications, a local company that had served the city for 30 years. The city had argued that Omega's system was filled with technical problems and that customer service was poor. Pat Grant, a Washington-based attorney who represented Rolla in franchise deliberations and who also has served as a lobbyist on cable issues for the National League of Cities, said the decision would "put some chills into the process" of franchise renewals for poorly run cable operations.

"Clearly, this decision establishes that cities do have some authority in their ability to deny a franchise," acknowledged Robert Sachs, senior vice president, corporate and legal affairs, for Boston-based Continental Cablevision Inc., the country's fourth-largest cable system operator.

The burden of proof still is on the local government that originally granted the franchise. Four major criteria exist for denying, or convincingly threatening to deny, franchise renewals:

• The cable company fails to comply with the "material terms" of the franchise, usually through gross violations such as failure to build out the system or reluctance to provide key components detailed in the franchise contract.

• The service is not "reasonable" in terms of customer service or signal quality.

• The company doesn't have the financial or technical means to keep the system running.

• The renewal proposal from the company fails to clear up problems found in analyses of system operations.

Experts have emphasized that if a government does not make the cable operator aware of alleged violations of the franchise agreement and fails to give the company an opportunity to correct them, there will be trouble denying franchise renewal.

Tom Weisner, government cable liaison for Aurora, Ill., a Chicago suburb that in 1989 went through a franchise renewal, said, "The No. 1 point I always stress is don't wait until the deadline nears to begin the official renewal process. It takes time, even years, to fully document the problems and begin to address your needs for the coming years." Mr. Weisner said Aurora cable subscribers had experienced some clear problems as franchise renewal time approached, such as a lack of public access channels and a rapidly aging infrastructure in the 20-year-old cable system. "But you don't come up with a wish list, either. You have to make a case for all the changes you want in the system."

Even the threat of non-renewal is enough to force big changes in cable operators' minds. Some municipalities underestimate the gravity with which cable operators take any hint of non-renewal.

Many cable franchises are owned by companies that incurred astounding amounts of debt when they bought up smaller systems. They cannot afford to contemplate losing their capital investments.

Local governments aren't always in control, though. Six months after winning renewal in Manhattan, Time Warner announced rate increases of $2 a month for basic service — an 11.8% hike. That's an example of why local governments pushed Congress to expand the 1984 cable act to give them greater powers over issues such as consumer services.

Governments hope telephone companies enter TV business

Mr. Bush's administration felt competition would increase, and cable TV rates would drop, if telephone companies were allowed to compete in the cable TV industry. In general, local governments and their representatives have favored telephone companies' participation in the cable business on the stipulation — agreed to by the Washington-based U.S. Telephone Association — that municipalities would be able to regulate phone companies at least as much as they regulate cable TV companies.

Phone companies want to fully utilize the expensive network of fiber-optic cables they have been laying across the country. Fiber-optic technology relies on hair-thin, flexible glass strands to transmit signals using pulses of laser light. Such technology, however, offers competition to a cable industry that already feels its profit margins are too low.

Phone companies have conducted tests in at least 20 markets, the largest being Cerritos, Calif. There, with permission from Cerritos government officials, about 700 participants received novel services, such as limited two-way programming, and they experienced the higher-quality sound reproduction of fiber-optics while company experts probed them on how much they would be willing to pay for the service. Thousand Oaks-based GTE California Inc. performed the test.

Revealingly, NATOA came out on April 23, 1991, with a survey showing a lack of competition in the cable marketplace and rising costs of service. The survey of 184 cable regulators overseeing 1,002 local franchises showed that cable rates were increasing at about 13% annually — more than twice the rate of inflation — and that competition existed in only 5% of service areas. One in four of the respondents to the survey stated that the local cable operator had reduced the number of channels on the least expensive, entry-level basic service and increased prices for services and premium channels that used to be considered basic.

Cable television as a source of local tax revenue

A U.S. Supreme Court decision upholding an Arkansas sales tax on cable television has opened the door for other states and municipalities to impose similar taxes.

"I imagine a lot of state legislators will be licking their chops over this one," said Bob Blount, director of the Arkansas Cable Television Association.

While those in the cable industry agreed the ruling may give state and local lawmakers the impetus to adopt cable tax bills, some government representatives were not sure this would be the case. "I don't think it should open the floodgates" to tax legislation, said Harley Duncan, executive director of the Federation of Tax Administrators, Washington.

The Arkansas Cable Television Association had opposed a 4% state sales tax that went into effect July 1, 1987. The association contended that the tax, which was not levied on other forms of media, violated cable operators' rights to free speech. The tax is added directly onto cable TV subscribers' monthly bills.

Supreme Court Justice Sandra Day O'Connor, writing for the majority in a 7-2 decision, stated, "There's no indication in this case that Arkansas has targeted cable television in a purposeful attempt to interfere with its First Amendment activities." Justices Thurgood Marshall and Harry Blackmun dissented in the April 16, 1991, decision.

Twenty-two states taxed cable TV at the time of the ruling, according to the Federation of Tax Administrators. Eighteen states imposed a sales tax on all cable services. Maine and Tennessee taxed only premium services, while Delaware and Washington had a gross receipts tax on cable services. Pennsylvania Gov. Robert P. Casey reportedly had proposed that cable be included in a number of services to be hit with a sales tax to balance the state's financially troubled budget. The city of Los Angeles was pushing for a 10% utility tax that would be levied on cable TV, telephone and public utility services.

Part of the Arkansas case was sent back to the Arkansas Supreme Court for a further ruling. It concerned the time period between 1987 and 1989, during which cable customers were taxed but satellite dish users were not. In 1989, the Arkansas Legislature amended its sales tax to include dish users. The Arkansas Cable Television Association argued that under the 14th Amendment to the U.S. Constitution, guaranteeing equal protection, cable TV operators should not have been taxed while satellite users were exempt. If the court were to rule in favor of the association, about $11 million would be refunded to customers, the association reported.

Issuing bonds to borrow money

When interest rates are low, state and local governments rush to the bond market to take advantage of lower borrowing costs. But when rates are high, governments try to get by with what little they have in their treasuries.

Double-digit interest rates and inflation during the late 1970s precluded hundreds of state and local governments from borrowing money in the municipal bond market to pay for major programs such as road construction, environmental protection and building rehabilitation. A decade later, the situation reversed. By the beginning of 1992, favorable interest rates were expected to continue well into the year, prompting states and localities to continue borrowing in near-record numbers despite a national recession that had weakened government finances.

Municipal bond volume surpassed $165 billion in 1991, a total second only to the $204 billion sold in 1985, the year governments rushed to the bond market to beat the restrictive provisions of the federal Tax Reform Act of 1986. But while bond issuance was booming in the early 1990s, the picture was not as rosy on the ratings front. The recession took its toll on credit ratings in 1991, with Standard & Poor's Corp. (S&P) of New York downgrading 601 municipal ratings while raising only 145. The downgrades affected some $53.1 billion in debt, while the upgrades involved only about $8 billion worth of bonds.

Budget woes caused that trend to continue in 1992 as struggling governments kept seeking to borrow at low interest rates. Driven primarily by the Federal Reserve's easing of key interest rates in hopes of spurring the sluggish national economy, most rates had fallen to their lowest levels in years. The Bond Buyer 20-Bond

Index, for example, a yield estimate based on a group of 20 general obligation bonds with an average rating of A on a scale that makes AAA the best possible rating, stood at 6.4% on Jan. 9, 1992, down from 7.09% one year earlier.

"With low rates, clearly everybody looks to access the market to the extent that they can," said Neal H. Attermann, vice president in the municipal finance department of Kidder, Peabody & Co. Inc., New York.

When a state, state agency, city, county, town, village, sewer district, fire protection district or any other government wants to borrow money to pay for a major project that will benefit its constituents, it turns to the tax-exempt municipal bond market to raise funds. In general, the interest paid by a government to investors who purchase its bonds is exempt from federal income taxes and state and local taxes in the state of issue. Municipal bonds carry a lower interest rate than bonds issued by, say, a for-profit corporation because the interest on corporate bonds is taxable. Investors are willing to settle for a lower interest rate on municipal bonds because, in most cases, they do not have to pay taxes on their investment earnings. An investor would have to pay taxes on municipal bond income, however, if he is covered by the federal government's alternative minimum tax, which requires some payment from every taxpayer with substantial income, even if all or part of that income would not ordinarily be taxed.

Governments normally try to enter the bond market only when they need to fund a major project, although occasionally they borrow for other reasons, including trying to prop up their finances. Any financially struggling government that enters the bond market is likely to see its debt rating downgraded; in other words, doubts remain as to whether that government has enough revenue, and will continue to garner enough revenue in the future, to pay off its debts. When the interest rate environment is low and officials realize they can borrow at less cost, struggling governments are tempted to issue more bonds than they should. In early 1992, Todd Whitestone, S&P managing director, predicted "a negative year in terms of more downgrades than upgrades. I would actually expect that '92 is going to be kind of a down year creditwise." Of all the factors weighed by the main rating agencies — S&P, Moody's Investors Service Inc. and Fitch Investors Service Inc. — in assessing issuer credit quality, financial operations were the most troublesome in the early 1990s.

Catherine L. Spain, director of the Government Finance Officers Association's federal liaison center in Washington, noted that the financial picture was gloomy for many governments in 1992. "Their one concern would just be what impact the fiscal situation has on financings," she said. "They may not be able to pay the debt service on the bonds." Still, Ms. Spain agreed that low interest rates drive issuers into the bond market, no matter what the financial picture.

That fact certainly was true in 1992, a year that saw state and local governments issue new bonds amounting to more than $232.5 billion — a record for the municipal bond market. Refundings, where governments save money on interest costs by replacing older bond issues carrying high interest rates with new issues at lower rates, represented nearly 40% of the market, up from 25% in 1991. The percentage of the municipal bond market backed by bond insurance ended up barely surpassing 1991's figure of 30%; state and local governments often buy insurance from bond insurance companies to guarantee to outside investors that the government will not default on the loan.

The overall pace of borrowing continued beyond 1992 as interest rates remained low; governments borrowed more than $65 billion during the first three months of 1993.

Some bond experts question the role refundings can play in a low-interest-rate environment. For one thing, the 1986 Tax Reform Act restricted the number of times issuers could refund bonds. In addition, interest rates can dip too low and affect governments' own investment earnings. For example, in early 1992 rates on U.S. government securities were down relative to rates on tax-exempt municipal bonds, leaving state and local governments in a negative arbitrage position. Five-year Treasury notes were yielding 5.92% in early January and one-year bills were yielding 4.09%, while the net interest cost on many municipal bonds coming to market was around 6% or more. "People look at refundings, but then you have the problem of the differential between Treasury rates and tax-exempt rates," Mr. Attermann said. When U.S. Treasury rates are that low, a municipal bond issuer would lose money when investing advance refunding proceeds in Treasury securities while waiting to legally call the refunded issue.

Ironically for bond issuers, low yields on municipal bonds failed to drive investors out of the marketplace in the early 1990s. The bonds remained more attractive than other fixed-income investments, especially when a comparison was made on a taxable-equivalent basis. Despite the fact that individuals had suffered "rate shock" because rates were so low, individuals kept buying municipal bonds, Mr. Attermann said.

Defaults loom large over municipal bond market

A wave of municipal bond defaults saturated the early 1990s, with most of the troublesome issues being conduit financings — debt sold through a government entity on behalf of a third party, such as an industrial development bond issued to finance a business expansion. Government officials, fearing defaults may taint investors' impressions of all municipal debt, claim distinctions must be made between conduit financings, which, though they carry the name of a government, are often the obligation of a private entity, and the lesser number of government purpose bonds in default.

Still, many believe the time has come for states to pay closer attention to bond activity within their borders and make greater efforts to ensure that investors receive adequate disclosure of information about debt issuers. Numbers compiled by the Bond Investors Association, a non-profit, bondholder-supported organization based in Miami Lakes, Fla., showed a whopping 127 municipal defaults totaled more than $3.49 billion through the first nine months of 1991. Richard Lehmann, the organization's president, pointed out that 1991 defaults were at least twice what they were the previous year. The organization counted 84 municipal bond defaults during the first three quarters of 1990 totaling $991 million. For all of 1990, the Bond Investors Association reported 150 defaults coming to more than $1.87 billion.

Mr. Lehmann believes the spate of bond defaults will change investors' attitudes toward municipal bonds. Such bonds over the years have been popular with investors primarily because the interest earned is exempt from federal taxation. The attitudes of less sophisticated retail investors might be particularly affected, Mr. Lehmann pointed out. "Investors have traditionally considered municipal bonds generically safe, and that's not the case anymore. That's unfortunate for municipalities," he said. "It's not the traditional municipal bonds that are the problem, it's the conduit financings." Improved disclosure of issuer information to investors would help head off a change in investors' attitudes, Mr. Lehmann believes. There typically has been a reluctance on the part of governments to accept additional disclosure requirements, "and they're shooting themselves in the foot by letting all these conduit financings in."

The bottom line, remarked Louisiana Treasurer Mary L. Landrieu, "is that every state needs to have a debt management plan that not only works at the state level but also helps the local governments with their financing needs." One big step toward developing and improving such plans could be the Debt Management Network, an effort to bring together officials from all 50 states who are involved in the debt issuance process. The group, co-chaired by Ms. Landrieu and Texas Treasurer Kay Bailey Hutchison, met for the first time in Austin, Texas, in December 1991. Besides giving issuers a forum for discussing technical aspects of debt issuance and "the big picture of debt policy," the group examines debt oversight models in use in some states, Ms. Landrieu said.

In Louisiana, the debt oversight mechanism centers on a 17-member State Bond Commission, chaired by the state treasurer. No debt can be issued in Louisiana without the commission's approval. Louisiana's system hasn't always worked well, Ms. Landrieu admitted, but "it's working better now." Two municipal revenue bond issues of $150 million, issued in 1986 under the auspices of the Louisiana Agricultural Finance Authority, went into default Oct. 1, 1991, because they were backed exclusively by guaranteed investment contracts (investments that typically promise a fixed rate of return for relatively short periods) written by the financially troubled Executive Life Insurance Co. The company in April 1991 was put into conservatorship by the California State Insurance Commission.

Ms. Landrieu notes that while in the past the Louisiana State Bond Commission frequently gave perfunctory approval to bond issues, the group has become more analytical in its approach since she took office in November 1987. "We've started in recent years to ask, 'Is this in the public's interest? Is there a better way to finance these facilities?' It's not an oppressive sort of oversight. It's very helpful," she said, adding that Louisiana's oversight focuses primarily on technical assistance. "The other thing it helps us do is keep accurate records of the debt. I'm a fairly strong proponent of some sort of state commission that will keep accurate records at the very least. I don't know how politicians can make good policy decisions without accurate information."

California often is viewed as a model for collecting data on debt issuance through its Debt Advisory Commission. The commission, chaired by the state treasurer, also provides technical assistance to bond issuers in the state. "We really don't see a great number of defaults among our issuers in California," said state Treasurer Kathleen Brown. "The two big ones we're aware of were caused by the Executive Life GICs (guaranteed investment contracts)." Ms. Brown said she is concerned about maintaining adequate oversight of capital planning and debt management at the state level, and she would like to see the same type of management and discipline brought to local governments.

A $400 million housing revenue bond issue sold by the Memphis Health, Education & Housing Facility Board is another Executive Life-backed deal in default; the board failed to make a Sept. 15 debt payment. Tennessee "has a concern with things that might not directly have to do with governments, some of the GIC-backed deals," said Ann V. Butterworth, director of the division of bond finance in the Tennessee comptroller's office. Of primary concern, she said, is the potential for some sort of federal response to what could be perceived as abusive transactions. "Our concern in these situations is that, when the federal government tries to eliminate abuse, they often take such a wide means that they eliminate government entities' ability to carry out government programs." Ms. Butterworth added that she has taken steps to keep potential problems with public purpose bonds to a minimum. "There's a strong feeling that timely disclosure is very important. We now have a provision where municipal issuers must file an informational statement within 45 days of the issuance of the debt. The better informed the market, the better off our governments are."

Tennessee officials responded to problems faced by some utility district bonds with the creation of two oversight boards in the late 1980s. The Wastewater Financing Board and the Utility Management Review Board have jurisdiction over governments that issue sewer system or other utility-related bonds. "We're hoping to head off any municipal defaults," said Bill Dobbins, environmental manager of the Tennessee Department of Environment and Conservation. About 200 wastewater systems and a like number of utility districts (mostly water systems) are subject to each board, and they are required to submit annual audits to the state comptroller's office. The comptroller looks for any of three red flags: an accumulated deficit, three consecutive years of net losses or a bond default. Any one of those three signs will trigger oversight by the appropriate board. The board then determines a method of curing the district's financial woes. "So far, there's only been about two or three utility districts that actually were in default on their bond instruments," Mr. Dobbins said. Cures have involved anything from increasing the rates the systems charge customers to mandating that certain steps be taken to improve operations. "The boards are the only ones we're aware of in the nation where a state entity can go into a community and have the authority to tell them what their rates should be," Mr. Dobbins said. That might sound like strong medicine to local officials, but it's hard to argue with success. When the boards were organized in 1987, more than 100 utility districts and 87 city operations were in "distressed condition" under state guidelines. Today, about 25 in each group are distressed, Mr. Dobbins said.

With investors increasingly concerned about reports of municipal bond defaults, state oversight of local bond activity could be the key to preventing serious erosion of investor confidence in the municipal bond market.

Strategies can help officials overcome market instability

As is the case with any financial market, unforeseen circumstances can boost or pummel the municipal bond market.

A case in point was Operation Desert Shield (President George Bush's stationing of U.S. troops in the Middle East to counter Iraq's invasion of Kuwait in late 1990) and Operation Desert Storm (the short-lived military conflict with Iraq in early 1991), both of which introduced volatility in the bond market and forced governments to think twice about borrowing money to fund capital projects and other revenue needs. The main concern among state and local officials was that investors were staying out of all markets — including the tax-exempt bond market — because of continuing tensions over Iraq's bellicose stance in the Middle East and signs of a softening U.S. economy. Governments feared that, if they issued bonds in such an unstable environment, not enough investors would be interested in buying the bonds or investors would demand interest rates that were higher than officials were willing to pay.

Stephanie Lewis, vice president in the Princeton, N.J., office of Government Finance Associates Inc., a financial advisory firm, called the market "volatile" at that time but "not disrupted." In other words, bond trading continued, although it slowed down a bit as war with Iraq appeared imminent.

Industry experts were unable to agree on whether issuers should wait out the volatility or take their chances by selling debt immediately. One thing upon which they could agree, however, was that flexibility was the key.

In any uncertain situation that affects the financial markets, governments can alleviate their own anxiety by adopting some of the following recommendations:

■ Sell short-term instead of long-term debt. Bonds with maturities of five years or less often draw better interest rates than 20- and 30-year bonds, explained Girard Miller, vice president at Fidelity Investment Corp. of America, Boston, a financial advisory firm.

■ Look to negotiated rather than competitive deals. When a bond issue is negotiated with an investment bank or a syndicate of banks, the government has the option of jumping into the bond market on any day the market seems agreeable to a new debt sale. For instance, a government would have been wise to go to market on a day when all parties in the Iraq dispute had come to an agreement — a move that would have benefited the shaky bond and stock markets. Competitive deals, in contrast, require a government to schedule a debt sale for a specific day far in advance, perhaps at a time when the market is down and interest rates up.

■ Stay in close contact with financial advisers or the senior managers on negotiated deals. Advisers and bankers have a stronger sense of what is acceptable in the market on a day-to-day basis, noted Louis Sprauer, vice president at bond dealer Chemical Securities Inc. of New York.

■ Consider credit enhancement through bond insurance or a letter of credit. Such financial backing reduces the bond issue's interest cost and makes the issue more attractive to bidders, Ms. Lewis said.

There's no way to guess how the market will react to a specific bond issue during volatile times. On Aug. 24, 1991, during Operation Desert Shield and four days before California came to market with $700 million in general obligation bonds, apprehensive market observers thought demand would be so low for tax-exempt bonds that the state would almost have to give its bonds away, said Bob Chamberlain, senior vice president at Dean Witter Reynolds Inc., New York. Dean Witter was part of a syndicate that purchased the issue. By the end of the sale, governments were able to relax as California's bonds — at that time rated triple-A, the strongest grade available, by the three major Wall Street credit-rating agencies — received a relatively low interest rate of 7.05% and sold out by the end of the trading session. Still, "bond traders would prefer not to take a position on bonds" under such conditions, Mr. Chamberlain said.

J. Chester Johnson, president of New York-based Government Finance Advisors Inc., which advises the likes of Boston, Detroit and Buffalo, N.Y., took a bullish approach. "As a financial adviser to urban credits, I have no reservations about suggesting they come to market now," he said just weeks before U.S.-led allied forces struck against Iraq. "This isn't the time to put your head in the sand. If you have an ongoing capital program, your interest rates will average out over the life of the program."

Governments must act together to protect bonds

Unfortunately, whenever public confidence diminishes in the bond market, federal agencies are tempted to step in with regulatory controls. In addition, the tax-exempt status of municipal bonds is at stake every time Capitol Hill determines that the U.S. budget is sinking into red ink and the Treasury needs more tax revenue. The bottom line is that, when it comes to state and local borrowing, the federal government is the enemy more often than the ally.

Financial experts like Robert J. Froehlich, vice president at Van Kampen Merritt Investment Advisory Corp., Lisle, Ill., believe government borrowers must act together to protect tax-free bonds. Mr. Froehlich has pointed out that two major events occurred in the late 1980s at the federal level that dramatically changed, and have the potential to continue to change, the tax-exempt municipal bond market. The first was passage of the Tax Reform Act of 1986. The second was a 1988 U.S. Supreme Court decision, *South Carolina vs. Baker.*

"Under the Tax Reform Act, half a corporation's tax-exempt income is included in book income in the calculation of the corporate alternative minimum tax," Mr. Froehlich pointed out. "This one component of the tax act greatly accelerated the changing market composition determining who holds municipal bonds. Historically, the market was dominated by commercial banks, with property and casualty insurers and households (including mutual funds) accounting for the rest of the market. The market now is increasingly dominated by individual purchasers. The percentage of the total municipal bonds outstanding held by households was approaching 60% in 1990. As institutions continue to move out, individual investors continue to move in."

In *South Carolina vs. Baker,* the Supreme Court ruled that the U.S. Constitution does not prohibit the federal government from taxing the interest on state and local government bonds. The decision overturned the court's 1895 decision in *Pollock vs. Farmers Loan & Trust Co.* "State and local government interest deductibility always has been an essential constitutional principle to protect the integrity and fiscal independence of the separate state and local governments," Mr. Froehlich noted. He added that eliminating this deductibility is not a new idea. Andrew J. Mellon, U.S. Treasury secretary under Presidents Warren G. Harding (1921 to 1923) and Calvin Coolidge (1923 to 1929), recommended that the interest on state and local government bonds be taxed. His ideas led to a proposed constitutional amendment permitting Congress to tax municipal bonds, adopted by the House of Representatives but defeated in the Senate.

"With the *South Carolina vs. Baker* decision on the books, there is no need for Mr. Mellon's amendment," Mr. Froehlich argued. "The Supreme Court has now clearly given Congress that right. As of yet, Congress has not acted on this new-found power to tax. If the states want to devise a strategy to fend off federal taxation of state and local municipal bonds, the time is now — not when Congress begins reviewing the actual proposed legislation to tax these bonds. One possible strategy would be to capitalize on the fact that municipal bonds are now predominantly held by individuals, the same individuals who elect and defeat congressmen.

"The municipal market needs to encourage more individuals to invest in municipal bonds. To do this effectively, the states need to unite and stop taxing the interest on out-of-state municipal bonds. Currently, 38 states have a state tax on the interest derived from out-of-state municipal bonds. If the states want to protect themselves, their local governments and their citizens from federal taxation, they must be willing to stop taxing each others' interest on out-of-state municipal bonds. The states do not have to fear that individuals would only buy bonds from other states if they revoke these taxes. There is typically a great degree of state loyalty as well as local knowledge that cannot be matched with an out-of-state bond. This action by the states would send a clear message to Congress: If the states are not going to tax municipal bonds, then Congress likewise should not impose a tax on such bonds.

"Tax-exempt status would increase the number of individuals that own municipal bonds. Also, it would have the indirect benefit of allowing better access to capital markets for local governments to fund their much-needed infrastructure repairs. The more buyers of municipal bonds there are, the easier it is for local governments to fund capital projects."

COPs arrest attention of finance officials

State and local governments often inadvertently thrust congressional oversight on themselves. Perceived abuses in the bond market led to the Tax Reform Act of 1986. The greatest abuse occurred when individual governments or pools of governments sold hundreds of millions of dollars in bonds for projects they never intended to build solely to invest the bond money and earn substantial profits on the interest. The Tax Reform Act in virtually all cases precluded governments from accumulating profits, known as arbitrage earnings, from bond proceeds. Still, governments go out of their ways in search of debt vehicles enabling them to bypass federal and state legislation. Recently, some of those vehicles, known as "bells-and-whistles deals" because alarms might — or should — go off when governments try to use them, are complicated forms of debt that go by nicknames like daily floaters and reverse floaters.

A more established form of debt that has raised the eyebrows of some federal officials is the certificate of participation (COP). There's a hackneyed political line that goes something like this: "If it walks like a duck and quacks like a duck, it must be a duck." But substitute the word "debt" for "duck" and you have COPs, that sneaky, not-quite-debt public finance tool.

COPs have come a long way from their beginnings in the late 1970s in tax-revolt, post-Proposition 13 California. More recently, they have become the predominant form of lease financing. While the structure of COP issues differs from state to state and even from jurisdiction to jurisdiction, slowly they have become standardized and have gained more acceptance among governments, debt-rating houses, bond insurance firms and investors. Anti-tax groups, though, generally view COPs as an underhanded method of bypassing voters and debt limits to obtain financing for extravagant or unwanted projects.

A manual released in the early 1990s, "A Guide to Certificates of Participation," from the New York-based Public Securities Association, was the first national survey to be released about COPs. The guide charted the phenomenal rise in COPs from 1982, when they started spreading outside of California, to the end of 1990, when 441 certificates totaling more than $5 billion were issued in 41 states. The guide also revealed how lease debt could be structured so it would not be categorized as debt, how to assure investors that a financed project would continue to be used (and, therefore, paid off) and how to avoid federal arbitrage rebate provisions.

Governments have used COPs to get around issuing general obligation debt (bonds backed by a government's general revenue) and revenue bond debt (bonds backed by specific revenue streams, including taxes on items ranging from cigarettes to airline tickets) in financing long-term capital projects such as new buildings, fleets of cars and heavy equipment. For their money, investors in COPs receive certificates that say they are "owners" of a project until the government benefiting from the project completes its periodic lease payments. Then the government purchases the project, usually years down the road, for a nominal sum.

COPs enable governments to avoid debt caps by making rent or lease payments that are subject to annual appropriations by the legislative body. Since COPs pay for public purpose projects, most certificates are considered safe investments, and the income investors earn from COP income generally is exempt from federal taxation. A local government is unlikely to miss payments on a new city hall or new police communications equipment, and bond insurers think enough of COPs to insure a majority of offerings.

The bottom line is that COPS enable governments to borrow money even when they are restricted from doing so, a fact that distresses tax-limitation advocates.

John Incorvaia, vice president in the southeast regional ratings division of Moody's Investors Service Inc., warned that, while COPs may not be listed as general obligation debt, they still constitute added financial obligations that a financially strapped county, city or other form of government may not be able to meet.

Mini-bonds allow residents to own a piece of their cities

Little bonds are making it in the big city.

Twice in 1992, New York City sold "mini-bonds" geared to individual investors as part of a general obligation bond sale. Called NYC Bonds, the low-cost bonds are designed to appeal to small investors saving for retirement, a child's education or other long-term goals. State governments in recent years have touted mini-bonds as a college savings instrument, but the appeal of these investments is broadening. Especially when interest rates for bank certificates of deposit are low, cities like New York and Denver can find a diverse market for mini-bonds, which in both cities finance capital projects. In the first sale of NYC Bonds in February 1992, the city government sold $100 million in bonds, or twice what it had expected. About $4 million in Denver mini-bonds sold in seven hours on Oct. 5, 1992, after city officials thought the sale would take an entire week.

The interest that investors earn from the mini-bonds generally is exempt from federal, state and, in New York City's case, local income taxes.

"It's only fair to give people of more moderate means the same opportunity to enjoy the tax-free advantages that larger investors can," said New York City Comptroller Elizabeth Holtzman.

It is not altruism alone that has pushed New York City and others into mini-bonds. New York officials say they save money with the bonds because they carry a lower interest rate than the city's typical general obligation bonds. New York's first sale saved approximately $2.2 million while diversifying the market for city bonds, Ms. Holtzman said.

NYC Bonds are zero-coupon bonds, meaning interest is paid only at maturity. The bonds, which are available in durations of five to 20 years, are purchased at a price well below the face value at maturity. For example, a 15-year NYC Bond that pays $5,000 at maturity might be available for a purchase price of about $2,000, assuming an annual interest rate of around 6.25%. The bonds are available in denominations of $5,000 and up. The bonds are uninsured, meaning that in 1992 they carried the city's moderately strong general obligation ratings of Baa1 from Moody's Investors Service Inc. and A- from Standard & Poor's Corp., both based in New York.

New York and Denver have successfully marketed mini-bonds as a way for investors to buy pieces of the cities.

In two sales — one in 1990 and the other in 1992 — Denver officials issued a total of $9.9 million in mini-bonds as part of two library bond issues approved by voters in 1989 and 1990. The second issue featured $500 tax-free bonds with a 12-year life span, paying $1,000 at maturity. Colorado residents seemed interested in a program that directly benefits projects like library construction, said Bob Osika, financial officer in Denver's Treasury Department. "It's a positive aspect for people to know they're putting their dollars to work for the city," Mr. Osika said. Denver's first mini-bond issue averaged $2,700 per investor order, Mr. Osika said. In 1992, the average order more than doubled to $6,000. City officials had planned to accept orders for the second mini-bond issue throughout the week of Oct. 5, 1992, but the sale ended on the first day when the city received orders for more than the $4 million remaining in library bonding authority. "We could have sold a lot more had we had the authorization," Mr. Osika said.

Mini-bonds are a concept newer to cities than they are to states. Illinois, for instance, began issuing college savings bonds in 1988 and does so once a year, said Jim Ofcarcik, special assistant in the state Comptroller's Office. The bonds, whose interest earnings are exempt from federal and state taxes, carry an interest rate close to that of traditional general obligation debt, Mr. Ofcarcik said. The investments, offered in denominations of $5,000 and up, have several built-in incentives for college savers.

Communities exploring the mini-bond idea should be aware of the potential costs. Interest costs may be comparable to those for traditional general obligation bonds, but selling the new concept has a price. For its second sale of NYC Bonds, New York spent an estimated $500,000 on advertising and marketing. The effort included a toll-free telephone information line that operated for three weeks prior to the sale.

Denver also makes a special effort to inform investors about the details of mini-bonds, hiring an outside marketing firm to do the work. As part of their marketing, officials try to explain the benefits and risks of mini-bonds. In most cases, the bonds may not be cashed in prior to maturity; investors face losses if they do so. As a result, the investment is not for everyone. "We make it clear to people that this is a long-term investment for those with long-term goals," Ms. Holtzman said.

Competition is hot between 3 major rating agencies

There was a new kid on the municipal ratings block in 1990, and Connecticut's Benson "Bud" Cohn, for one, was delighted. Though his state's bonds already were rated by Moody's Investors

Service Inc. and Standard & Poor's Corp., the assistant treasurer for debt management said Connecticut sought a credit rating from the new kid, Fitch Investors Service Inc., for a couple of reasons. "First," Mr. Cohn explained, "we have a great deal of respect for Claire Cohen," the doyenne of state credits who followed Connecticut while she was at Moody's and now does so as Fitch's executive managing director of government finance. "Second," he went on, "it's worthwhile to have three rating agencies. It introduces a little more competition into the industry."

Indeed, Fitch's service proved to be a bargain, Mr. Cohn said: $35,000 for a year's worth of ratings of general obligation bonds. That compared, Mr. Cohn said, with Moody's fees of $62,000 for the year and S&P's fees of $7,000 to $10,000 an issue, with at least five issues expected for the year. And if all that wasn't enough, there was this not-so-little extra: When Moody's and S&P downgraded Connecticut's ratings last spring to double-A, Fitch refused to do so, saying the state still merited its Fitch rating of AA+.

Experienced analysts, lower rating fees and, most important, the possibility of higher credit ratings and lower interest costs have prompted municipal bond issuers to take heed of "the new Fitch" and have roiled the once placid waters of the municipal ratings business.

Ms. Cohen said more than 40 major municipal bond issuers requested and received new Fitch ratings in 1990, ranging from Maryland to the Washington Public Power Service Co. to the Los Angeles public schools. There was no recent similar effort for comparison, so it was hard to say how good that was. But H. Russell Fraser, an outspoken maverick and Fitch's chairman and chief executive officer, has boasted that "in terms of our acceptance in the marketplace, we're way ahead of where we expected to be." If true, that might not be good for Moody's and S&P, the giants of the ratings business. But Fitch's push could be very good news for state and local governments, finance experts say.

Mr. Lehmann of the Bond Investors Association is among those who welcomed the newly aggressive Fitch. For one thing, he said, charges for ratings, though still a small part of bond issuance costs, "have become a problem" with a number of governments, particularly smaller ones. He added that Fitch's presence eventually "will make it more economical" to get a rating, which not only helps determine the issuer's interest costs but is critical to finding a market in the first place. "We see them as an up-and-comer trying to break into a close-knit circle," said Dick Cohee, an assistant financial director for the city of Jacksonville, Fla., which recently received a Fitch rating.

Publicly, at least, officials from both Moody's and S&P have pooh-poohed the new Fitch's significance as a competitor. "Obviously, they're rating some things," said Hyman Grossman, S&P

managing director of municipal finance. But mostly, he said, referring to Fitch's 45-city public relations tour in early 1990 and Mr. Fraser's penchant for controversial statements, "they've made a lot of noises."

"We're going about our business the way we've done in the past," said William deSante, a Moody's managing director. "We're not spending a lot of time watching what Fitch is doing."

A bond rating is important because it gives investors an indication of a government's ability to pay debt. The agencies offer similar grades on bonds, although Moody's often will add the number 1, and Fitch and S&P will add a positive or negative sign, to further define rating strength. The basic ratings include the following:

■ Aaa (Moody's) and AAA (Fitch, S&P) are the highest ratings available and signify strong financial condition.

■ Aa (Moody's) and AA (Fitch, S&P) are high-grade bonds, although long-term risk of debt pay-back is higher than with triple-A bonds.

■ A (Moody's, Fitch, S&P) signifies upper-medium-grade bonds, where government finances are secure but could suffer from negative activity in the future, such as an economic downturn.

■ Baa (Moody's) and BBB (Fitch, S&P) are medium-grade bonds showing that a government can cover debt payments, although finances are somewhat precarious and could become unstable in the future.

■ Ba, B, Caa and below (Moody's) and BB, B, CCC and below (Fitch, S&P) are speculative, non-investment-grade bonds, commonly known in the corporate sector as junk bonds. Uncertainties remain over whether the government has the ability to repay long-term debt.

Investors won't touch a sizable bond issue without a rating to guide them. Thus, when a government wants to borrow money, its officials notify a rating agency six to eight weeks before the planned bond sale. Next, the government's financial adviser or investment bank underwriter sends relevant financial documents to the rating agency. The government, adviser and underwriter maintain a dialogue with the agency until about four weeks before the bond sale, when the government makes a presentation to the agency. A rating analyst discusses his evaluation of the government with the area manager of ratings about three weeks before the sale. One to two weeks prior to the official bond sale, the rating analyst presents a recommendation to his or her agency's senior department officials; the analyst then notifies the government of the agency's decision and releases the rating to the public.

Fitch's Mr. Fraser, a former S&P analyst who went on to head AMBAC Indemnity Corp., a municipal bond insurer, joined with Robert D. Van Kampen, founder of bond house Van Kampen

Merritt Inc., to acquire the family-owned Fitch in April 1989. Though Fitch had been rating corporate and government debt since 1913, it had become a moribund also-ran, particularly in municipals, where it sold only a few major ratings. Fitch's lethargy allowed Moody's and S&P to obtain near total control of the municipal ratings market, resulting in what some critics described as a cozy "duopoly." Mr. Fraser said only one state had paid for Fitch ratings and that Fitch's annual revenue from municipal ratings before the ownership change was less than $1 million, compared with his estimates of $50 million for Moody's and $35 million for S&P. Municipal ratings accounted for about one-third of Fitch's estimated revenue of $10 million in 1990.

Moody's, owned by Dun & Bradstreet Corp., has been rating government debt since 1919 and recently reported 42,000 municipal ratings outstanding. S&P, a unit of McGraw Hill Inc., has been in the municipals business since 1950 and reportedly had 8,000 ratings outstanding. Mr. Fraser argues that the two agencies have grown indifferent over the years and are ripe for competition. "We had been customers, and we just didn't think the two rating agencies were actively serving the market," he said, referring to his AMBAC days.

Fitch's early strategy, in municipals as well as corporate debt, was to build instant credibility by hiring top analysts from its competitors and elsewhere, luring them with the chance to acquire equity in Fitch. Employees own 35% of the company. In addition to Ms. Cohen, who had been doing ratings for more than three decades, Fitch hired such highly regarded municipal analysts as Alan Spen from Drexel Burnham Lambert Inc.; Colleen Woodell, also from Moody's; Fred Martucci from Municipal Bond Insurance Association; and Richard Raphael from S&P. Byron D. Klapper, Fitch managing director of information products, also came from S&P, where he spearheaded its well-received credit publications.

Fitch argues — somewhat contradictorily, critics note — that S&P and Moody's are slow to respond to changing conditions and that their ratings often don't reflect the value placed on issues by the marketplace.

The presence of well-known analysts at Fitch obviously has made a difference. "We knew (the Fitch analysts) from Moody's and, after talking to them at several events, we approached them for a rating on a new, somewhat complicated program," said Larry Thornton, Iowa's deputy treasurer. "Also, our investment banker and attorneys suggested that we use Fitch."

"They indicated by the questions they asked that they weren't rookies," said Kenneth Wissman, treasurer of the Massachusetts Water Resources Authority, which requested a Fitch rating. "The write-up they did afterward was very detailed and well-written."

Fitch has touted itself as more conservative than its competitors, but one critic, who didn't want to be named, said it was much ado about nothing. The more "conservative" ratings didn't materialize, he said. If anything, Fitch's ratings have proven higher than existing ones at S&P and Moody's.

A celebrated case in point was Fitch's affirmation in April 1990 of its A rating on Massachusetts debt, which Moody's and S&P downgraded to near junk bond status (though much too late, according to some critics). Fitch says its Massachusetts rating reflected a long-term orientation. "This is not a poor state," Mr. Fraser said. "It has a well-diversified, very sophisticated economy. Smart investors are buying the bonds." An unscientific sample of Fitch ratings recently found many of them to be equal to, or a notch better than, those of Moody's and S&P. Ms. Cohen said she doesn't think there is an overall pattern of higher ratings at Fitch.

Some issuers admit they see in Fitch at least the possibility of what they tend to call "fairer" (translation: higher) ratings. "We were anxious to get a better rating than Moody's had given us (Baa), and we thought we deserved a better rating," said Joseph R. Caputo, comptroller of Suffolk County, N.Y. Fitch gave the county an A rating, the same as S&P. "Two out of three ain't bad," added Mr. Caputo, who was impressed with Fitch's attentiveness.

Fitch's first step is to attain parity with the other two rating agencies. When — and if — that happens, it could begin to replace Moody's or S&P on some ratings.

"I would certainly hope that Fitch will become an increasingly accepted rating and increasingly important in the marketplace," Ms. Cohen said. "As that happens, I think you'll see more shifting around, where we might be one of two ratings." Mr. Fraser, who likes to ride quarter horses on his Wyoming dude ranch when he isn't riding herd at Fitch, is, not surprisingly, less circumspect. "Fitch is going to become a household name," he predicted. "If you're doing an issue and you really want your credit story told, you'll come to Fitch. And if you want major institutions to buy your bonds, you'll come to Fitch."

Government pension systems

As the repository for money used to cover pension payments to current and future government retirees, public pension systems hold hundreds of billions of dollars in money that is invested in everything from U.S. Treasury bills and other safe securities to the more volatile stock market. In late 1991, the three largest state and municipal pension funds were the second, third and fourth largest in the country — the California Public Employees' Retirement System ($64.66 billion in assets), New York State and Local Retirement Systems ($50.08 billion) and New York City Retirement Systems ($48.88 billion) — surpassing the funds of private sector giants like AT&T, General Motors and IBM Corp. The only larger pension system was the Teachers Insurance & Annuity Association-College Retirement Equities Fund, with $99.61 billion in assets.

No wonder large state and local pension funds carry so much weight. As the primary investors in many major companies, the funds have been known to pressure executives into making decisions they normally wouldn't make. For instance, some funds have taken socially responsible stances and divested money from companies that maintained business presences in South Africa in an attempt to overturn, through financial force, that country's anti-black, pro-apartheid policies. Other funds have tried overturning corporate policies and ousting company executives at stockholder meetings.

Large or small, a pension system must be run by capable managers who understand the ins and outs of investments.

The only rule on how to assemble an efficient pension fund management team may be to realistically determine — and compensate for — the individual members' strong and weak points. Though it sounds simplistic, such general guidance reflects the tremendous diversity inherent in public sector pension funds. This diversity stems from various statutory requirements, fund sizes and peculiar membership on the boards of trustees, which bear ultimate fiduciary responsibility. What plays in the $20 billion-plus State of Michigan Retirement Systems may not work with a small county or a fire-protection district.

"The differences between public sector and private sector asset management are fast disappearing, but in the public sector there are still more bells and whistles to respond to," noted Charles Mathis, a consultant with Callan Associates Inc., an Atlanta-based financial consulting firm.

Typically, the core members of a pension fund management team are the elected or appointed board of trustees, staff members (in some cases the state treasurer), a team of outside consultants, outside auditors and attorneys, and investment management firms, also known as outside money managers.

Consultants and money managers say that public funds, especially small ones, require more education and a different style of interaction. They also shop around for the best fee structures far more often than comparable private sector funds. But smaller, public sector funds also tend to be loyal (once a relationship has been established) and recession-proof as far as paying their bills, explained Fred Shick, manager of the Chicago office of Noble Lowndes Inc., a national consulting firm. For smaller, relatively unsophisticated pension funds, hiring a consultant is generally considered a good first move.

"When we are invited to make a presentation, the trustees already have a consultant and they have at least taken a stab at defining their investment policy," said Carolyn Hughes, director of marketing for INVESCO Capital Management of Atlanta.

Another good starting move when formulating an investment policy is to examine statutory requirements. During the past decade, states and other large funds have repealed so-called legal lists of permitted investments in favor of the prudent-person rule, which allows fiduciaries to design investment strategies according to common-sense prudence. But the centerpiece of a pension fund investment strategy is an actuarial determination of what benefits will be payable and when. Such calculations can be like a cold shower to the unsuspecting.

Natalka Bukalo, director of asset consulting services for Noble Lowndes, East Orange, N.J., recalled the situation of a municipality facing bankruptcy. "All they wanted to talk about was long-term strategy when, in fact, they faced the possibility of large short-term payouts."

Past that hurdle, the next step is to devise an asset-allocation policy by the trustees — the mix of equities, bonds, real estate and other instruments in the portfolio. Here, conflict-of-interest problems can crop up, particularly in small funds. Bill Mattingly, chief of the employee benefits practice of Katten Muchin & Zavis, a law firm with headquarters in Chicago, has advised small funds to pool assets or invest in mutual funds or bank-sponsored commingled funds whenever possible.

Another problem for small funds is fees, notes William Miller, a founder and managing director of Renaissance Investment Management Inc., Cincinnati, an investment firm with $1.3 billion under management. Typically, investment fees are a percentage of the total funds invested. "A money manager can invest $200 million for one-fourth of 1%, but it cannot break even on that fraction when managing $200,000," Mr. Miller said. Ideally, an independent consultant remains a permanent part of the team, monitoring the performance of outside managers.

Such checkups typically occur every quarter. Some small towns still require monthly reports, however, and Ms. Bukalo pointed out that simplification of reporting requirements is something trustees may be able to manage administratively rather than through legislation.

Finding compatible managers for small funds usually is a matter of communication, Mr. Miller said. "The investment strategy may be exactly the same for a small as a large plan, but it must be communicated differently," he noted. Appointed boards frequently consist of local officials such as fire chiefs, public works directors and others who are not experts in the field but who resent dealing with condescending outsiders.

Finally, Mr. Miller said, it is sometimes difficult to focus the attention of elected officials on the long-term goals that a pension plan entails. Elected officials, for example, might be tempted to maximize performance during their terms in office rather than for the distant future.

But experts add that sophistication in these and other matters seems to be percolating down to the smaller from the larger funds. Former Michigan State Treasurer Robert A. Bowman reported that a growing number of small players in the pension arena are keeping in close contact with larger, state-level colleagues or with other small funds.

But there are limits to cooperation, pointed out Utah State Treasurer Edward T. Alter. Sometimes it's easier to admit ignorance to an outside consultant than to a public sector colleague.

Pensions fend off attacks from deficit-ridden governments

In the day-to-day workings of pension funds, administrators generally are free from the influence of city councilmen, state legislators, county freeholders and other politicians who would like to get their hands on the money to further their own causes. Occasionally, however, pension money is kicked around like a political football.

Whenever bad financial times hit governments, public pension administrators find their funds under attack by officials looking to balance their budgets. Pension fund leaders fired a couple rounds in a counterattack in late 1991. One was a meeting in Washington sponsored by the National Conference on Public Employee Retirement Systems (NCPERS) that brought together pension fund officials and congressional officials. The gathering was meant as a strategy session aimed at drawing up a battle plan for fighting future raids of pension assets, including winning federal legislative protection for the pension funds. The other shot was an amicus brief that the NCPERS filed in the California Court of Appeals, Third Appellate District Court, supporting a lawsuit that sought to block Gov. Pete Wilson's effort to tap the California Public Employees' Retirement System (CalPERS) for $1.6 billion to help balance the state budget.

"We are concerned that over the course of the next decade the public pension funds are going to be under serious attack," said Harold Schaitberger, legislative counsel to the NCPERS. "It's the last pot of untapped assets that are left in our economy," said Mr. Schaitberger, who also has served as executive assistant to the president of the International Association of Firefighters in Washington.

"I think the problem is pretty extreme. It has occurred in at least 19 different jurisdictions," said Carlos Resendez, executive secretary of the NCPERS and executive director of the San Antonio Firemen's and Policemen's Pension Fund. "There's no question that every jurisdiction that has an ailing economy is going to look to the pension funds to try to offset their ailing economy and not concern themselves with the long-term liabilities."

NCPERS officials said their organization, which represents 400 public employee funds and 5 million public employees, chose to enter its friend-of-the-court brief in support of the lawsuit filed by California public employee fund participants because Mr. Wilson's action represented a "highly dangerous precedent. On the forefront of current issues impacting the public pension plan industry, none is more threatening than the raid of pension assets by state and local governments," the brief contended.

"It's a real quick Band-Aid approach to an ailing economy," Mr. Resendez said of tapping pension assets to balance budgets. "It will jeopardize the future benefits of the retirees, and that's the bottom line."

According to Mr. Schaitberger, the strategy for fending off future raids is a "three-legged stool" of education, litigation and legislation. The NCPERS educates members on "some of the tools of the trade" that governments are using to raid funds, he said, including adjusting earnings assumptions, "which is certainly becoming a popular method to allow the employer to adjust its contributions." Indeed, of the 28 funds that responded to a *City & State* survey of the 50 largest public pension funds, 11 indicated actuarial assumptions had been adjusted upward over the past two years. In other words, if economists and pension administrators believe a pension system can earn an 8% return in a given fiscal year, but if they are pushed to raise that assumption to 10%, the government will not have to put as much money into the pension system to meet its obligations to retirees; in effect, the government saves money, sometimes tens of millions of dollars. "It's something that can occur without a lot of fanfare but the effect can be significant," Mr. Schaitberger said.

In 1990, New York City Comptroller Elizabeth Holtzman wanted to allow the $10 billion New York City Teachers' Retirement System and the city's smaller $600 million Board of Education retirement fund to diversify their investments into stocks as well as fixed-income bonds. The comptroller said the move could generate an additional $3.4 billion in earnings for the two funds over 10 years. The recommendation concerning the teachers' fund was implemented. "The objective was to basically reduce the contribution and to provide portfolio-type returns," said Charles Moses, Ms. Holtzman's deputy press secretary. The increased earnings assumption on the teachers' fund to 9% from 8.25% and the corresponding decrease in contributions helped fund a 5.5% pay raise for New York teachers. Three other funds run by the comptroller's office — police officers, firefighters and other city employees — were similarly diversified in early 1988.

Not everyone is convinced there will be a widespread move toward increased earning assumptions by governments looking to decrease pension contributions. "I've not seen wholesale change in actuarial rate assumptions," said Marilyn Wood, president of the Online Pension Network, a data base service of the Institute for Fiduciary Education, Sacramento, Calif.

Added Gary Findlay of Gabriel, Roeder, Smith & Co., Detroit, an actuarial and benefits consulting firm, "It probably is quite reasonable to expect that governments will explore activities where they have expenditures, and I wouldn't think they would look at pension funds or fringe benefits any more or any less than other areas where they have expenditures. But has there been any widespread switch to the New York approach? I'm not seeing it." Mr. Findlay speculates that officials of most pension plans are unlikely to be swayed into overestimating interest assumptions by short-term political pressures in recession-ravaged cities and states. "Ultimately, the cost of the pension plan is the dollars you pay out," he said. "By changing methods and changing assumptions, you change the flow of money into the system and the flow of money out of the employer's general fund. But, ultimately, you can't change the cost."

Politicians and other government officials also can take advantage of pension money simply by delaying whatever their government's required contribution is determined to be. "It goes on paper as saying they'll make it, but then they delay," Mr. Schaitberger said.

151

Of the funds surveyed by *City & State,* six — including CalPERS — indicated their sponsoring governments tapped pension assets or reduced contributions to balance budgets in 1991. A seventh, the California State Teachers' Retirement System, faced a possible hit before the end of that year.

When they face tough fiscal times, state and local governments look at other ways to use their pension funds to bail themselves out of financial trouble. Borrowing from pension funds is one of those options. Government Finance Associates Inc., New York, advised the City of Philadelphia Board of Pensions and Retirement in 1991 on whether to make a short-term cash-flow loan to the city. The firm's president, J. Chester Johnson, said the financial advisory firm had been approached by other governments looking to borrow from their pension funds. His advice: Don't. Besides his work on the Philadelphia financing, Mr. Johnson closely observed other financial maneuvers of this sort. He worked at the U.S. Treasury when New York City tapped its employee pension funds for loans as the city faced its fiscal crisis in the 1970s. Later, Government Finance Associates was the financial adviser to Detroit when that city touched its employee pension funds for similar loans during its own fiscal crisis in the early 1980s.

As in New York and Detroit, Philadelphia's decision to look to its pension board for financial help stemmed from the city's inability to gain access to normal credit markets. Ultimately, the Philadelphia fund contributed 25% of a $150 million short-term borrowing package the city assembled in January and February 1991. The notes were repaid in April. According to Mr. Johnson, the pension board was "extremely concerned" about the loan, wanting to ensure that any financing met federal regulations governing the fund's tax-exempt status, and that assets were repaid in a timely fashion and at a rate adequate for investments. "I would caution any government against (borrowing from its pension fund) except in the absence of (credit) market access," Mr. Johnson said. "It's very, very costly to do that."

Even governments that never have been in Philadelphia's dire financial straits have looked to their pension funds for financial help. "We have been approached by certain governments that still remain investment-grade and we have routinely said that it's only in the most extraordinary circumstances that you should even consider doing this," Mr. Johnson said. "I don't think it's a very fruitful area of exploration when you have access to the credit markets."

With officials of strapped governments looking more and more to their pension funds, the likelihood of federal action grows. Congressional committees have held hearings on a possible federal role in protecting public pension funds from raids by their sponsoring governments.

Historically, there has been a split between pension fund participants, who look favorably on federal involvement, and those on the plans' administrative and fiduciary side, who have been reluctant to accept a federal role, but Mr. Schaitberger believes that might have changed. "I think the recent history and California may have been the straw that broke the camel's back to convince the side that has resisted federal intervention to at least allow the pendulum to move and to say, 'Let's look at it and decide what the federal role might be,' " Mr. Schaitberger said.

The influence of pensions on social and political issues

In mid-1991, U.S. President George Bush was convinced that the days of apartheid were ending in South Africa, but state and local governments embracing South Africa divestment policies weren't so sure. The president had announced he was lifting federal sanctions against South Africa that originally were designed to pressure the white apartheid government into giving the black majority a greater voice.

Only the public pension fund in Oregon immediately repealed its policy of not investing in companies that do business with South Africa. Oregon's action resulted from a unanimous vote in the state Legislature, ending the state's nearly 4-year-old divestment policy. According to Oregon Treasurer Tony Meeker, legislators had approved a mechanism tying the end of divestment to South Africa's ability to meet the five conditions of a federal sanctions act. Mr. Bush's announcement that he was satisfied South Africa had met the conditions — release of all political prisoners, repeal of a state of emergency, legalization of all political parties, repeal of major apartheid laws and an agreement to hold so-called good-faith negotiations with black leaders — triggered the repeal of Oregon's divestment. "We then went through a process of determining the appropriate procedural kinds of things," the treasurer explained. He wrote the money managers handling state funds to advise them that Oregon, which at the time possessed an $18 billion pension portfolio, was lifting its policy against companies doing business in South Africa.

Oregon found itself in "a very peculiar situation" because the state had conditions paralleling the federal legislation, said Richard Knight, research associate with the Africa Fund, a nonprofit, anti-apartheid organization based in New York. "Because their Legislature meets only once every two years, the power rested with their treasurer, and he elected to lift the divestment."

Most other cities and states with divestment policies, however, indicated no intention to follow Oregon's lead. Mr. Knight noted that New York Mayor David N. Dinkins, who was in South Africa in November 1991, about five months after Mr. Bush's decision, announced that the United States' most populous city was going to retain its divestment policies. Other public officials, notably Boston Mayor Raymond L. Flynn, had been outspoken in holding that same position. Mr. Knight pointed out that Mr. Flynn, as then-president of the Washington-based U.S. Conference of Mayors, had made conference policy "very clear" that sanctions should stay in place.

In late 1991, the Africa Fund counted 27 states, 24 counties and 92 cities with divestment policies. Most of those, Mr. Knight said, would look to black South African leaders like activist Archbishop Desmond Tutu and revolutionary African National Congress President Nelson Mandela to determine when to lift divestment policies.

"The president's decision did not have as much of an impact as one might think," agreed Mr. Resendez of the NCPERS. Despite Mr. Bush's action, there was little immediate state or local movement one way or the other. "Divestiture made a big hit back four or five years ago and then it died down," Mr. Resendez observed. As for Mr. Resendez's own San Antonio fund, it never implemented a South Africa divestment policy. "We feel that if we keep social and political issues out and concentrate on the best (investment) return for participants, that's the best manner of operation. It also keeps you from being controversial."

Peter Kinder, president of Kinder, Lydenberg, Domini & Co. Inc., a Cambridge, Mass., firm that compiles a social investment index of 400 stocks screened with regard to social criteria (including South Africa divestment), believed President Bush was wrong and the state of Oregon was "way out of step. I don't think any government is going to move strongly in this area until Mr. Tutu and Mr. Mandela say it's OK to do so. Those are two very sophisticated politicians and they are not going to be swept up by any waves of enthusiasm."

Diane Bratcher, director of communications for the Interfaith Center on Corporate Responsibility, said state and local officials in jurisdictions with divestment policies were looking for concrete signs of change, including high-level negotiations between the white-led South Africa government and black leaders. The center is a national coalition of about 250 Protestant and Roman Catholic institutional investors. The New York-based organization was formed about 20 years ago when churches began to push corporations to meet certain social guidelines. "The churches kind of pioneered the whole effort to divest and pressure corporations' social responsibility," Ms. Bratcher said. But it was the entry of state and local governments into the divestment picture in the mid-1980s, led by New York City, that forced corporations' hands in South Africa, she added.

Controversies over government divestment policies climaxed in the late 1980s. Proponents of such policies argued that governments had a social obligation to use financial pressure to end South Africa's system of strict racial segregation and discrimination favoring the minority white population. Opponents emphasized that divestiture was merely a political issue or would erode the fiduciary responsibilities of pension fund officials.

Overall, state and local action expanded the universe of socially screened institutional investments dramatically, taking the portfolio of such investments to about $600 billion in 1991 from $40 billion in 1984. Massive funds like CalPERS have proven their effectiveness at bringing pressure on corporations — and at times even on countries — with their investment policies. The California fund implemented a South Africa divestment policy in September 1986.

Michigan Treasurer Douglas Roberts announced Nov. 1, 1991, that Gov. John Engler's investment advisory committee had asked him to discuss Michigan's South Africa divestiture laws with the state Legislature. Mr. Roberts complied but indicated that he supported the state's laws prohibiting investments in companies doing business with South Africa. Mr. Roberts denied a report that Mr. Engler's administration wanted to relax Michigan's ban on such investments. Michigan's original policy set a Dec. 31, 1993, deadline for eliminating pension fund investments in companies that transact business with South Africa. The ban was to remain in effect until the treasurer determined that all South Africans had full political and civil rights. The investment advisory committee had suggested state officials revisit the issue because divestment policy blocked Michigan's pension fund from investing in 123 of the stocks in the Standard & Poor's 500 Composite Stock Index, which is an index of stock prices composed of 400 industrials and a smattering of utilities, financial firms and transportation companies.

Oregon's Mr. Meeker pointed out that, under South Africa divestment policies, finding replacements for all the stocks a fund eliminates from its portfolio isn't easy. In 1987, the start of the divestment program, Oregon had $950 million sunk into securities of companies that did business in South Africa. When President Bush made his July 10, 1991, announcement, the state held less than $300 million in such securities. "Now, obviously, there are administrative costs as well," Mr. Meeker explained, "because when you get rid of a stock you have to replace it. There are two transactions there." It cost Oregon $250,000 a year to administer the divestment program, Mr. Meeker said.

According to Mr. Resendez, however, it was not difficult for local governments to implement divestment policies. "Contrary to a lot of the initial apprehension that they were going to lose tons of money, that in fact did not occur," he said, noting that the development of such investment vehicles as Africa-free funds made pension funds' divestment efforts easier.

Shaking off the shackles of investment restrictions

Looking for higher returns with minimal risks, guardians of state and local pension fund assets are intensifying their fights against age-old restrictions that limit their investment options. Officials in several states, driven by the chance to earn higher yields achieved by many of today's corporate pension funds, are more openly criticizing legal lists of acceptable investments that governed the early days of public pension management.

Even in more liberal states like Connecticut, where up to 50% of the state's pension fund assets already may be invested in stocks, there are those who long for more flexibility.

"Modern portfolio management theory has changed," explained Bob Toigo, president of the Institute for Fiduciary Education, Sacramento, Calif. "To get higher rates of return, you need more diversified portfolios."

Only a handful of state pension systems still don't invest in the stock market, although officials continuously work to liberalize those investment policies.

Connecticut treasury officials want the General Assembly to give them more leeway to take advantage of shifts in the financial markets. Since they are restricted from investing more than half of their pension fund assets in stocks, the treasury officials have proposed that the limit be raised to 60%. "We think in going to 60% there is a significant potential to increase rates of return," said Frank P. McDermott, Connecticut's assistant treasurer for investments. He said such a change would give officials greater flexibility in moving money from one investment to another based on market factors. The $8 billion in Connecticut's state-managed pension assets in early 1990 was divided among about a dozen investments, with the highest percentages invested in domestic stocks and bonds, international stocks and bonds, and real estate.

According to statistics provided by Constitution Capital Management, a Boston-based public pension fund manager and a division of the Bank of New England, stock investments far outperform bonds over the long term. Through 1989, stocks listed on the Standard & Poor's 500 Index yielded a 10.22% annualized rate of return for a 30-year investment. In comparison, bonds in the Shearson Lehman Government/Corporate Bond Index produced a 6.69% return, and U.S. Treasury bills brought in 6.66% during the same period. The annualized rate of inflation for that period was 4.79%.

Indiana's pension fund managers have had to cope with a 138-year-old state ban on any investments in businesses — a ban that applies to all state funds. Some state legislators had hoped voters would help change that in the fall of 1990 in wake of an Indiana General Assembly proposal for a constitutional amendment to allow state funds to be invested in stocks. Indiana voters, however, disagreed and defeated the statewide referendum. Voters narrowly rejected a similar measure in 1986. Such a change would have had a significant effect on state pension funds, primarily the Public Employees' Retirement Fund of Indiana, which has been forced to invest primarily in government securities. As of Sept. 30, 1991, the $3.8 billion fund had 99% of its assets in conservative fixed income investments; in comparison, neighboring Illinois'

$3.5 billion State Board of Investment held 39.3% of its mix in the fixed income category and 41.8% in stocks.

"There is concern on the part of many that the risks involved (in stock investments) are greater than what the state should assume," said Phil Smith, executive secretary of the Public Employees' Retirement Fund of Indiana.

According to today's experts, failing to diversify one's investment portfolio poses a far greater risk than staying with traditionally safe investments such as bonds. States that divide their pension dollars among a variety of investments are hedging their bets against a sudden downturn in one category.

"It's all part of the general trend of increased sophistication among public pension funds," Mr. Toigo said.

Some governments have been loosening their investment restrictions for years, but only recently they have discovered that the flexibility has paid off. A legal list of accepted investments dating back to the 1930s — once a bible for local governments in Massachusetts — fast is becoming a dinosaur as pension funds that have stuck to the list have lagged behind funds that abandoned it. A December 1989 report from the state's Division of Public Employee Retirement Administration stated that government funds still operating according to the legal list in 1988 achieved an average investment return of 8.95%, while funds that operated more like private pension systems yielded 11.76%. A survey of 1,455 large corporate funds and 370 large public funds by Greenwich Associates of Greenwich, Conn., showed that in 1989 nearly 51% of the corporate funds' asset mixes consisted of stocks, while only 42.6% of the public funds' portfolios were in stocks. According to the survey, public funds invested much more heavily in lower-risk bonds than private funds did (43.6% to 28.8%, respectively).

Kansas doesn't believe there's no place like home

Some investments are far riskier than others. For instance, directing public pension fund assets to investments with local economic development potential sounds like a great idea, but, if it's done without an eye toward a fund's fundamental goals, it can spell disaster.

Just ask the folks in the state of Kansas. The Kansas Public Employees Retirement System (KPERS) embarked on a backyard investing program in 1985, clearly with economic development objectives in mind. The plan was to invest pension assets directly in in-state businesses to help boost the Kansas economy. In May 1991, six years and possibly hundreds of millions of dollars in losses later, the KPERS board clamped a moratorium on the investments and began focusing on getting out of those still in place.

"Out of about $500 million in direct placements, we think there's a loss of about $230 million," said Republican state Sen.

Wint Winter Jr., co-chairman of a special legislative committee formed early in 1991 to investigate KPERS's investment practices and recommend policies for the future.

"We have written off a total of $121 million in investments that were in the direct placement portfolio," said Elizabeth B.A. Miller, who joined KPERS in August 1991 as the fund's first in-house investment officer.

As of Sept. 30 of that same year, $193.5 million of KPERS's $4.2 billion in assets were still in the direct placement investments. KPERS officials were trying to maximize the amount they could recover from their backyard investments, but, given the nature of the investments, that can be difficult. Since the fund invests directly in the businesses instead of buying their stock, investments are not liquidated easily.

At one time, most people in Kansas seemed to agree the KPERS program was a good one. "If you were to meet with our board and the Legislature, you would hear the comment that it was a good idea but rather poorly executed," Ms. Miller said. "I think the lack of control and oversight by the retirement system staff was certainly a factor." Essentially, the backyard investing program failed because state officials took their eyes off two key criteria for successful investments: risk and return.

"If you just go after trying to help the local economy in one form or another and you don't go about trying to get adequate return for your pension fund and you don't avoid excessive risk, you're going to get into trouble," said Mr. Toigo, whose institute has been developing a handbook on economically targeted investments (ETIs). "We're not advocating that states should be doing these or not. It is happening increasingly. Minimally, the people who are doing it need to know what the pros and cons are." The institute conducted a study of ETIs in 1989 under a grant from the Ford Foundation, New York. Ninety-nine funds responded to the institute's survey of 126 of the country's largest public pension funds. Of the respondents, 40 indicated they were involved in some sort of economically targeted investing. "If you examine the ones that have failed, it's because they haven't examined all the goals," Mr. Toigo said. "Sometimes these programs don't work because they try to do too much, and they tend to be very complex. There's due diligence that needs to be applied."

Mr. Winter, who admits he once thought the KPERS program was a fine idea, now seems to share much of Mr. Toigo's point of view. The legislation that Mr. Winter's special committee recommended to the full Kansas Legislature in January 1992 reflected that perspective. Over the past few years, Mr. Winter has come full-cycle on the issue. "Four years ago I thought, 'Great idea. Use pension money for economically targeted uses,' " Mr. Winter said. "After seeing the things we've seen, my sense was, 'Can't be done. Prohibit it entirely.' " He believes that, while direct placements are possible — and even prudent — for the state retirement system, focusing solely on economic development is wrong.

State legislatures

To many observers, the ugly partisan standoff that held California's budget hostage for two months in mid-1992 adds yet another count to the growing indictment of divided government. Just as Democratic President Bill Clinton and former Republican President George Bush derided the gridlock in Congress during the 1992 election campaign and hoped for what ultimately took place — one-party rule (Democratic) in the federal government — many political experts believe state governments can overcome their fiscal and policy chaos only if they enjoy the same fate.

But an examination of many states thought to be plagued by divided government shows that gridlock is often more a result of a clash of personalities or of a failure of executive leadership than of partisan divisions.

"It's an excuse, quite frankly, to say that divided government causes all of these problems," said Sherry Jeffe, senior associate at the Center for Politics and Policy, Claremont Graduate School in Claremont, Calif. Divided government "may not be the best of all possible worlds, but when you have leaders who are willing to work together to solve problems, there shouldn't be gridlock."

The debate over divided government takes on added significance when one realizes just how pervasive it is. From 1984 to 1993, more than half of the 50 states always had one political party in control of at least one half of the legislature and the opposing party controlling the governor's mansion. Reaching a high of 31 states from 1990 to 1992, the number declined slightly to 27 states in January 1993.

As a result of the Nov. 3, 1992, elections, Democrats controlled both houses in 25 states and 64 chambers; Republicans controlled both chambers in nine states, and a total of 30 chambers. In 15 states control of the legislature was split, with each party controlling a chamber.

In a handful of states, divided government seems to have become permanent. New York has been divided for more than 20 years, Colorado for 19 years and Illinois for 16 years. In some states, voters cannot even make up their minds which party should control a single legislative chamber. Florida's Senate in 1993 was tied at 20 Democrats and 20 Republicans. Michigan's House of Representatives was deadlocked at 55 Democrats and 55 Republicans.

Or, maybe the voters *do* know what they want. Voters in states that have suffered from some of the worst legislative logjams have been consistent in continuing to support divided government. Take the case of New York. The Democrats have been in firm command of the Assembly and the Republicans have controlled the Senate for two decades; the governor has been left to try to bring the warring sides together. If voters ever watched in dismay as budget after budget came out late and legislators squabbled over election law reform, the death penalty and a host of other concerns, they certainly failed to show it. Of course, Gov. Mario M. Cuomo and legislative leaders said they wanted to end the division, but Mr. Cuomo rarely went out of his way to help fellow Democrats win the Senate. Rather, he appeared to enjoy a role as the Great Conciliator.

Morris Fiorina, professor of government at Harvard University, Cambridge, Mass., argues that gubernatorial and legislative elections have become separate issues in voters' minds. Winning the governorship has almost no statistical relationship to winning the legislature in many states. He added that in some states where one party has dominated the legislative process, voters tend to favor gubernatorial candidates of the minority party. This has been true in Colorado, Idaho, Illinois, Rhode Island, Utah and Wyoming.

Still, legislative sessions in a number of states with divided government were marked during the early 1990s by strong and frequently partisan differences. Spending cuts, tax increases and property tax caps caused heated stalemates in states like California, Connecticut, Illinois, Maine, Michigan, New Jersey and Pennsylvania; those states gave rise to more complaints about divided government than usual.

Divided government undoubtedly plays a role in increasing tensions, but leadership skills, public opinion, ideology and timing are equally important in making a difficult situation worse or better.

"Partisan splits within state governments simply don't equate to legislative stalemates," said Karl Kurtz, director of state services for the National Conference of State Legislatures, Denver. "The general conclusion of those who have studied this is that leadership, or a lack of it, is what makes the difference."

Blair Horner, a lobbyist with the New York Public Interest Research Group, Albany, N.Y., said the budget gridlock seen in the state capital of Albany is "less partisanship or even personality than regional differences within the state. What really happens is that if an issue has only regional appeal, its representatives will hold it to trade for another issue of regional appeal elsewhere." But because of rifts within both parties over local concerns, the process of conciliation sometimes breaks down.

Former Minnesota Gov. Rudy Perpich, a Democratic Farmer Labor Party member, always enjoyed a majority in both houses of the Legislature. He had some early successes in his first term. But when he came back to power in 1982 after having been defeated in 1978, he concentrated on economic development and began a gradually worsening relationship with legislative leaders. "The Perpich problem was one of style, it wasn't a philosophical dispute with the Legislature," explained Charles Backstrom, professor of political science at the University of Minnesota, St. Paul. "He isolated himself from the legislative process and then would step in and veto a carefully crafted bill, not telling anyone what he was doing or that he was about to do it." In stark contrast, Independent-Republican Gov. Arne H. Carlson, who defeated Mr. Perpich in the November 1990 election, has learned how to work with a Minnesota Legislature that could have simply railroaded through its own agenda. In 1992, major initiatives on health care and workers' compensation were worked out by Mr. Carlson and the opposition.

"The whole issue of divided government being a cause of gridlock is just an excuse for the executive not showing leadership," said Paul Green, professor of political science at Governors State University, University Park, Ill. "In fact, it is easier to negotiate solutions to regional conflicts when you have divided government." A governor can essentially use the cover of having to deal with the opposite party to solve statewide problems by horse-trading with the opposite party, Mr. Green argues. Dan Walker, Democratic Illinois governor from 1972 to 1976, failed to get along with the Democratic Legislature and compiled the worst legislative record of the post-World War II era. By contrast, two Republican governors from Illinois, William Stratton in the 1950s and James R. Thompson in the 1980s, had strong legislative achievements working with legislatures dominated by Democrats.

Many political observers, however, still believe divided government is a major cause of gridlock. Alan Rosenthal, director of the Eagleton Institute of Politics at Rutgers University, New Brunswick, N.J., said partisan splits make life more difficult for everyone in the legislative process. "The more competitive the politics are in a given state, the easier it is for any natural conflict to become exacerbated," he said. "Given the fact that campaigning never ends these days, you have continual jockeying for advan-

161

tage that makes cooperation more difficult. Having one party in control of the legislature and the executive would tend to minimize this kind of dissension."

Another, more important factor in legislative gridlock may be what Mr. Kurtz identified as a lack of public consensus on the solutions to major public policy problems. "Some societal problems, like the crisis in health care, have become so complex and unwieldy that even the most unified of governments would have difficulty in agreeing on the best solutions," he said.

Not understanding or knowing how to solve these problems, it seems voters in many states have decided they want both parties to come to the table to solve them, each with control of a branch of government.

Term limits for legislators are here to stay

Love 'em or hate 'em, term limits for state legislators began sweeping the country in the early 1990s. Voters on Nov. 3, 1992, passed term limits for legislators in 12 states: Arizona, Arkansas, Florida, Michigan, Missouri, Montana, Nebraska, Ohio, Oregon, South Dakota, Washington and Wyoming. Within weeks, new term limit proposals came forth in Georgia and New Jersey. Proposals already were working their way toward ballots in Maine, Idaho, Utah and Massachusetts. Movements were growing in New York and Texas. And three states — California, Colorado and Oklahoma — already had adopted legislative limits.

Typical of the proposals was one from Georgia Lt. Gov. Pierre Howard, who pledged Nov. 9, 1992, to seek a limit to terms equal to eight years for state executive officers and 12 years for legislators. Mr. Howard said the difference between a state government without term limits and one with term limits "is the difference between fishing in a stagnant pond and fishing in a trout stream where the water's running through."

Voters, some attention-seeking politicians and taxpayer groups say they love term limits because the measures relax partisan gridlock and put an end to career politicians and their cozy, money-driven relationships with special interests.

By and large, legislative leaders and public policy analysts hate term limits, saying they will lead to more gridlock as leadership loses control of crowded government institutions. The loss of institutional and policy memory and fealty to leadership will lead to numerous agendas in constant conflict, they claim.

One of the major goals of the limits, "throwing the bums out," was realized almost immediately in California, which adopted term limits in 1990. A California Assembly member is allowed to serve no more than six years, or three two-year terms, in his or her lifetime. On the other side of the Legislature, senators get eight years, or two four-year terms. The departure of Democrat Barry Keene, the one-time Senate majority leader who said he resigned out of frustration with gridlock in California's legislative process, was hastened by the knowledge that he would get to serve only his current term, which was scheduled to expire in 1996. Bruce Bronzan, a Democrat considered one of the country's most experienced health policy experts and chairman of the California Assembly's Health Committee, left for an academic post, saying he couldn't pass up the opportunity; the knowledge that he would be out on his ear in just two years influenced his decision, according to insiders in the state capital of Sacramento.

The 28 new people who entered the 80-member California Assembly in early 1993 (in wake of the 1992 election) represented the first crop of elected lawmakers who knew they could serve no more than six years, assuming that each would be re-elected twice. New Democratic Assemblyman Louis Caldera of central Los Angeles said, "People have a sense that they've been elected to do a job and they have only a short period of time to do it. I'm not going there to occupy space."

Lewis K. Uhler, co-author of California's term limit initiative, said 1992's candidates were different because they knew before running that they could not make a career out of legislative service. He said the group was more experienced and older and represented a broader cross-section of the populace than past legislative classes. "This seems to be a group of people with more concern for solving the issues than simply getting re-elected, which is what we thought this process was all about," Mr. Uhler said.

But others don't want to see experienced lawmakers disappear. By the middle 1990s, "we are going to see entire leaderships being thrown out," said Mr. Kurtz of the National Conference of State Legislatures. Without seniority, "people will have only a few years to become and serve as legislative leaders. You will likely see one-term speakers, with their successors already in line before they take charge."

Mr. Rosenthal of Rutgers University argues that term limits eliminate institutional memory, causing a new kind of policy gridlock. "You have legislators who have honed their political expertise over many, many years, who know what has been tried and worked and what has been tried and didn't work," he said. "What will probably happen under term limits is that, as new people keep coming in, policy will be rewritten and rewritten. The real question will be whether local governments will be able to absorb all of these policy changes."

If power shifts away from legislatures, it will go to executive branch agencies, which will have far more institutional memory. Governors will seem to be more effective than weak legislative leaders, Mr. Rosenthal argues.

Two State University of New York professors, Gerald Benjamin and Michael J. Malbin, who both work with the Rockefeller Institute of Government, Albany, N.Y., pointed out in their book, "Limiting Legislative Terms," that not all term limits are alike. For instance, California caps lifetime service at six and eight years in the Assembly and Senate, respectively, while Colorado opted for a limit on continuous service in one chamber. Once a person hits the limit of eight consecutive years, he or she must do something else for four years before serving again in that body. Those four years, however, may be spent in the other house of the Legislature. The majority of term limit plans adopted in 1992 followed the Colorado method. This would have the effect of allowing career politicians to stay in business. Legislatures and other government offices will become involved in games of musical chairs, Messrs. Benjamin and Malbin speculated.

Conservative think tanks influence state lawmakers

For most of the 1980s, Don E. Eberly cut his conservative teeth in Washington. He organized briefings for citizens' groups visiting the White House, then held several congressional staff roles. Today, the 38-year-old still wages the Reagan Revolution, but on a different battlefield. Mr. Eberly moved to Harrisburg, Pa., in 1987 and established the Commonwealth Foundation for Public Policy Alternatives. In September 1991, Mr. Eberly fired a warning shot from the right that rocked the Pennsylvania establishment. After years of mostly bemoaning the sick state of public education, his organization suddenly helped guide a state Senate vote allowing parents broad authority to look outside their traditional public school districts in choosing their children's schools. "All hell broke loose after that," Mr. Eberly recalled, with more than a hint of glee. Once-smug teachers' unions immediately launched a media campaign that, with the support of liberal legislators, helped narrowly defeat a similar measure in the House. But the message was clear. The conservative movement in Pennsylvania had arrived.

Conservatives who took Washington, D.C., by storm in the 1980s, preaching lean and mean government, today are scoring tactical victories in state capitals over the issues of school choice, privatization (paying companies to run services, such as garbage pickup and parking ticket collections, that usually are performed by governments) and business-friendly regulation. Conservative governors and state legislators are the visible winners and may be quick to take credit. But the strategists in this state-level ideological struggle are right-wing public policy groups operating in the shadows of the statehouses. Most commonly labeled "think tanks," these groups share one guiding principle: Government is not the ultimate answer to society's problems. Refusing to accept the size of government preferred by liberals, the free-market think tanks fight to eliminate onerous government regulation and red tape, and they welcome the private sector when it can do the public's business better and cheaper.

The accomplishments of these groups, which have sprouted since the mid-1980s in half the states, do not yet translate to scores of legislative bills or executive orders. But, through a flood of written research, media placements, staff-sponsored workshops and support from a few influential politicians, movement conservatives are legitimizing their agenda in many of the states whose governments are ideologically divided and ripe for new ideas. Liberals, meanwhile, show few signs of mounting an organized counterattack.

"The liberal mentality is for a strong central government," said Pennsylvania state Rep. Fred C. Noye, a Republican who chairs the conservative American Legislative Exchange Council (ALEC), Washington. "Liberals are living in the past, wanting the federal government to control everything."

When conservatives look at Washington, all they see is a largely entrenched and bureaucratized Congress with little appetite for innovation. In most states, however, the policy debate looks wide open.

In many ways, the recent emergence of state-based conservative think tanks is an outgrowth of the success of national and regional conservative groups like ALEC, the Washington-based Heritage Foundation and the Santa Monica, Calif.-based Reason Foundation. Several of the larger national groups have offered their smaller brethren funding and technical aid. In fact, staff lists at the state-based think tanks read like a directory of former Beltway conservatives.

Charting a career path similar to Mr. Eberly is John Andrews, president of the Golden, Colo.-based Independence Institute, the 1990 Republican candidate for governor of Colorado and a former speech writer for President Richard Nixon in the 1970s. John W. Cooper, president of the James Madison Institute for Public Policy Studies, Tallahassee, Fla., served stints with both the conservative American Enterprise Institute and the Ethics in Public Policy Center. Some state think tank staff members once toiled for ALEC, the Washington-based conservative group numbering 2,400 state legislators sympathetic to the needs of business. One former ALEC official is current South Carolina Policy Council chief William Myers, who recently welcomed another ALEC staff member, Timothy Beauchemin, to the Columbia think tank staff.

"This all started in the mid-1980s with (President Ronald) Reagan's decentralizing initiative," Mr. Andrews recalled. "As movement conservatives, we were looking to extend the Reagan Revolution to the state and local level."

Though the universe of state-based think tanks is overwhelmingly conservative, leaders of some groups prefer the libertarian moniker, the free-market designation or no label at all.

Twenty-seven of the state-based groups, ranging from the California Public Policy Foundation in Sherman Oaks to the John Locke Foundation in Raleigh, N.C., belong to a trade association housed at the offices of the Chicago-based Heartland Institute. The association, once known as the Madison Group, has reorganized as the State Policy Network, emphasizing its state-level focus.

The think tanks generally advocate a leaner state government, limits on business regulation, more experiments with privatization and education overhauls emphasizing school choice. Most think tanks avoid divisive social issues like abortion, preferring topics with potentially broader appeal.

Considering their agenda, it is not surprising that many are financed by a combination of conservative-leaning foundations and big business, with less support from individual donors. In most cases, these are not organizations with deep pockets. Many run on annual budgets of less than $250,000 (though donations have picked up for some of the more influential groups) and staffs of fewer than 10 people. Mr. Eberly's Commonwealth Foundation for Public Policy Alternatives, for instance, has a staff of five full-time-equivalent employees and, in 1991, had a budget of $325,000.

Because the state-based groups register as non-profit corporations, they cannot lobby directly. Instead, they preach their gospels in writing, with reports that find their ways into lawmakers' hands and newspaper columns that community leaders scan over their morning coffee. Think tanks like the Heartland Institute, which has branch offices in Cleveland, Detroit, Milwaukee, St. Louis and Kansas City, Mo., are apt to measure their successes in newspaper citations rather than in legislative bills. The Heartland Institute, founded in 1984, is one of the more influential conservative think tanks in the United States, with a full-time-equivalent staff of 13 people and, in 1991, a budget of $631,270.

"We don't go to Springfield (Ill.), Lansing (Mich.) or Madison (Wis.)," said Joseph L. Bast, president of the Heartland Institute, one of the few conservative think tanks choosing to locate outside state capitals.

Critics of the state-level conservative movement offer a different perspective.

"I don't think these groups have any other agenda but to be influential at the legislative level," said Robert Bothwell, executive director of the National Committee for Responsive Philanthropy, Washington. Mr. Bothwell, whose organization urges charitable foundations to support liberal aims, has ominously warned his givers about the rapid growth of conservative state policy groups.

Expert opinions help give think tanks some pull

Though most state think tanks are staffed by only a handful of full-time employees (some are derisively called "one-man bands" by detractors), most retain a list of consultants from the civic, business and academic communities to pen reports as needed. Advisers to the Heartland Institute include experts from Amoco Corp., Chicago; General Motors Corp., Detroit; New York University; and Northwestern University, Evanston, Ill. Having access to

166

these resources means that the think tanks can respond quickly to developing policy debates.

"We want to change policy," Mr. Myers said. "We provide folks who share our ideology with the ammunition they need to do battle."

In a growing number of states, the ammunition is finding its desired target. In Pennsylvania, for instance, the Commonwealth Foundation helped transform school choice from an issue with practically no constituency to one with broad appeal.

"We don't see school choice as a panacea, but we criticize the more traditional approaches to school reform," said Mr. Eberly, reserving special scorn for the ideas espoused by teachers' unions.

It is hardly unusual for these conservatives to find themselves facing off with unions. Think tank officials list unions among the liberal-leaning groups they claim have dominated state debate for too long. Others on that list include environmentalists, professional trade groups, academics and the media. Now that the school choice issue has received its first serious legislative hearing in Pennsylvania, Mr. Eberly believes a bill including government-subsidy vouchers for parents who want to send their children to private schools could become law by the mid-1990s. "Now we have some negotiating strength for the future," he said.

Arizona policy-makers also are beginning to consider school choice seriously, partly because of the research effort of the Phoenix-based Barry Goldwater Institute for Public Policy Research, founded in 1988. The institute, led by President Michael K. Block, in 1991 had an annual budget of $120,000 and two full-time-equivalent staff members. In the late 1980s, under former president Michael Sanera, the institute began to use research to shatter a variety of assumptions reinforced by a bipartisan establishment. One of its most provocative reports showed that, despite the prevailing wisdom, Arizona residents were not undertaxed in relation to taxpayers in other states. A stronger anti-tax view has since begun to take hold among state policy-makers, particularly with the February 1991 election of Republican J. Fife Symington as governor.

In Colorado, the Independence Institute, with an annual budget of $200,000 and 3.5 full-time-equivalent staff members, has contributed to building a constituency for privatization. The institute, founded in 1985, gave momentum to a 1988 law requiring the Regional Transportation District in the Denver area to place one-fifth of its service in the hands of privately owned companies. Gradually, more Colorado legislators are jumping on the privatization bandwagon, maintains state Rep. Phil Pankey, a Republican and an enthusiastic user of Independence Institute research. Mr. Pankey believes his colleagues are more inclined to embrace the institute's free-market agenda than they were when he arrived as a legislator 10 years ago.

"The social programs that we're dumping money on aren't

working," Mr. Pankey insisted. "We've got to look at something different."

Fellow GOP Rep. Jeff Shoemaker applauds the Independence Institute for generating thought on issues, but he wonders whether his more liberal colleagues pay much attention to the group's writings. "I'd say they're effective because I agree with them most of the time," Mr. Shoemaker said. "But, on the other hand, I would have their opinions anyway."

Indeed, some liberals and centrists have questioned the legislative accomplishments of conservative think tanks. H. William DeWeese, a Democrat and the House majority leader in Pennsylvania, calls the Commonwealth Foundation "a fire-breathing team of highly financed right-wing thinkers."

In 1991, the South Carolina Policy Council, with four full-time-equivalent staff members and an annual budget of $165,000, reacted swiftly to the release of proposed state wetlands regulations that it believed would unfairly burden developers. The council, founded in 1986, issued a point-by-point analysis of the regulations and an op-ed piece that was published in 40 newspapers. The publicity resulted in a barrage of citizen letters to state environmental officials, who tabled the rules. The South Carolina think tank recently turned its attention to the state budget, urging the governor and legislators not to fall back on one-shot revenue-raisers. Mr. Myers, the council's executive vice president, would like legislators from both parties to rethink their assumptions about government. He constantly asks why there are so many sacred cows in the state budget — items that Republicans and Democrats alike fail to challenge. But he insists he wants his group to remain above the electoral fray. To ensure that goal, he has tried to create distance between the South Carolina Policy Council and a political action committee that the think tank created to rate the performance of individual legislators.

Other conservative state think tanks are finding a cordial reception from the new breed of governors of the 1990s. In Illinois, Republican Gov. Jim Edgar in 1991 quoted from a Heartland Institute book, "Coming Out of the Ice," to bolster his argument for steep spending cuts as an alternative to major tax increases. The two governors most inclined to adopt the conservative think tank agenda as their own are Republicans John Engler in Michigan and William F. Weld in Massachusetts. Their elections in the fall of 1990 placed the goals of the Midland, Mich.-based Mackinac Center and the Boston-based Pioneer Institute for Public Policy Research at the forefront of state-level debate. Critics of Mr. Engler believe the governor has gained immeasurable political advantage from the Mackinac Center, which had a 1991 budget of $290,000 and four full-time-equivalent staff members.

"A lot of the reports they issue are even farther to the right than where the governor wants to go," said Olivia Maynard, director of former Democratic Gov. James J. Blanchard's Office on Aging.

"He can then react to that and seem more moderate than he is."

Ms. Maynard wonders whether Mr. Engler's next crusade will be for drastic changes in welfare policy now that the Mackinac Center, founded in 1987 and currently led by President Lawrence W. Reed, has published material calling for an overhaul of the system. Welfare changes, including punitive measures directed at clients who have more children or whose children do not attend school, stood to receive attention from the conservative think tanks in the mid-1990s. Market-oriented solutions to the health-care crisis also promised to be a hot-button issue. Concerned about the Mackinac Center's spin on such topics, Ms. Maynard and a group of Michigan liberals and moderates have been fighting back behind a new policy group to promote what they consider government's rightful place in solving problems.

"We don't say government is always the answer, but that it has a role to play," said Ms. Maynard, who in the fall of 1992 began leading the Michigan Prospect for Renewed Citizenship.

Statistics from the Denver-based National Conference of State Legislatures (NCSL) show little change in the partisan composition of legislatures since 1983. Nationally, Republicans have achieved net gains of 199 House seats — an average of four per state — and 32 Senate seats from 1984 to 1992. Think tank supporters take heart from the fact that 14 states have split control of their legislatures, with Democrats dominating one house and Republicans the other. And in 17 states where one party controls both chambers, the governor is of another party. Combined with redistricting efforts that will dilute the power of liberal, urban state legislators, it's no wonder that conservative think tanks have shifted their attention from gridlocked Washington to the states.

"This is seed activity that the think tanks are getting into," said Jack Van Der Slik, director of the Illinois Legislative Studies Center at Sangamon State University, Springfield. "It's a campaign of ideas that may very well evolve into something more later. I don't think they've gotten there yet."

Like a juggernaut, the conservative movement continues its march from Washington in search of 50 ripe territories.

"Washington in general is approaching the point of irrelevance," Mr. Eberly said. "If you're concerned with major public policy issues, chances are you're focusing as much on state policy as anything else." And how does Mr. Eberly want policy-makers to react to the presence of himself and his colleagues? "We want the power structure to rethink how it confronts public problems," he said. "We're in the business of developing ideas over time, not pushing bills."

But if the conservatives' path to the state capitals remains largely unimpeded — by liberals or anyone else — it won't be long before people like Mr. Eberly move from developing ideas to claiming full-scale victories in the state policy war.

State legislatures listen to a smart ALEC

As a Pennsylvania legislator, Rep. George E. Saurman is automatically invited to meetings of the NCSL. But don't bother to look for him there. Mr. Saurman prefers to network with fellow conservatives through ALEC, an organization that is accomplishing nationally what state-based conservative think tanks seek locally.

"My feeling is that NCSL is more liberal than I would like," said Mr. Saurman, a Republican who chairs an ALEC task force on environmental issues.

Created by a small bipartisan group of legislators in 1973, ALEC has grown into the leading pro-business, limited-government advocate at the legislative level, with 2,400 member lawmakers. And with age and experience comes clout. Unlike state-based think tanks, which hesitate to measure their successes in bills passed, ALEC revels in the score-card approach. Every two years, ALEC sends to all 7,400 state legislators a multivolume set of model bills on topics ranging from victims' rights to plastic packaging. ALEC then compiles an annual summary of which model bills were introduced and enacted in the 50 states. 1991's count: 240 model bills introduced, with 92 becoming law. Of the 49 states with legislative sessions in 1991 (Kentucky lawmakers did not meet), only New Jersey, Vermont and Washington failed to enact any bills patterned after ALEC models.

"I don't know if getting model legislation adopted is our most important goal, but it has to be a major objective," said Mr. Saurman. "The private sector's interest in ALEC would not be retained if we didn't accomplish anything."

And what a private sector interest it is. About 70% of ALEC's $3.7 million budget for calendar year 1992 came from corporate donations, with Fortune 500 names scattered all over its donor list. Foundation money accounted for the rest of the budget.

No national liberal group has undertaken the kind of legislative effort that ALEC has. The NCSL — whose officials scoff at suggestions of any liberal bias — says it acts more as an information resource than as a bill advocate.

ALEC, on the other hand, wears its politics on its sleeve. After every state legislative election, ALEC members recruit freshman legislators who appear to carry pro-business philosophies. The issues ALEC pushes tend to mirror topics dominating the current state legislative debate, said Duane Parde, a senior policy analyst with the group. Among recent hot issues are pro-business environmental measures, anti-crime bills, health-care reform and taxation. Model bills range from the innocuous to the incendiary. Some receive a warm welcome in many states, while ALEC officials admit others don't have a prayer in most places.

Creating an image

The image projected by a government or by one of its officials is all-important to constituents. The way the news media portray politicians can make or break careers. The way a city, county or state is perceived by the rest of the world — a spectrum of adjectives running from crime-ridden to Arcadian — can determine a region's future. That is why public officials must concentrate on forging positive images for both themselves and their home communities.

Dealing with the media is one of the more difficult aspects of public service. Mayor Richard J. Daley had a way of distancing himself from reporters with comments like, "I don't answer to the twisted, polluted imagination of the journalistic enterprise." In other words, no comment. The mayor, who died in 1976, didn't think highly of the press, and it's no wonder. Reporters always were writing and broadcasting the very things he wished they would leave alone, "making mountains out of moles," as he put it, "deliberately" misunderstanding him.

The late mayor, the last of the big-city bosses, had his own philosophy about the power role of the press. Not so much emphasis on the bad news, he recommended: "My mother said, God love her, 'If you're broke, get out your best suit and your straw hat and put on the greatest front (you can).'" Mr. Daley reigned in an era when putting on "your greatest front" was a practical strategy for a public official. Press coverage was less pervasive then, in the years before Watergate, and reporters less likely to peel back a front and peer beneath it.

Feeling the heat of the media spotlight

These days, public officials must cope with constant scrutiny from the media. They cannot afford to be contentious. Reporters are the main link to the taxpayers. Failure to relate to the press in constructive ways can cost officials their jobs.

"One of the most creative things journalists and public officials have to do is to develop an ongoing, positive relationship," said Richard Schwarzlose, associate dean of the Medill School of Journalism at Northwestern University, Evanston, Ill. "Officials and reporters don't always have the same goals in mind, yet they rely on each other in a variety of ways. It's really crucial that they be able to look one another in the eye, sit down and work out a system wherein the public is served by both the official and the reporter."

Mr. Schwarzlose suggested that a mutual dose of trust is key. Reporters must be fair and honest. Officials must be open and accessible to the press. The responsibility for a constructive relationship belongs to both participants. Mr. Schwarzlose's recipe for a good relationship makes a lot of sense on paper but, out in the world where embarrassing, even incriminating, mistakes are made, being open and honest is not always easy.

"There are times when I wish I could write those stories," admitted City Manager George Hanbury of Portsmouth, Va. Then he added, "In the 22 years I've worked as a city manager, I've learned you can't fabricate one day and be truthful on the next. You've got to be truthful even when it hurts. The worst thing in the world is for a reporter to catch you in a lie. He'll never trust you again, and he'll second-guess every statement you make."

It's very much in a government's interest to reveal mistakes and bad news up-front, agreed Coleman Warner, City Hall reporter for the *New Orleans Times-Picayune*. "A reporter who has been lied to has twice the incentive to dig for the truth. Once he finds it, you can count on the information being represented in full color," he said.

The New Orleans city government paid dearly for failing to reveal a burgeoning budget deficit before the 1988 Republican National Convention in New Orleans, Mr. Warner recalled. City officials kept mum about the budget to avoid bad publicity from the hundreds of reporters in town covering the convention. When the multimillion-dollar deficit finally was made public in the fall, the city's only option was to approve numerous budget cuts, special fees and other unpopular measures. The administration "very easily could have been faced with a number of stories that read, 'Meanwhile, New Orleans goes down the tubes.' And in that sense they saved themselves some grief from the national press corps," Mr. Warner said. "But locally the cuts were twice as painful as they might have been if the deficit had been dealt with sooner, and the administration looked really bad. It was a major controversy when council members accused the city of sitting on that information."

On the other hand, Mr. Warner said New Orleans' regional

transportation administrators were quick to respond to the press when a group of city bus drivers was arrested for filing false insurance claims. "By jumping on the issue quickly, they came off looking like they were trying to take care of things. The (newspaper) story read like any news story. It wasn't a finger-pointing story that asked, 'Where were you and why were you asleep on the watch?' It was just another breaking news story. It was reported and then it was over."

Steve Marantz, City Hall reporter for the *Boston Globe,* said officials are reluctant to reveal mistakes because they do not want to demonstrate their shortcomings. "While making mistakes is a natural thing for a government to do — everybody's fallible — there seems to be this determination among government officials to maintain an image of infallibility," Mr. Marantz said. "It's part of the packaging and selling of politics. Mistakes don't sell. My own feeling is that acknowledging mistakes might actually increase the credibility of an administration. People tend to be sympathetic when someone admits to making a mistake."

Attempts to avoid the attention of the media usually backfire, said Idris Diaz, City Hall reporter for the *Philadelphia Inquirer.* "I've seen so many situations where press coverage is prolonged because of the unwillingness to talk about a mistake," Mr. Diaz said.

W. Wilson Goode, mayor of Philadelphia for two terms until 1991, once said he didn't recall who had appointed a local commission that was scouting a site for a new mayor's mansion. In fact, the mayor had appointed the commission himself. Plans for the new mansion were controversial, Mr. Diaz said, because finances were tight in Philadelphia and many residents viewed the mansion as an extravagance. "The mayor ended up looking pretty foolish in print. Had he simply said, 'Yes, I appointed the commission but the timing is wrong now,' or, 'We screwed up,' it would have been better."

How to deal with news organizations

Public officials cannot choose the reporters who cover them and, unfortunately, at some point, it is likely they will be the targets of reporters who refuse to play fair. But for the most part, experts report there are several steps public officials can take to foster positive relationships with reporters and to promote fair coverage:

• *Don't lie or try to shade the truth.*

"There is no rock big enough to hide under," remarked Susan Silk, president of Chicago-based Media Strategy Inc. Ms. Silk, a former print reporter and television reporter-producer, helps her clients earn free media coverage. Media Strategy services include a variety of seminars on how to deal with the press. "Let's say someone has embezzled nine zillion dollars from the town fund. You say, 'We've got trouble here in River City and I, as your city manager, am going to get to the bottom of it.' There's no lying here. You tell the truth. You give reporters all of the information you can. If it's a situation that's going to unfold over four or five days, you schedule daily briefings around the deadlines of your local press. The easiest way to put a lid on any fallout is to take control. It may be a town crisis, but, if you've done your building of media relationships, it should only be a media problem. The reporters know you. They trust you. You've given them straight answers in the past. They're still going to report the story, but without that frenzy, that shark-like mentality."

● *Know your local and state Freedom of Information laws.*

Experts agree that it is in everyone's interest — officials, reporters and the public — to allow reporters access to the documents they need to report stories fully and accurately. States have specific laws defining what is and isn't public record. It is never wise to withhold documents that the public has a legal right to see, explained Mr. Schwarzlose. "The only time to say no is when you're on firm ground to say no," he said. "The minute a reporter has any inkling that your answer is the wrong one, he or she is going to pursue you. They're going to come after you with everything they've got."

● *Do your homework before you talk to reporters.*

The obvious reason to prepare for an interview is to avoid looking ignorant. But preparation also allows an official to play a pro-active role in the interview process, said Jim Bergfalk, public affairs consultant and partner with Sherman, Coelz & Bergfalk, a public relations firm in Kansas City, Mo. Instead of following a reporter's lead, Mr. Bergfalk suggests that officials begin interviews with the points or issues that are important to them. "Reporters tend to have the best memory for the things you say first," he said. Officials also should take time to consider the interview format. "For example, if it's a television interview, pick the setting if you can. The backdrop is as important as the message. And recognize that you're restricted to short, catchy phrases."

● *Answer each question directly.*

If you don't have an answer, admit it. An evasive answer or no answer at all only will serve to draw attention to an issue, Mr. Schwarzlose said. But an honest "I don't know" is acceptable. "If you're the kind of official who is open and honest in your press dealings, then 'I don't know' can serve as a temporary stopgap until the answer can be found. It's perfectly appropriate."

● *Go off-the-record with care.*

Get permission to go off-the-record before giving information, Mr. Bergfalk advised. "Where a lot of people get into trouble is they say, 'I'm going to tell you a little bit of something off-the-record,' and then they go right into it. They don't wait for the reporters to agree. What you're really saying is, 'I'm going off-the-record if you'll give me permission, so I can give you some background understanding of this issue.' Good reporters clearly understand this." On the other hand, Ms. Silk tells her clients there is no such thing as off-the-record. "If you don't want to be quoted, the easiest rule in the world is don't say it," she said.

- *Speak from the perspective of what will interest the public.*

It is a mistake to think of an interview as a conversation with a reporter. Instead, it's a conversation with the reporter's readers, listeners or viewers. Therefore, comments should be shaped with that audience in mind. "Think about what you'd like to hear or read," Mr. Bergfalk said.

- *Try to avoid using technical jargon and buzzwords.*

Technical terms are meaningless to the vast majority of the public, not because people are stupid but because they are not in the business of running governments. If it is absolutely necessary to use an obscure term, define it in a way the average person can understand. Mr. Bergfalk said one classic example of simplifying a complicated subject matter is a presentation George Romney made when he was governor of Michigan. "The governor kept talking about this billion-dollar budget and he never once used any zeros. He talked about 'one of these and one of those and two of these' and people understood it."

- *Set aside certain times to be available to reporters.*

A public official's willingness to be available to the press fosters trust. The failure to return reporters' telephone calls or be accessible after a press conference implies an attempt to cover up.

- *Recognize that you won't be given a chance to edit or correct a story.*

Virtually all print and broadcast news organizations have strict policies against allowing sources to see stories in advance of publication or broadcast.

- *Take time to follow up with reporters on stories.*

Following up with both criticism and praise is part of a positive relationship with the press. If an official thinks a reporter has written a particularly good story, he should take time to let the reporter know. If the story is misleading or factually wrong, the reporter needs to know that, too, so the mistakes are not repeated.

Cities put on the glitz through marketing

A government official's own image inevitably is intertwined with the image of the community he or she serves. Thus, city officials in Brea, southeast of Los Angeles, wanted to transform the suburb's blighted downtown strip into a trendier, more upscale enclave. It was time for some marketing — not to outsiders, but to Brea's own 28,000 residents and its business community. Internal marketing of the revitalization plan, business-minded city officials reasoned, would make the plan far easier to finance and implement. In October 1989, about 150 Brea residents participated in a weekend-long design and brainstorm session, aided by a team of outside design consultants. City officials used extensive marketing techniques to involve residents in the process and help reshape their image of the city and its eventual repositioning in the regional commercial marketplace.

"More and more issues cannot be solved by government alone," observed Frank Benest, Brea's city manager and born-again marketer. Mr. Benest, who eschews government-speak in favor of the patter of a marketing man, said governments' "customers" must be converted into partners in the process of determining how a city will sell its "products." "If you want to provide a particular service, but it's clear the customers don't want it, maybe it's a product government ought not to be offering."

Public officials have begun to learn Mr. Benest's marketing language. In the tough competitive market, with its shifting and costly demands for "improved quality of life," government officials need to adapt and hustle.

"Cities that want to really compete for the finite amount of economic development out there realize that they must first invest in their quality of life, adding cultural and economic development, improving the educational system, attracting cultural activities, invigorating the urban center," said John T. Bailey, a Cleveland-based municipal consultant and former urban scholar at Cleveland State University.

In the late 1980s, Mr. Bailey authored a major study for the American Economic Development Council, Rosemont, Ill., that identified three stages of economic development and marketing by cities. In the 1970s, chasing jobs and smokestacks through economic incentives was the rage. Cities next went after specific industries, ideally, cleaner, high-technology firms. "Nowadays, you see many cities with forward-looking marketing programs entering a third phase, what I call the product-development phase," Mr. Bailey said. "This is when the objectives of the city are defined. Basically, it is doing the things that make the city a good place for investment."

"There must be ongoing communications with your stockholders (residents)," said Bill Guerrant, director of the Charlotte (N.C.) Public Information Department. "You have to tell people the bad with the good. You have to get out there and define for the public what are the situations and choices and then see if they want that product or that solution." Mr. Guerrant, also the president of the City-County Communications and Marketing Association (3CMA), Washington, heads what may be the most complete marketing apparatus of any mid-size city. In addition to a public information staff of 12, many of whom are former print and television reporters, Charlotte has four video producers and four printers in its state-of-the-art facilities at the gleaming new 15-story Charlotte-Mecklenburg County Building. "We've had a centralized public information office for 20 years."

Too many marketing campaigns are "one-shot deals" for whipping up public interest, followed by a back-to-business-as-usual letdown. "If you don't have an ongoing two-way communication with the people, you will be in trouble when things go wrong," Mr. Guerrant warned.

Many campaigns amount to little more than sloganeering, Mr. Bailey added. "Some cities waste a lot of money promoting themselves to their residents with meaningless catch phrases. A classic example is Houston, with its 'Houston is Hot' campaign. That's just a cliche not tied to any coherent program."

Richard Lillquist, executive director of the 3CMA, said the real change taking place in both marketing and government is that officials now know that the market determines what the city produces in the way of services, "instead of a monopolistic attitude of telling people what services they ought to purchase."

Not all new marketing techniques target development. In 1986, Colorado Springs, Colo., was booming with tens of thousands of new residents and new electronics companies. A downturn in the oil industry, the financial crash of savings-and-loan institutions and the collapse of the real-estate market have dampened the euphoria, but the city still is growing and grappling with urban sprawl. Colorado Springs also has lacked a coherent self-image. It changed too quickly from a small operation whose economy heavily depended on nearby military installations into a high-technology mecca with a population of nearly 300,000 people. The public-private Partnership for Community Design sponsored a series of focus groups in Colorado Springs. Some of the questions that were brought up: What should the city look like? How is it going to bring together a sprawling and booming patchwork of smaller communities? As a result, a group called Citizens' Goals came up with a visionary plan called Project 2000. The plan called for unifying themes such as elaborate new welcoming archways on roads leading into town, focusing public attention on the great outdoor assets of the community and revitalizing the downtown. In 1990, the Community Design Forum, a related effort, unveiled a green-and-white logo using Pikes Peak and a new slogan: "Colorado Springs: Reaching Higher."

In Brea, public marketing was used to promote a new recycling program. Rather than decreeing how it would be carried out, the City Council first measured public opinion on what residents would prefer. They opted for a voluntary, instead of a mandatory, program. Residents also wanted businesses and industrial firms to take part. Videos at public events, door fliers, inserts in garbage bills, recycling promotions and publicity through neighborhood groups became part of the marketing offensive for recycling. After four months, the program had an 80% participation rate, and 27% of the community's waste was being recycled — enviable statistics even for mandatory efforts.

New image paves the way for Wichita

The mid-1980s were worrisome years for business leaders, public officials and economic planners in Wichita, Kan. The city of

290,000 residents historically had held a leading spot in the agriculture and oil and gas production industries, in addition to a healthy share of business from aviation-related firms such as the Boeing Co. and Beech Aircraft Corp. The bad news was that all these economic sectors were in trouble. Wichita needed to diversify its economy, reposition itself vis-a-vis other urban areas and update its image. So local officials launched a long-term economic expansion effort that tapped the talents of residents as well as those of the best and brightest from government, business, labor and education.

The results were impressive. From mid-1987 to mid-1990, Wichita had become a corporate home to the telemarketing and franchising industries. Some 23 local businesses expanded, creating nearly 2,000 jobs. Nine companies relocated or established satellite offices in Sedgwick County, bringing in another 2,750 jobs. City officials hoped to spend the rest of the 1990s trying to bring home a $375 million cornucopia of special projects highlighted by a revitalized downtown and an invigorated regional transportation system. Thanks to the program's ongoing success — and $2.5 million spent to advertise that success over a four-year period — the city had generated some 50 laudatory articles in national publications.

Mr. Bailey of the American Economic Development Council pointed to Wichita as an example of a new generation of marketing "in which community investment or 'product development' activities in education, technology, capital access and infrastructure are being undertaken to support long-range strategies aimed at the jobs of the 1990s and 21st century. The logic that more jobs make a city better is giving way to a realization that making a city better attracts more good jobs."

Before they went national with one of the most successful marketing campaigns of any mid-size city in recent years, Wichita officials knew they had to mobilize the community. "We were in a position with the economy that we had to evaluate our entire economic development strategy," said City Manager Chris Churches. "The problem was that everyone was doing their own thing. The city had an economic development program, the county had one, the chamber of commerce had one. So we in the city approached the others to see what we could do."

Their first step was to hire Stanford Research Institute Inc. of Palo Alto, Calif., to take a comprehensive look at Wichita and suggest changes to improve the city's economy and image. Out of the study came a $9 million, five-year plan aimed at developing new business technology, improving the local education system and redeveloping Wichita's downtown area. In one 45-day period in 1986, business and municipal leaders raised about $9 million in pledges from residents and the private sector to develop and implement the Blueprint 2000 plan. The city and Sedgwick County each ponied up $250,000 per year for the program, but it was

178

clear that eventually a far greater commitment would be necessary. A public-private effort called Wichita Sedgwick County Partnership for Growth Inc., nicknamed WISE, tapped top talent from the city, suburbs, county, business community, labor and the local education system. The city and county both phased out their economic development programs in favor of WISE.

The most expensive part of the seven-pronged program was a variety of proposed downtown projects: a science center, a major hotel, an amphitheater, a retail complex, expansion of the public library, an art museum and an 18,000-seat arena for conventions and Wichita State University sports. WISE also planned to improve Wichita's transportation network and create a business-education compact for schools, a program to support new small businesses and a world-class biomedical research center. The city and private sector intended to share the $375 million cost over the decade.

Tourism promoters make do with less cash

Officials also try to promote their regions through standard tourism campaigns, although, at least on the state level, tight budgets make such efforts difficult if not impossible. From New York to Alaska, shrinking or flat state tourism-promotion budgets have sent officials scrambling for cheaper alternatives to television commercials and for ways to develop new markets and capitalize on emerging trends in travel. For many states, tourism ranks second or third in revenue generation and employment, often providing windfalls of billions of dollars to otherwise lethargic post-industrial economies. Among the six top states in tourism spending, second-place New York (Illinois ranks first) has faced the most serious ad spending cutbacks.

"Almost all (state department budgets) have to be cut" because of New York's financial problems, said Bern Rotman, director of communications for the state Department of Economic Development. New York spent close to $7 million on tourism promotion for the fiscal year that ended March 30, 1991, down 41.3% from fiscal 1990. Of the state's four annual efforts, the two largest — a spring campaign and a campaign promoting New York City — suffered the biggest cuts.

In the early 1990s, Alaska's tourism budget headed for a deep freeze, even though the number of visitors was up 3% annually. In fiscal 1990, the tourism budget was slashed to $5.2 million from $8 million.

New Jersey's plans to spend $5 million in fiscal 1991 to attract visitors included celebrity television spots with entertainers Bill Cosby and Brooke Shields. Although the new budget represented a slight increase over fiscal 1990, the state was seeking corporate advertising partners.

Illinois used its expected $11.5 million budget — flat for two years — to increase the number of domestic visitors by advertising across 30% of the country, including neighboring states. Illinois had initiated co-op ad programs with corporate partners such as American Express Co., British Airways, and other foreign and domestic airlines in an attempt to cut costs and increase exposure. Illinois' program is an example of a noticeable trend in state tourism spending nationwide to lure international visitors.

There is more to tourism promotion than just dollars. States with comparatively limited budgets are attracting more visitors. Susan Edwards, secretary of South Dakota's Department of Tourism, reported an "excellent" tourism market. "Though we don't have a lot of dollars, we're careful about the way we spend them," she explained. "For every $250,000 increase, we know exactly where that money will go. It's not how much we have to spend, but how smart we spend it." South Dakota spends most of its yearly $3.1 million tourism marketing budget in surrounding states, which "give us the most bang for our buck."

Massachusetts overflows with historical and arts attractions that lure traveling culture vultures. According to Deborah Firth, a Massachusetts tourism official, the state tries to capitalize on that wealth, despite a limited tourism budget. To supplement its budget, Massachusetts turned to co-op advertising arrangements with the private sector, and a national promotion of the state as the "birthplace of Thanksgiving" was scheduled to segue into a successful "The Spirit of Massachusetts is the Spirit of America" campaign.

Despite tighter budgets and additional competition, states are not about to give up on tourism marketing. Whether they are from the state next door or from overseas, travelers have become too important for most states to ignore.

Public-private ventures help states sell themselves

In 1990, Indiana officials discovered they had no business image to market to out-of-state corporations. It wasn't that the state's economy was so bad. It was just that when people thought of Indiana, well, not much came to mind.

Indiana has an image now, emphasizing its strong business climate of relatively low taxes and a well-trained labor force. In developing and marketing that theme, Indiana followed the lead of many states in what is becoming a growing trend: To sell itself, a state must form a strong alliance with businesses and other representatives of the private sector.

In recent years, states have become more like many cities in creating public-private partnerships for economic development. Alabama, Florida, Ohio and Utah are among states that have similar partnerships or are busy developing them. A 1987 survey, commissioned by the city of Lakeland, Fla., of several hundred cities found that two-thirds of local economic development campaigns were run by some form of independent agency that received funding from both the public (government) and private sectors.

Now, following an example laid down by Utah in 1987, states are privatizing some marketing campaigns as well. "The trend over the past two years has generally been not-for-profit entities contracting with the public sector for economic development activities," said Rich Thrasher, president of the Economic Development Corp. of Utah in Salt Lake City. "That trend is moving from the local level to the state level."

In putting together the new marketing plan for Indiana, Gov. Evan Bayh agreed to increase the state's marketing budget to $1.5 million from about $600,000 a year, but he also set a goal of raising $1 million from the private sector to help fund the initiative. That goal was met in September 1991. Under the plan, chairmen of Indiana corporations help sell the state's image to their counterparts in other states. The Indiana Economic Development Council, Indianapolis, is working with the Indiana Commerce Department's marketing and tourism development division on aspects of the plan. At a series of luncheons in Indianapolis, out-of-state business leaders heard Hoosier businessmen recount success stories; those out-of-state leaders then networked with the local executives and some local mayors and state officials.

"We looked at where other states have been successful in marketing themselves, and the common theme for those programs was public-private partnerships," said Denise Miller, director of Indiana's marketing and tourism division. "The partnership brings the business people into the planning of the campaign and uses them to sell the state directly to their counterparts."

"What you get in purely public sector economic development campaigns is a fragmentation of effort," said Ted Levine, president of Development Counsellors International, a New York-based consulting firm that has worked with dozens of state and local economic development agencies. "You have politicians competing with each other over prospects and everybody doing the same research. Many government officials also don't understand the factors businesses use in making relocation decisions."

Utah was the first to have a statewide not-for-profit organization, created after dozens of local governments agreed they needed to stop fighting each other and begin to pool their resources to get noticed outside the state, said Mr. Thrasher, whose non-profit agency was created in 1986 by a group of municipalities. "The advantage of privately run efforts is that the activities and priorities are not changing over time due to partisan political developments," Mr. Thrasher said. "You need government involved, of course, because it sets the parameters for economic growth and what the focus of the campaign should be. But government should leave the ongoing marketing work to the private sector."

Mr. Levine agrees: "Only the public sector knows what all of the resources you have to work with are. They have to be involved in deciding what image you are going to sell. They need people like us to help them define the image and help sell it."

Dave Cooley, president of the Memphis-area Chamber of Commerce, said a public-private partnership is essential if geographic bias is to be eliminated from sales efforts. "Increasingly, you are seeing economic development becoming a regional, even a multi-state, effort. It's essential to have the private sector help coordinate that," he said. Memphis is participating in a new organization called the Mid-South Common Market, an entity representing western Tennessee, Arkansas and Mississippi in attracting new industry. "If you don't have the private sector, an organization like that will fall apart because of political interests," Mr. Cooley added. The Memphis-area chamber shares office space and sales calls with Memphis Light, Gas & Water, the publicly owned utility company in the metropolitan area. "It used to be that when I went to meet a prospect, there waiting in the office would be someone from Light, Gas & Water. Now, we travel together," Mr. Cooley said. Part of Mr. Cooley's budget comes from the Memphis-Shelby County government, which has an Office of Planning and Development, "but we do most of the selling."

Mr. Levine said one problem many public sector people have is creating what he calls the "unique selling proposition" for their regions. His organization and other private sector groups help governments determine what it is about their areas that can set them apart in a crowded marketplace. He used the example of Dayton, Ohio, which was not known for anything until officials determined, with Mr. Levine's help, that the area had more patents granted per capita than any other. From that came the selling theme: Dayton, Innovation Location.

Model public officials

One of the best ways to learn how to run a government is to examine the successes of public officials who are known nationally for their superior management styles. *City & State*, the twice-monthly newspaper on state and local government with news offices in Chicago, New York and Washington, annually presents its Most Valuable Public Official Awards to elected and appointed officials who excel in serving the public. The following five people — a mayor, former mayor, county executive, city manager and governor — are recent award-winners who are worthy of emulation. Each has his own style, approaches government in a different way and wrestles with a unique set of problems.

From minister to pol to scholar, Hudnut's career stands out

From a perch in an ivy-covered think tank in Indianapolis, William H. "Bill" Hudnut III reflects on two decades in government, one chapter in a life of service. Minister, congressman, four-term mayor of Indianapolis and now senior fellow at the Hudson Institute, a conservative research organization based in the leafy northeastern part of Indianapolis, Mr. Hudnut has turned the page again, this time to work on education.

Fresh from a semester-long fellowship at Harvard University's John F. Kennedy School of Government in Cambridge, Mass., Mr. Hudnut works with scholars at the institute and at Indiana University-Purdue University-Indianapolis on a book about his city as a case study in urban management. He also works on a project on how to revitalize education in the United States. The institute wants to broaden its scope of interests to include more work on state and local government issues. For Mr. Hudnut, who wrote an autobiographical book, "Minister Mayor," that was published by The Westminster Press of Philadelphia in 1987, it is a perfect fit because he is interested in a position close to home in Indianapolis.

But wherever he lands, Mr. Hudnut, who was born in 1933, is sure to have an impact. During his time as mayor of Indianapolis, from 1976 until early in 1992, he raised his city's profile, both literally and figuratively, higher than any mayor of any other U.S. city. Once a sleepy Rust Belt outpost stirred to life each year by the Indianapolis 500 auto race, this central Indiana city, whose municipal government is consolidated with Marion County government, was transformed into a booming metropolis. Major corporations, financial institutions and computer firms established regional headquarters, warehouses, back offices or distribution centers in Indianapolis. New office towers, cultural developments and many sporting venues popped up in the downtown. Indiana University-Purdue University-Indianapolis became a major research institution and presence.

Continuing a strategy started under Richard G. Lugar, the former Indianapolis mayor who became a Republican U.S. senator, Mr. Hudnut was the point man for this transformation, even if many of the ideas behind it came from the city's active business and civic leadership. New office buildings and a railroad station that was turned into a unique several-block-long retailing and restaurant arcade launched the process.

But sports, both amateur and professional, were the glue that held it together. Mr. Hudnut led the charge for the building of a tennis complex, the $90 million Hoosier Dome (to which he lured the Colts professional football franchise from Baltimore), the Market Square Arena for professional basketball's Pacers, and a series of smaller sports facilities that ultimately won the city the 1982 National Sports Festival and the 1987 Pan-American Games, among many other events.

Then, in October 1991, the Republican mayor capped his career with back-to-back wins in the ever more competitive sport of business recruitment. Working in tandem with Democratic Indiana Gov. Evan Bayh, Indianapolis beat out more than 100 cities to land United Airlines' planned $1 billion maintenance facility and a $100 million U.S. Postal Service sorting center. Before the year 2000, the two facilities are expected to bring in 7,700 jobs that pay, on average, more than $40,000 a year.

The projects were typical of Mr. Hudnut's years in office. For one thing, they involved competition between cities, a situation Mr. Hudnut clearly loves. In addition, both facilities were given strong doses of tax incentives, which Mr. Hudnut used liberally on many projects, and the deals were consummated through the exuberance of a mayor who thrills for the big-ticket project.

"I probably haven't been as choked up with anything since I walked into the Hoosier Dome with (Colts owner) Bob Irsay in

April of 1984," a teary-eyed Mr. Hudnut crowed after United Airlines' decision.

"Bill Hudnut's impact was profound and permanent in Indianapolis," said Mitch Daniels, vice president for corporate affairs at Eli Lilly & Co., the city's top employer. "It was his irrepressible optimism and bridge-building that made many projects, such as downtown reconstruction and the amateur sports strategy, come to fruition," said Mr. Daniels, former political adviser to President Ronald Reagan and past president of the Hudson Institute.

Added Harrison Ullmann, publisher of the *Indiana Letter,* a political insider's newsletter, "As a Republican, Hudnut was naturally close to the business community. But he also had good rapport with labor, particularly the construction trade. He kept a lot of momentum going when things could have fallen apart."

Mr. Hudnut sees himself as a prototype for the entrepreneurial mayors now found in cities around the country. "An entrepreneurial mayor is a risk-taker, but you have to take prudent risks," he said. "Building the Hoosier Dome was a risk, but it was not something that was going to go up or down just based on whether we landed the Colts or not. Instead, it was done first as an expansion of our convention center, as a way to attract meetings and conventions. We didn't sit around sucking our fingers and letting the type of deterioration that was occurring around that site continue. We got lucky when the Colts decided to come, but we had that facility in place to make it happen, too."

Also risked in most of these ventures were significant amounts of public dollars committed to leveraging private dollars. In some cases public money was the majority of the investment, as in the Hoosier Dome and the tennis center. The United Airlines project came at a staggering cost, with a total of $291 million in tax breaks and other financial incentives. Of that amount, the city invested $111.5 million and the state put up $171 million. The rest came from other sources. "The big question is this: Did we pay too much? I don't think so, but time will tell," Mr. Hudnut said.

Not every vision translates into successful reality. Union Station, the renovated downtown rail facility that houses dozens of retail operations, did not immediately meet financial expectations. The unfinished piece of business of Mr. Hudnut's record is a planned but not yet completed $500 million Circle Centre Mall. Mr. Hudnut indicated it will be a needed supplement to his vision of downtown. "We got hit by the recession," he said. "A lot of investors backed off, but that doesn't mean it isn't a good plan. People want a 45-second solution these days on the evening news and then move on to the next thing. You have to have patience."

Without the commitment of city dollars, Mr. Hudnut said, Indianapolis would still be "India-No-Place," its former nickname. "Let's face it, this is the Rust Belt. Indianapolis is not a city that had success just drop into its lap. If we don't go out and hustle the Colts, hustle United Airlines, they aren't going to be here. Without Union Station and a $60 million revitalization program, you are going to keep on sinking into the swamp of deterioration in that neighborhood. If you don't reverse this exodus of the middle class from the central city and the concentration of poor people in the inner city, the centrifugal forces that are hurting so many cities will tear us apart."

Mr. Hudnut declined to seek re-election, opening the way for Steven Goldsmith, a fellow Republican, to enter the mayor's office. Mr. Hudnut was supportive of a major effort on the part of the new mayor in 1992 to trim the city work force and make the provision of services more competitive — two issues that Mr. Hudnut thinks other cities ought to study seriously.

"That's another characteristic of the entrepreneurial city, managing efficiently and downsizing in an era of ever tighter resources and opposition to tax increases," Mr. Hudnut said. "In particular, I see no reason that cities ought to treat water or even provide it. They can contract out services like water and wastewater. Why do we need to manage golf courses, or have this huge capacity of city workers to remove snow a few times a year? What city governments have to do is make sure that the essential city services are done well, but not necessarily to provide all these services themselves."

Disseminating views like these will be a key feature of Mr. Hudnut's tenure at the Hudson Institute. Being at the institute allows him more time to be with his wife, Beverly, who gave birth to the couple's first child in September 1992; Mr. Hudnut has five children from two previous marriages.

Working at a think tank, no matter how prestigious, is a far cry from the rough-and-tumble of high elected office, as Mr. Hudnut is the first to admit. "I miss it," he said. "It's not just the importance of it all, but that job was fun, it was action all the time. At the same time, there are only three ways to leave public office, only one of them a good way," he said with a laugh. "I left the good way, alive and voluntarily."

It's difficult to imagine Mr. Hudnut away from the fray for long. He freely admits his ultimate goal was to be governor of Indiana, but he stumbled before he got started, losing by a wide margin in a race for secretary of state in 1990.

Dallas city manager keeps cool during hot budget battles

In the steamy dog days of August, City Manager Jan Hart takes an annual risk of raising the temperature further in Dallas' council chambers with the task she must perform — presenting the budget. If anyone can maintain a cool head, it's Ms. Hart. The first woman appointed to the position in Dallas, which is the eighth largest city in the country, Ms. Hart manages a $1 billion budget and 13,000 employees in 34 departments. She keeps a low profile, carrying out the council's policies under the city's council-manager form of government.

"She manages in an exemplary manner," said Max Wells, a councilman who chairs the City Council's finance committee. "She is faced with the test of a slightly reducing tax base each year."

The city is sweeping up after the party times of the early 1980s, when a building boom led to an explosion of growth in the tax base. Since taking office in March 1990, Ms. Hart, who was born in 1948, has been managing a city that has come up shorter on revenue each year than the previous year. Excluding public safety, which is considered a priority public service, the Dallas city work force was reduced 20% during the   five years   up to fiscal 1992, Ms. Hart said.

Although it has been a scramble to keep revenue coming in to compensate for a shrinking tax base, Wall Street bond rating agencies are pleased with Ms. Hart's skills. "She has taken the necessary steps to maintain reserves, make the necessary cuts on the expense side and enhance revenue," said Peter J. D'Erchia, director of Standard & Poor's Corp.'s tax-backed group.

"We never spend beyond our means," said Ms. Hart, who holds a master's degree in public affairs from the Lyndon B. Johnson School of Public Affairs at the University of Texas, Austin.

A series of internal financial controls assures that the city stays on sound financial footing. One of those controls disallows debt payments on borrowed funds to exceed 20% of total locally generated revenue.

Ms. Hart worked her way through the ranks of the Dallas city work force. She has served the city since 1974 as city manager, first assistant city manager, assistant city manager, budget director and city controller. Along the way, she became a certified public accountant, a certified internal auditor and a certified management accountant. When she became city manager, she got hit with a $71.2 million budget shortfall, and property taxes had to be raised 7%.

Ms. Hart fashions plans and proposals for the council on the fourth floor of a modernistic I.M. Pei building that houses City Hall. The inverted triangle-shaped structure has a wall of windows with a spectacular view of the glass-and-concrete canyons of the downtown Dallas business district.

The business community gives the city manager high marks for her economic development efforts and the attention she pays to existing businesses. "She's so accessible," said E. Larry Fonts, president of the Central Dallas Association, a group of 200 major city property owners. "If you have a need to get in touch with her, she will drop what she's doing. You will hear from her within a business day."

The city has embarked on an aggressive economic development program to market Dallas and retain business. Ms. Hart and Mr. Wells came up with the idea of a Dallas Business Leaders Council, an advisory group of top business leaders that has been active since early 1991. The leaders offer guidance to the city on the best programs for retaining and attracting business. "They're helping us re-evaluate and design a marketing program," Ms. Hart said. The Dallas business community respects Ms. Hart's style. "She has approached very complex and controversial issues in a very systematic way," said Dan S. Petty, who serves on the executive committee and board of the Greater Dallas Chamber of Commerce. "She's not timid at all in making the tough decisions and she stands by them once they're made."

One of those decisions, however, became a major controversy. Ms. Hart fired the police chief in 1990 after a grand jury indicted him on a misdemeanor perjury charge relating to testimony on a complaint registered against the chief by an assistant police chief. A jury later acquitted the chief. Some council members questioned why Ms. Hart got the district attorney involved when the matter could have been dealt with internally. But the city manager had the support of the majority of council members. "Under the circumstances it was the right thing to do," said Glenn Box, a council member who supported her decision.

Ms. Hart has had several votes of confidence from two different city councils. When her predecessor resigned in 1990, she served as acting city manager. "Three weeks later the council unanimously named her city manager without even discussing a search," Mr. Wells said. That same day, the city's election system was struck down by a federal judge. Ms. Hart weathered the subsequent redistricting and overhaul of the City Council system. The council originally had eight members elected from at-large districts and three members from single districts. Now 14 members are from single districts and only the mayor is elected at-large.

Ms. Hart offers credit to the newly formed council for Dallas' continuing accomplishments. "We now have more balanced input from all parts of the community and a better ethnic and geographic representation," she pointed out. "They all have a common mission — to make Dallas the best city it can be. They're good, hard-working people."

One of the projects Ms. Hart has been working on is privatization, where private sector companies take over the operation of services normally controlled by government. The concept has helped keep the cost of services down in Dallas, she said. "We regularly compare services with other cities. We're always looking for ways of doing things better," she said.

The consultant who counseled her on the city's privatization effort was impressed with how well she used her staff and worked with the council. Even though the city in the early 1990s already was highly privatized in services such as fleet management, park services and city telephone system management, the council gave Ms. Hart a mandate to find more services to privatize, said John

D. Donahue, associate professor of public policy at Harvard University's John F. Kennedy School of Government, Cambridge, Mass. "There wasn't an enormous amount of neglected opportunity," he said. "The bottom line is they weren't going to solve the city's fiscal problems by a major push at privatization." In the research process, Ms. Hart promised the council that members of her staff would complete the analysis. Mr. Donahue said his role was to review their work. "She got the best people who know how the city works and had me take a look to see if there was anything missing," he recalled. "She trusted her people. She sent a message that she had confidence in them."

They call Wayne County's executive 'Mr. Ideas'

When Wayne County, Mich., Executive Edward H. McNamara talks of the Detroit-area county's economic development director, he says Dewitt "Dewey" Henry is a man of a million ideas. "He said that about me?" Mr. Henry asked with a laugh. "He's the man of ideas. The guy has so many ideas he wears me out."

When Mr. McNamara talks of the transformation in Wayne County from a debt-ridden, poorly rated, poorly operated jurisdiction to a casebook example of a well-run urban county, he uses the word "we," as in "we did this" or "we did that." That "we" is not an imperious pronoun. Mr. McNamara is talking of his team members, and he drops their names frequently as he tells the story of his tenure, which began in 1986.

When others talk of the turnaround in Wayne County, though, they speak of the triumph of Ed McNamara, a superb leader with lots of ideas that keep paying off. "The facts speak for themselves," said J. Chester Johnson of Government Finance Associates, New York, financial advisers to the county since 1987. "Ed has superlative — and that's a word I don't use normally — financial and political acumen."

After all, it was a combination of Mr. McNamara's ideas and his team that launched Made in America for the World, a three-day exposition in Detroit during the fall of 1992 that spotlighted American-made goods for export; that stanched the hemorrhaging red ink in the county's budget and passed four consecutive balanced budgets leading into fiscal 1992; that created a financial environment which impressed the Wall Street bond rating agencies enough to raise the county's rating to investment grade; that created the Alternative Community Workforce of non-violent criminals to work on projects like cleaning freeway berms and the Rouge River; that implemented an economic development policy throughout the county aimed at creating jobs; and that worked to keep the Detroit Tigers professional baseball team in town. As Mr. McNamara says as he points to architectural drawings in his office for the upgrading of Detroit Metropolitan Wayne County Airport and a proposed new Tigers stadium, "Lots of things are going on."

Wayne County is the 95th most populous government jurisdiction in the United States, with more than 2.1 million people and 43 municipal governments. But when Mr. McNamara took office in 1986, the county was suffering from severe economic difficulties. As the newly elected county executive — one of the few elected county executives in the country — Mr. McNamara faced a $135 million deficit that quickly zoomed to $200 million. "We were bleeding badly," he said, but by working with "very talented people," costs were brought under control.

The team did it by cutting department costs. Where the Sheriff's Department once controlled the county jail and overtime wages were running sky-high, Mr. McNamara's office took over, armed with a court order.

With health-care spending   out-of-sight, the county government identified 50,000 indigents, sought bids for health care and agreed to pay a fixed rate per month per person to each of four health-care providers. "The plan encouraged the providers to seek out and address health needs," Mr. McNamara said. "If a person has high blood pressure, the provider will give them medicine; then the person won't have a stroke." The program of preventive health care for indigents, CountyCare, ensured that the county knew exactly how much it would spend. "It was one of the major reasons we whipped the budget into shape," Mr. McNamara said.

The county had an old poor farm and, under Mr. McNamara, the commissary was converted to a shelter for homeless families. "We feed them, get schooling for the children, find out the skills of the parents," he explained. "We hope to keep them long enough for them to find a house and a job."

Is Mr. McNamara, who was born in 1927, a New Deal Democrat? Labels are unfortunate, he said. "People have needs and we must recognize them. The Republicans don't," said the man who was President Bill Clinton's Michigan co-chairman during the 1992 election with   Democrat   James J. Blanchard, former Michigan governor.

Mr. McNamara came to public service via a school board election in Dearborn Township, where he and his wife, Lucille, moved after he was finished with a stint in the Navy and education at the University of Detroit. Mr. McNamara and his wife have five children and two grandchildren. After school taxes got him upset enough to run in 1953 for the school board — where he served 5½ years, the last two as president — the family moved to Livonia, Mich., in 1960. He was elected to the City Council in 1962. He became council president six years later. He unsuccessfully ran for lieutenant governor in 1970; in an ironic role reversal, Mr. Blanchard was his driver during that campaign. In 1970, Mr. McNamara ran against and beat the incumbent Livonia mayor, then served as mayor of that western Detroit suburb for 17 years.

Today, Mr. McNamara's not ready to slow down. He brushes off speculation that he may run for governor, although the political grapevine in Michigan buzzes about it.

Mr. McNamara takes pride in his aid program that benefits distressed local governments within Wayne County, such as Ecorse, a town that went bankrupt and through receivership beginning in the late 1980s. As Mr. McNamara explains it, "We told them, 'You stay in line and we'll help you.' We told them they couldn't give contracts to their brothers-in-law. They had to have clean personnel and purchasing policies and we'd help them. If they don't stay on the straight path, we call and remind them." The county offered $8 million in urban revitalization projects, including social services.

Ed Jeep, regional director of economic development administration for the U.S. Department of Commerce, with offices in Chicago, called Wayne County's economic development programs "quite innovative. What was done in Ecorse is a useful model for elsewhere. They focus on the disadvantaged communities within the county. They do exemplary work, aggressively working to solve the problems of the poor. It is remarkable for an urban county."

The Wayne County team is working hard on a proposed $1 billion overhaul of Metropolitan Airport. By using revenue from a passenger facility charge, the county in the early 1990s began constructing berms to control noise; buying land for new runways and runway expansions to offer greater landing space to larger, international planes; and working on a six-lane access road that will go under a runway to relieve congestion at the entrance. A new, high-technology control tower and additional parking facilities also are in place. The goal is to make Metro an airport equal to any international facility.

James struggles for a renaissance in Newark

A visit from schoolchildren often gives a mayor a respite from tough questions. But in Newark, N.J., kids have more on their minds than how much the mayor earns or whether he ever takes off that necktie.

"How do you stop someone from using drugs?" one student asks Mayor Sharpe James.

"Why do people hurt other people?" a smaller child whispers as the mayor bends over to hear.

Mr. James barely flinches, repeating words like "pride" and "respect" to make his points. His is not the voice of a condescending adult. He weaves in witty stories and references to pop culture to elicit smiles as well as attention from his young crowd.

Since becoming mayor in 1986, Mr. James has reached out to Newark's grown-ups in the same way. Admirers say he deserves as much credit as anyone for the renaissance about which Newark boasts after the city spent years trying to overcome the televised images of 1967 riots that left its business district in ruin. Mr. James' supporters say his uncanny ability to bring people to-

191

gether is what has turned things around.

"Sharpe is a man who illuminates a room when he walks in," said Saul K. Fenster, president of the New Jersey Institute of Technology, one of a quartet of Newark colleges comprising 45,000 students, faculty and staff. "If people didn't walk into the room ready to agree, they come out feeling different after hearing him."

Elected mayor after 16 years on the City Council, the Jacksonville, Fla., native, who was born in 1936, has managed to win the predominant support of Newark's neighborhoods, business community and media. In a job he clearly enjoys, that is probably the achievement of which he is most proud.

"The excitement of Newark is to be in a room with CEOs (chief executive officers), community-based organizations, elected officials, clergy and even welfare recipients and find common ground," said Mr. James, echoing the themes of the Rev. Jesse Jackson, whose 1988 Democratic presidential campaign was chaired by Mr. James.

Things did not always appear so harmonious. After a divisive 1986 election campaign in which Mr. James unseated the city's first black mayor, Kenneth Gibson, Newark's movers and shakers openly wondered how they would relate to the new city leader.

"Many of the corporate giants had supported the incumbent," recalled Mr. James, whose athletic appearance belies his age. "But when people told them I cheat in tennis, they said, 'This is someone we can work with.' "

In reality, an important symbolic action he took at the start of his administration had a lot more to do with it. After a couple of daylong summit meetings with business leaders, Mr. James recommended the hiring of a deputy mayor for economic development. What was more startling at the time was the person he had in mind for the job: Everett Shaw, president of Renaissance Newark Inc., the economic development arm of the city's largest corporations. Mr. Shaw wears both hats, even to the extent of maintaining two offices. He is paid with private funds and believes his is the only such arrangement among large cities in the country. "A lot of urban centers talk about the public-private partnership," Mr. Shaw said, "but the mayor said we were going to be wedded in Newark. Our goals and purposes are one and the same."

Mr. Shaw has had plenty of projects to sink his teeth into in recent years. Bucking the trend of urban centers watching large corporations relocate to suburbs, Newark officials in 1989 began negotiations that resulted in Blue Cross and Blue Shield of New Jersey's decision to consolidate its 4,000-employee operation in the city. Newark also landed a $200 million, 2,500-seat performing arts center for its downtown, despite early warnings from project planners that they would be unlikely to choose the city as their site. Newark's first new movie theater in 50 years opened in the fall of 1991. A major developer began constructing market-rate, single-family housing in the downtown area, offering hope in a city with a history of public housing problems.

The city has received some welcome assistance from the state government of New Jersey. Experts have pointed to the state's 7-year-old enterprise zone program as a successful model for urban revitalization, with Newark being the prime beneficiary. According to a May report from the state Department of Commerce and Economic Development, Newark's enterprise zone, which offers tax breaks and other incentives to businesses that expand in, or relocate to, the area, has helped the city attract 3,000 jobs and $800 million in private investment.

While some large cities saw a leveling-off or decline in employment as the 1980s ended, Newark's fortunes began changing for the better. The unemployment rate dipped to 5.4% in 1990 from 8.5% in 1989.

Private sector leaders applaud Mr. James' effort to include them in the governmental process. "The mayor, in dealing with the business community, is a decent communicator," said Richard Schoon, president of the Metro Newark Chamber of Commerce. "He realizes he has not been able to do this by himself." Added Mr. Fenster, who with other academics is working with the city on plans for a research and development park, "We feel very strongly that we are not just responding to government's ideas, but that people in government are responding to ours. There's a sharing." In reaching out to private business, Mr. James has had to avoid pitting its interests against those of city neighborhoods. Not only has he insisted to business leaders that the neighborhoods are an equal priority, but he has urged neighborhood leaders to support downtown projects. "Like many cities, our corporate base is predominantly white and our political base is overwhelmingly black," Mr. Shaw said. "I don't think there is another place where there is such camaraderie and trust between the two." The mayor's balancing act has succeeded in that few controversies have erupted over local development projects, Mr. Shaw said. Also, in a city not unfamiliar with bitter politics, Mr. James ran unopposed for his second term in 1990.

That doesn't mean there aren't urban problems eating away at Newark's psyche. The realities of drug use among youths, pressing housing needs and lagging economic growth in minority communities affect Newark as they do most urban centers. Moreover, the city's credit ratings from Wall Street financial institutions rank it lower than most cities of similar size (about 275,000 people).

Added to that is the burden of a national image problem that won't go away. Despite winning a "Triple Crown" of city awards from the U.S. Conference of Mayors, National Civic League and Environmental Protection Agency in 1991, too many outsiders still associate Newark with urban blight, not urban rebirth.

193

"When other cities comment on us out of ignorance, because all they remember is Newark was burning in 1967, I get angry," Mr. James admitted. "We send a response demanding an apology, or at least urging a visit."

Sometimes the stereotypes are played over the national airwaves. When youngster Samantha Smith described her favorable impressions of a visit to the Soviet Union several years ago, talk-show host Phil Donahue said she might have received a sanitized look at life there — much as a foreigner visiting the United States would not be shown a place like Newark. The city also made national news in 1989 when Newark, Calif., Mayor David Smith suggested changing his city's name so as not to be associated with the more infamous Newark. Mr. Smith changed his mind after he and mayors of other Newarks around the country visited New Jersey and saw both the city's progress and its problems, Mr. James said.

"I don't think we will ever live down our past completely," the mayor said. "People will simply come to see us and be amazed at what we have done."

Mr. James isn't sure how much longer he would like to serve as mayor. He does know, however, that after leaving elective office he would like to fulfill his other passion: teaching. A graduate of Newark public schools and the New Jersey state college system, Mr. James taught at Essex County College and in the Newark schools for 25 years before becoming mayor. He also has coached track and cross country, having been a star runner himself in the early 1960s. His office trophy case proudly displays a 1961 time of 1:51.5 in the 800-meter run; he narrowly missed qualifying for the 1960 Summer Olympics in that event. Among his present athletic exploits, his tennis doubles matches against longtime friend and New York Mayor David N. Dinkins are legendary; Mr. James boasts of holding an edge in their on-court confrontations.

In 1994, Mr. James was slated to become president of the National League of Cities, whose offices are located in the nation's capital. An eloquent spokesman for urban issues, Mr. James vowed to give the league the high profile that the U.S. Conference of Mayors enjoyed during the 1991-1992 presidency of Boston Mayor Raymond L. Flynn. National League of Cities Executive Director Donald J. Borut said colleagues consider Mr. James to be among urban America's most motivating figures. "He does things large and small in his city," Mr. Borut said. "He has been able to lead Newark in some dramatic ways, then he has been able to turn around and work with Continental Airlines to take kids to the beach in Puerto Rico for the day." Mr. James also is one of a handful of city officials active in the leadership of both major municipal public interest associations.

Despite the typical urban problems that Newark must face, the city holds several assets that Mr. James believes will serve it well. He never tires of discussing the city's transportation amenities, including the largest containerized port on the East Coast and the fast-growing Newark International Airport, which many travelers consider preferable to the two congested airports in New York City.

"We've given Newark mouth-to-mouth resuscitation and gotten it off the critical list," Mr. James said. "Cities can depreciate in their quality of life, but cities do not die."

National spotlight begins to shine on Georgia's governor

Georgia Gov. Zell Miller became a political overnight sensation due to his head-turning July 13, 1992, keynote address at the Democratic National Convention that nominated future President Clinton as the Democratic candidate for the White House. As is the case with many celebrities, however, it took Mr. Miller decades to achieve instant stardom. Mr. Miller had prepared for years for his convention moment. In 1956, he missed the birth of his second son because he was watching Tennessee Gov. Frank Clement's 1956 convention address on television.

"The reaction I received to my speech was a huge surprise to me," Mr. Miller said. "I was just hoping I would not embarrass myself, the state of Georgia or the party."

Few Georgians could have been too surprised. In his political career spanning nearly four decades, including his election as governor in November 1990 and a 16-year period as lieutenant governor, Mr. Miller has grown into a walking textbook on Georgia-style politics. While some governors try to sidestep the political side of their jobs when things seem messy, Mr. Miller swims knee-deep in it.

"If you had sat me in some state like Kansas, I couldn't have achieved anything," he said. "A governor can have the greatest program, but if he doesn't know what he needs to do to translate it to reality, it's worthless."

Upon his inauguration as governor, Mr. Miller, who was born in 1932, had a clearly defined agenda and the political means to achieve it, with education heading his list of priorities. What he wasn't prepared for was the magnitude of the state's fiscal problems at the time. A campaign for economic growth and excellence in education suddenly became an act in budget-balancing. Double-digit revenue growth in the late 1980s had led to a state spending spree that could not go on; the state had added 12% to its payroll in the five years before Mr. Miller took office. In his first legislative year, the governor succeeded in cutting $415 million in state spending, including the elimination of 2,000 state jobs. Some of the cuts were driven by recommendations of a business-led Commission on Effectiveness and Economy in Government, which Mr. Miller had appointed to study state agencies and recommend ways to improve efficiency. Commission members had expected to spend at least 18 months on their task, but because of state budget problems they were asked to make initial recommendations after just three months of work.

"I'd have to say what got it done was having a motivating governor," said Virgil Williams, an Atlanta business executive who chaired the commission.

In the first two years of Mr. Miller's four-year term, the state adopted nearly half of the commission's 400 recommendations. Included were a tax amnesty program expected to raise $30 million, a requirement that all state tax payments over $10,000 be made electronically, and a master bank account for all state agency cash balances, expected to generate $6.8 million in annual interest. "The governor allowed the commission's work to be a totally independent analysis," Mr. Williams said, "but once the recommendations were made they were tailored to his policy goals. He has a strong agenda and he knows what it is."

Mr. Miller's Georgia Rebound package, an infrastructure plan anticipated to create 29,000 jobs, was approved almost in full by the Democrat-dominated Legislature in the spring of 1992. The package was highlighted by $300 million in capital projects for education, $103 million in borrowed money for road improvements, and $70 million for 6,090 new prison and boot-camp beds.

Still, education tops the list of priorities. "Like most Southern states, we have great needs in the area of education," said Mr. Miller, who has taught history and political science at the university level. "I don't want the state to get farther behind." The governor's personal education started as a child in the tiny village of Young Harris, Ga., in the southern Appalachians. His story shares many similarities with Mr. Clinton. Both men came from families of modest means in the small-town South, and both have no memory of their fathers. Mr. Miller's father died just days after his son's birth.

It is likely that Mr. Miller sees something of himself in the younger Democrat. "In Bill Clinton I see a person who has been on the front lines of governing," Mr. Miller said of the former Arkansas governor who won the presidential election against Republican incumbent George Bush in November 1992. "He's as well-prepared for the presidency as anyone I've ever met."

While the young Mr. Clinton was moved by meeting President John F. Kennedy in the 1960s, Mr. Miller has been guided by the words and deeds of the late President Franklin D. Roosevelt. Mr. Miller's inauguration speech featured a favorite Rooseveltism: "Try something. If it works, try more of it. If it doesn't work, try something else. But for God's sake, try something."

Not all of the governor's tries have been received warmly. A political brouhaha erupted in his first year over his crusade against the state Department of Transportation. A favorite story of Georgia politicians concerns a luncheon meeting between the governor and members of the independent Transportation Board. On that day during the summer of 1991, the ex-Marine allegedly used drill-sergeant tactics to intimidate board members into dumping commissioner Hal Rives. With a voice that observers have described as "more barbed wire than honeysuckle," Mr. Miller made it clear that he would hold transportation funds in abeyance if the board did not act. The board acted.

Reminded of the event, Mr. Miller smiles but does not flinch from the political implications. "Any governor who gets a program through has to exert whatever pressure he can in terms of incentives or withholding favors," he said. "It's just the way the process works." A spokesman for the Department of Transportation said any ill will from the controversy has subsided. "The governor's effort to replace the commissioner hinged on the department needing to have more input from the political establishment, and thereby from the people," said Jerry Stargel, the department's director of public affairs. "Transportation is so important to Atlanta and to Georgia. The department head should be someone the governor can work with." Since the controversy, the transportation agency's focus has shifted to more important matters, like upgrading state port facilities and accelerating road projects.

Mr. Miller has led efforts to remove the Confederate battle symbol from the Georgia flag. He admits this is not the most pressing issue facing the state, though he acknowledges it probably has received the most national attention of any Georgia issue in a long time. Still, Mr. Miller believes many Georgians are ashamed of their state flag, a product of the segregationist movement in the 1950s. He also thinks the flag hurts the state economically. Mr. Miller reminds his opponents that the world will be watching Georgia during the Atlanta Summer Olympics in 1996. He would prefer that viewers not receive a mixed message about race.

Georgians are familiar with Mr. Miller's willingness to go for the jugular, but the rest of the country had not heard a sample until his convention keynote address. His speech contained some of the event's most memorable lines, including, "We can't all be born rich, handsome and lucky . . . and that's why we have a Democratic Party," and, "We've got us a race between an aristocrat, an autocrat and a Democrat" (independent H. Ross Perot was the "autocrat").

Phillip Jones, the Democratic National Committee's political director for the Southern region, said that, immediately after the convention, Mr. Miller and Texas Gov. Ann W. Richards are the two Democrats sought after most by local party groups holding events. "Some of the people at the convention who didn't know him didn't know what to expect," Mr. Jones said. "It was an emotional speech for a guy who's a former Marine."

Part of Mr. Miller's unfinished business involves expanding opportunities for minorities in state government. During his first two years as governor he added six black judges to the ranks of the state Superior Court, and he asked every state agency to designate a contact person for minority-owned businesses.

INDEX

200

Environment, 44, 45, 55-56, 63, 64-65, 66-68, 69, 71, 122, 131, 167, 168, 170
Environmental Systems Research Institute Inc., 31
Ernst & Young, 21-22, 35
Escambia County (Fla.), 42-43
Essex County (N.J.) College, 194
Ethics in Public Policy Center, 165
Evans, Dick, 64
Executive Life Insurance Co., 135

Fagnani, Lynne, 104-105
Fairfax County (Va.), 86
Fallon (Nev.), 49
Federal Aviation Administration, 51-52
Federal Communications Commission, 124, 125, 126
Federal Deposit Insurance Corp., 18, 19
Federal Energy Regulatory Commission, 49-50
Federal Housing Administration, 104-105
Federal Reserve System, 131
Federation of Tax Administrators, 15, 130
Feldman, Roger, 43-44
Fenster, Saul K., 192, 193
Ferguson & Co., 19
Ferrari, Dave, 17-18
Ferraro, John, 52
Fiber-optic technology, 22
Fidelity Investment Corp. of America, 137
Filippine, Edward, 128
Financial World, 18
Findlay, Gary, 151
Fiorina, Morris, 160
Fire protection, 2, 5, 36, 39
Firth, Deborah, 180
Fitch Investors Service Inc., 132, 142-146
Fixler, Philip, 47-48
Flateau, Jim, 85
Flint (Mich.), 76, 119
Flood control
    See *infrastructure, special districts*
Florida, 11, 16, 27-28, 58-60, 81, 84, 88, 94, 99, 102-103, 109, 160, 162, 180
Florida League of Cities, 59
Flynn, Raymond L., 105, 153-154, 194
Fonts, E. Larry, 187
Football, 117, 184, 185
Ford Foundation, 158
Forest preserves, 4
Fort Drum, 48
Fort Lauderdale (Fla.), 118-119
Fort Pillow, 93
Fort Worth (Texas), 5
Fountain Square Plaza, 117
Fourth Ware Technologies Inc., 34-35
Fraser, H. Russell, 143-146
Freedom of Information Act, 174
Freestone, Tom, 31
French Quarter, 119
Froehlich, Robert J., 9-10, 138-139
Frutiger, David, 66
Fuller & Co., 113
Fulwood, Isaac, 78

Gabriel, Roeder, Smith & Co., 151
Gage, Larry, 106-107
Gainesville (Fla.), 59
Gambling (government-run), 15, 119
Gangs, 74
Gaon, David, 113
Garbage collection, 8, 39, 40, 41-43, 55-72, 90
    See also *recycling*
Garcia, Manuel, 27-28
Gardiner, Mark S., 12-13
Garland (Texas), 20
Gates, Daryl F., 79
General Accounting Office, 124
Generally accepted accounting principles, 16-18
General Motors Corp., 147, 166
Geographic information systems
    See *property*
Georgia, 30, 162, 195-198
Georgia Rebound, 196
Gibson, Kenneth, 192
Giese, Thomas, 93-94
Goldsmith, Steven, 186
Golf, 186
Gonzalez, Henry B., 18
Goode, W. Wilson, 173
Goodman, Chris, 47-48
Government
    See *city government, county government, municipalities, special districts, state government, towns and townships, U.S. Government, village government*
Government access, 24-25
Governmental Accounting Standards Board, 16, 18
Government Finance Advisors Inc., 138
Government Finance Associates Inc., 137, 152, 189
Governmental Leadership Award, 46, 48
Governmental Refuse Collection and Disposal Association, 43
Government Finance Officers Association, 7, 17, 19, 132
Governors State University, 161
Granger, Brent, 42
Granger Container Service Inc., 42
Grant, Pat, 128
Green, Paul, 161
Greenberg, Sheldon, 78-79
Greene, Richard, 120
Greenwich Associates, 157
Grizzle, Charles, 44
Gronevelt, Russell, 46
Gronkowski, Roman, 19
Grossman, Hyman, 143-144
Growe, Joan, 29
GTE California Inc., 129
Guaranteed investment contracts, 135
Guardian Technologies, 89
Guerrant, Bill, 176-177
Guns, 73, 85

Hamilton County (Tenn.), 90
Hampden County (Mass.), 85-86
Hanbury, George, 172

205

206

Raleigh (N.C.), 120
Ramirez, Richard, 80
Ramsey County (Minn.), 13
Raphael, Richard, 145
ReActs-HMA, 61
Reagan, Ronald, 39-40, 164, 165, 185
Real estate
    See *property*
Reason Foundation, 48, 165
Rebuild LA, 60-61
ReClaim Inc., 60-61
Records, 25-28
Recycling, 8, 55-72, 177
Reed, Lawrence W., 169
Regional Medical Center at Memphis, 106-108
Regional Transportation District (Denver), 167
Reinhardt, William G., 44
Renaissance Investment Management Inc., 149
Renaissance Newark Inc., 192
Rensselaer Polytechnic Institute, 122
Rensselaer Technology Park, 122
Renzema, Mark, 89
RePave, 61
Republican Party, 6, 45, 159-162, 167-169, 172, 185, 190
Research and development facilities
    See *technology parks*
Research Triangle Park, 120
Resendez, Carlos, 150, 154, 155
Resource Conservation Research House, 61
Rhode Island, 3, 22, 70, 89, 160
Richards, Ann W., 197
Richmond (Va.), 3, 75-76
Richmond, Philip, 42-43
Rigby, Richard, 118-119
Riverfront Stadium, 117
Rives, Hal, 197
Roads
    See *infrastructure*
Roberts, Douglas, 155
Rock and Roll Hall of Fame, 115
Rockefeller Institute of Government, 163
Rolla (Mo.), 128
Romney, George, 175
Rooney, Phillip B., 55-56
Roosevelt, Franklin D., 39, 196
Rosenthal, Alan, 161, 163
Rotman, Bern, 179
Rouge River, 189
Rout, Jim, 106, 107
Ruppel, Ronald, 104-105
Rutgers University, 161, 163
Ryan, Allan, 52-53

Sachs, Robert, 128
St. Joseph's Hospital, 103
St. Lawrence County (N.Y.), 48
St. Louis, 3, 73, 77
St. Louis County (Mo.), 3
St. Paul (Minn.), 13
Sales tax
    See *taxation*
Salt Lake County (Utah), 3

Samuels, Gary, 34-35
San Antonio, 118, 120
San Antonio Firemen's and Policemen's
    Pension Fund, 150, 154
San Diego, 3
Sanera, Michael, 167
San Francisco, 18, 19, 77
Sangamon State University, 169
San Jose (Calif.), 77, 121
Santa Barbara County (Calif.), 13
Santa Clara County (Calif.), 121
Satellite dishes, 124, 130
Saurman, George E., 170
Savard, Marguerite, 44
Schaitberger, Harold, 150-151, 153
Schlatter, Gary, 88-89
Schools
    See *education*
Schoon, Richard, 193
Schuler, David, 20
Schwarzlose, Richard, 172, 174
Scotland, 52
Scott, Dave, 19-20
Seattle, 57, 58, 74, 100
Sedgwick County (Kan.), 178-179
Seidel, Ray, 24-25
Sewers
    See *infrastructure, special districts*
Shaw, Everett, 192, 193
Shearson Lehman Brothers Inc., 156
Shelby County (Tenn.), 105-108, 182
Sherman, Coelz & Bergfalk, 174
Sheshunoff Information Services Inc., 19
Shick, Fred, 148
Shields, Brooke, 179
Shoemaker, Jeff, 168
Shreveport (La.), 118
Sierra Pacific Power Co., 50
Signs, 7, 31
Sikes, Alfred C., 124, 126
Silicon Valley, 121, 122
Silk, Susan, 173-175
Sixteenth Street Mall, 112
Skokie (Ill.), 7
Skumatz, Lisa, 57-58
Sloan, Ron, 74-75
Small, Ken, 59
Smith, David, 194
Smith, Paul M., 95-96
Smith, Phil, 157
Smith, Samantha, 194
Smith, Verenda, 15
Smith Barney, Harris Upham & Co. Inc., 52
Socialism, 6
Social Security, 97
Social services, 3, 5, 21, 23, 32-33, 47, 74-75, 169, 191
Solid Waste Association of North America, 56
Solon (Ohio), 62-64
South Africa, 147, 153-155
South Carolina, 93, 138-139, 168
South Carolina Policy Council, 165, 168
South Carolina vs. Baker, 138-139

207

South Dakota, 162, 180
Southfield (Mich.), 19, 46
Soviet Union, 194
Spain, Catherine L., 132
Special districts (general), 4, 5-6, 49-50, 56, 103, 105, 106, 107, 132, 136
Spen, Alan, 145
Spencer, Steven, 92
Sprauer, Louis, 137
Springfield (Ohio), 74-75
Standard & Poor's Corp., 102, 131, 132, 142, 143-146, 187
Standard & Poor's 500 Composite Stock Index, 155, 156
Stanford University, 120-122
Stanford Research Institute Inc., 178
Stargel, Jerry, 197
State government (general), 2, 10, 35, 39-40, 83, 86, 108-110, 130, 132, 141, 159-170, 171, 179
State of Michigan Retirement Systems, 148
State Policy Network, 166
State University of New York, 163
Steelman, Bradley, 125
Steinhurst, William, 34
Stewart, D. Michael, 3
Stocks, 147, 154, 155-157
Stouffer Foods Corp., 63
Stratton, William, 161
Streets
            See *infrastructure*
Subdivisions, 6
Suffolk County (Mass.), 95
Suffolk County (N.Y.), 146
Sullivan, Mike, 17-18
Superfund, 66-67
Survey of Cable Television Rates and Services, 124
Surveyors, 4
Symington, J. Fife, 167
Synergic Resources Corp., 57
Synergics Inc., 49-50

Tabor Center, 112
Tacoma (Wash.), 66-68
Tampa (Fla.), 102
Tampa General Hospital, 102-103
Tarr, Nancy, 10
Tallahassee (Fla.), 59
Taxation (general), 75, 101, 107, 120, 168, 170
            Bond-interest tax, 138-139
            Collection, 15-16, 196
            Incentives, 184-186, 193
            Income tax, 10, 15, 99, 130, 141
            Property tax, 3, 4, 6, 7, 12-16, 47, 105, 117, 121, 160, 187
            Sales tax, 7, 9, 10, 15, 17-18, 104, 105, 108, 111-112, 121, 129-130
            Severance tax, 17-18
            User fees, 7, 25, 27, 28, 172
            Utilities, 130
Tax increment financing, 120
Tax Reform Act, 131, 138, 139-140

Tax revolts, 12, 14, 140-141, 167
Teachers Insurance & Annuity Association, 147
Technology parks, 120-122, 193
Telecommunications
            See *information technology*
TeleTalk, 33-34
Television
            See *mass media*
Tennessee, 30, 92-94, 107, 130, 135-136, 182, 195
Term limits, 162-164
Texas, 5-6, 18, 22, 30, 38, 84, 87, 90, 94, 98, 107, 134, 162
Texas Rangers (baseball team), 120
Think tanks, 164-170, 183, 185, 186
Thompson, James R., 161
Thornton, Larry, 145
Thrasher, Rich, 181
Time-Warner Inc., 127, 129
Toigo, Bob, 156-158
Toledo (Ohio), 40, 119
Toregas, Costis, 35-37
Tourism, 39, 105, 111, 112, 115, 119, 179-180
Towns and townships (general), 4-5, 56, 123, 132
            Assessor, 5
            Clerk, 5
            Selectmen, 4
            Treasurer, 4
TRACS, 23-24
Trade, 2
Trademark Register, 24
Transportation, 2, 5, 39, 41, 44, 51-54, 112, 118-119, 167, 173, 178, 179, 191, 194-195, 196-197
Trojanowicz, Robert, 74-76, 77
Troy (N.Y.), 122
Truckee-Carson Irrigation District, 49-50
Truscott, John, 45-46
Tucker, Kimberly, 94-96
Turner Broadcasting System Inc., 126-127
Tutu, Desmond, 154
Twenty-four-Hour City Hall/County Court House, 36

Uhler, Lewis K., 163
Ullmann, Harrison, 185
Unions, 40-41, 90-91, 107-108, 164, 167
Union Station, 185-186
Unisys, 29
United Airlines, 184-185
United Graphics Consultants, 26
U.S. Conference of Mayors, 153-154, 193, 194
U.S. Government (general), 4, 39-40, 83, 85, 86, 94, 97, 108, 123-124, 132, 135, 138
            Bureau of Land Reclamation, 49
            Census Bureau, 6, 12, 86
            Constitution, 127, 130, 138
            Department of Commerce, 191
            Department of Health and Human Services, 99
            Department of Housing and Urban Development, 44

Would you like to purchase another copy of this book as a gift for a relative or friend? Did you borrow this book at a library and, after reading it, decide you would like a copy of your own? This order form makes purchase of additional copies of "Issues Confronting City & State Governments" possible. Please do *not* tear this page from the book. Instead, make a photocopy, or write down the information. A discount schedule for bulk orders also is available by writing to the publisher.

I would like to receive _____ copies of "Issues Confronting City & State Governments" at $24.95 per copy, plus $4 per book to cover shipping charges. Make check payable to P.O. Publishing Company.

Name: _____

Street address: _____

City: _____ State: _____ ZIP code: _____

P.O. Publishing Company
P.O. Box 3333
Skokie, Illinois 60076-6333
(708) 329-7929